The sniper's rifle spit leaden death into the Marine ranks again, and another youngster cried out in pain and mortal fear. Loren Kleppe raised his rifle above the bunker's lip and sighted in on a dark shadow that lay facing his bleeding brothers. The smoke and debris that had filtered over the battlefield made a clear sighting impossible. The Viet Cong sharpshooter no doubt felt a degree of safety, with the Marines bloodied and confused by mortar rounds still tearing into the sand dunes as they lay stunned and weary.

Loren took up the trigger slack, and the M1-D bucked hard against his shoulder. The heavy match bullet tore through the short hundred-meter distance between friend and foe. Kleppe couldn't see clearly through the smoke as the Viet Cong sniper's head blew apart like a pumpkin smashed by a mallet during a Halloween prank back home. No more shots were fired from the enemy bank, and Kleppe slumped down like a drugged animal into the bottom of his bunker. . . .

By John J. Culbertson

OPERATION TUSCALOOSA: *2nd Battalion, 5th Marines, at An Hoa, 1967*

A SNIPER IN THE ARIZONA: *2nd Battalion, 5th Marines, in the Arizona Territory, 1967*

Books published by The Random House Publishing Group are available at quantity discounts on bulk purchases for premium, educational, fund-raising, and special sales use. For details, please call 1-800-733-3000.

13 CENT KILLERS

The 5th Marine Snipers in Vietnam

John J. Culbertson

PRESIDIO PRESS

BALLANTINE BOOKS • NEW YORK

A Presidio Press Book
Published by The Random House Publishing Group
Copyright © 2003 by John J. Culbertson
Foreword and map on p. xvi copyright © 2003 by Ronald J. Brown

Published in the United States by Presidio Press, an imprint of The Random House Publishing Group, a division of Random House, Inc., New York, and simultaneously in Canada by Random House of Canada Limited, Toronto.

Presidio Press and colophon are trademarks of Random House, Inc.

www.presidiopress.com

ISBN 0-345-45914-8

Manufactured in the United States of America

First Edition: January 2003

20 19 18 17 16 15 14 13 12

In every great military unit there exists an outstanding leader who unites and motivates the men. In the "13 Cent Killers" of the 5th Marine Snipers Platoon that standout warrior was Thomas Casey. Casey was not only the finest sniper team leader, but he was also the epitome of the "13 Cent Killers" on his own skill and merit. Sergeant Casey led over forty night ambushes personally and was responsible for the deployment and record number of enemy WIA/KIAs during Vietnam's bloodiest and hardest fought battles in the pivotal year of 1967. Sergeant Tom Casey has emerged as the most deadly of all American Snipers in Vietnam and the heroic example of what it means to be a combat Marine.

CONTENTS

Foreword

Musketry, the ability of riflemen to hit their target with aimed fire, is a very important skill in the United States Marine Corps even in this modern age of stealth fighters and laser-guided bombs. This tradition carries back to the age of sail when leathernecks were posted in the foretops with orders to pick out and shoot enemy leaders during ship-to-ship fighting on the high seas. The "steel-and-steam" navy of the late nineteenth century eliminated this mission, but the Marines still retained their emphasis upon sharpshooting.

In 1917, the 5th Marine Regiment was part of the initial component of the American Expeditionary Force sent to France during the First World War. When the Marines began to prepare for combat under the tutelage of French veterans, the American commander was astonished to find no time on the training syllabus for rifle marksmanship. He was smugly told that there was no place for the individual rifleman in modern warfare because machine guns and massed artillery firing from deep trench lines were the arms of decision on the Western Front. The stubborn Marines, however, rejected this tenet and quickly added rifle marksmanship to the training schedule even though French officers shook their heads in disbelief at such a waste of time. Not long thereafter, the Allied defense lines were shattered by a surprise German offensive. Soon, the French Army was in full retreat and a German juggernaut was headed straight for Paris with its way unblocked by trenchlines, machine-guns pits, or artillery batteries. Into this breach marched the 5th Marines. When a distraught French major ordered the 51st Company to fall back, Marine captain Lloyd Williams replied, "Retreat, hell! We just got here."

The next day the lead units of the Kaiser's army approached Belleau Wood located less than forty miles from the suburbs of Paris, so close that German artillery spotters could pick out the Eiffel Tower and the spires of Notre Dame cathedral with their binoculars. German scouts were suddenly taken under fire and more than a few fell to the ground, victims of astoundingly accurate rifle fire, as they neared Les Mares Farm. The German commander then did what had worked so well for the last few weeks; he ordered a frontal assault, expecting the inexperienced and out-gunned Americans to turn tail and run. Wave after wave of Feld Grau–clad Prussian Guards were cut down as they advanced through the wheat by well-placed shots from American M1903 Springfield rifles. Les Mares Farm turned out to be the closest the Germans got to Paris during the First World War. The tide of the war had been turned with the help of God and a few Marines—men who knew how to make every shot count.

This book also tells the story of a few good men who knew how to make every shot count. In its pages we learn about the men of the 5th Marines Sniper Platoon who worked the blood-soaked ground south of Da Nang in 1966 and 1967. Their stories are skillfully told by John J. Culbertson, himself one of their number during that time. Culbertson offers a moving testament to the forgotten heroes of a misunderstood war—men who unflinchingly placed themselves in harm's way only to have their efforts belittled by many who refused to serve. Culbertson lovingly and respectfully documents the exploits of these few brave and humble men, but at the same time, he paints a larger picture, giving the reader the full context of time and place, enumerating tactical lessons learned, and debunking many myths as he recounts the 1st Marine Division's initial year in the Republic of Vietnam. We follow men like Tom Casey, Ron Willoughby, and Vaughn Nickell as they fight the Viet Cong and North Vietnamese in the An Hoa Basin and the Que Son Valley. Culberston details how the men were trained, describes the equipment they carried, and explains the tactics they used while serving in the Marine Corps's most decorated regiment, the Fighting Fifth Marines.

Although Private First Class Culberston and I served in Vietnam at different times, by virtue of serving in the same unit—the Fighting Fifth Marines—we certainly walked a lot of the same ground and there can be little doubt that we fought many of the same people. John Culbertson is well qualified to tell this story. He lived parts of it and gained firsthand testimony about the rest from his comrades-in-arms. Thus, this book is not a distant historical tome whose facts were pulled from some musty long-forgotten documents, nor is it the retelling of some self-serving sea stories by a wannabe hero. *Thirteen Cent Killers,* just like John's two previous memoirs, *Operation Tuscaloosa* and *A Sniper in the Arizona,* contains the authentic memories of someone who was there and experienced firsthand the heat and mud of battle. Culbertson once again splendidly mixes personal experiences with historical fact to present the unvarnished truth about what the war in Vietnam was like for those who fought it.

Our paths first crossed when I was researching my own history of the 5th Marines. John was forthright in his criticism and accurate in his assessments so I frequently used information he provided in that book, *A*

Few Good Men: The Story of the Fighting Fifth Marines, the USMC's Most Decorated Regiment. John joined the Marines in 1965, volunteered for combat duty in Vietnam, and was eventually assigned as a rifleman with Company H, 2nd Battalion, 5th Marines, in 1966. The highlight of his tour of duty was two weeks spent at the 1st Marine Division Sniper School, an experience he describes as both enjoyable and educational. The friendships he made during that time and the lessons he learned there are the bedrock upon which this book is built. Culbertson's last Purple Heart Medal doubled as his ticket home (Marines were sent stateside after receiving a third wound) for duty at Quantico, where he quarterbacked the all-Marine football team in 1968. Following his separation from the service in 1969, former Sergeant Culbertson used his G.I. Bill benefits to get a college degree, but it took many years and a lot of soul-searching before John finally took pen to paper to chronicle his experiences as a combat Marine. We are all better off because he decided to do that, and this book is one more fine addition to his outstanding body of literary work.

Semper Fi

Ronald J. Brown
Author, *A Few Good Men*

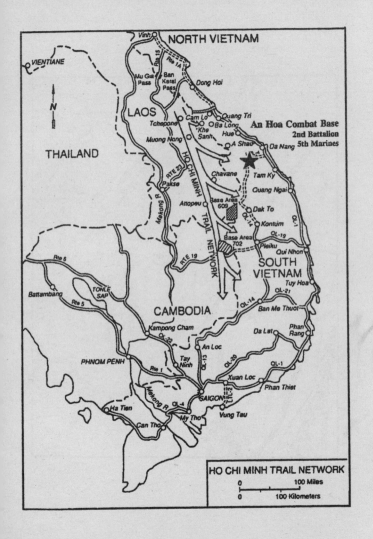

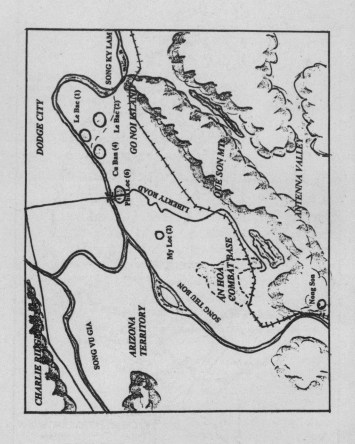

Prologue

Hurst, Texas

It was a lazy Sunday afternoon in October 2000 when our small group of former Marine Corps snipers sat around the glass-topped table on Pat Montgomery's patio on the sunlit banks of Lake Henderson, just east of Dallas, Texas. The conversation centered on the reflected memories of our days as combat Marines in Vietnam while attached to the most decorated regimental sniper platoon in the Vietnam War. From October 1966 through the battle for Hue City in February 1968, there were forty-three members of the platoon. Three were killed in action (KIA), and there were twenty-one other Purple Hearts awarded, two Silver Stars, three Bronze Stars, and one individual Vietnamese Cross of Gallantry, along with two Presidential Unit Citations.

The fabled 5th Marine Regiment of Guadalcanal and Pelileu fame had set the standards for combat valor on the bloody beaches of Okinawa and the frozen, blood-spattered banks of the Chosin Reservoir in Korea. In Vietnam, by 1966, the Marine Corps was introducing sniper teams into the TO (table of organization) of rifle companies and battalions as attached support elements during major operations. And in the summer of that year, the 5th Marines had moved their TAOR (Tactical Area of Responsibility) to the Demilitarized Zone (DMZ).

The 1st, 2nd, and 3rd Battalions of the 5th Marine Regiment operated in the area surrounding the Marine firebase at Con Thien and as far east as Phu Bai. The new platoon of snipers would be assigned to the various rifle companies for OPCON (Operational Control for Combat Operations), reporting directly to the Headquarters section of rifle companies taking the field.

It was amazing to sit around the deck of a beautiful home in total security, hearing my fellow Marines reminisce about the days when life was anything but secure and all of us felt bulletproof. We discussed the way rumors get started after wars are long over and the details get fuzzy. Sniper stories and supposedly official accounts of snipers had been published in books promoting the art of combat marksmen—or sniping—to a level of "deadly performance" far beyond the actual deeds of snipers in combat. These reports grossly exaggerated the actual tactics employed, as well as claims of the number of enemy confirmed dead, or "kills."

Pat Montgomery mentioned that he had never seen a sniper operate alone. Why in hell would anyone go out alone anyway? If you twisted your ankle in the field, you'd be done for, not to mention that the Vietnamese peasantry would relay a patrol's size and weapons complement to the first Viet Cong cell or unit in the immediate vicinity. Some eighty percent of all Vietnamese peasants in I Corps were sympathetic to the Viet Cong. In the instance of my battalion—the 2nd of the 5th Marine Regiment—no patrol ever passed through the first village toward the Thu Bon River without seeing the mamma-sans and other villagers counting our numbers for a thorough "intel" report to local Communist forces. Often the patrol would be ambushed, or at the least encounter some booby traps along the trail soon after its patrol route was compromised.

We all agreed that a single sniper would be picked up

and killed immediately once he'd been identified. Since it was obvious that Americans looked strikingly different from Vietnamese, it was a foregone conclusion that no Marine ever, at any time, snuck out of his base and traversed enemy territory without being sighted. That includes the gutsy lance corporal, Luther Hamilton, of Hotel Company, 2nd Battalion, 5th Marines, who ran six miles from a blocking force positioned along the Thu Bon River west of An Hoa to Phu Loc 6, at night and alone. In late January 1967, Luther had run for help to save the life of PFC Cross, who was bleeding to death from shrapnel wounds back in his bunker. Luther was sighted, pursued by the Viet Cong, and almost killed.

Pat Montgomery looked me in the eye. I had attended 1st Marine Division Sniper School, which was headed by Gunnery Sergeant Vernon D. Mitchell of Chula Vista, California. At different times in 1967, the school had been attended by all four of us gathered at Pat Montgomery's house. Kenny Barden from Jackson, Mississippi, attended the sniper school in early March, I was there in late March, and Eddie Rackow had gone in April. Montgomery, Barden, and Rackow had been assigned to the 5th Marine Sniper Platoon as part of Headquarters Company of the 5th Marine Regiment. I had merely returned to my unit, the 2nd Battalion, 5th Marines, and was assigned as company sniper and point scout in Hotel Company. The other three, along with their fellow snipers in the 5th Marines Sniper Platoon, seldom operated with the 2nd Battalion, 5th Marines, at An Hoa.

Sniper teams were not popular among many infantry or "line" officers early in 1967. The officers whom I walked point scout for always said that they wanted the expert marksmen up front, and that no "sniper platoon" was going to rob the 2nd Battalion of its shooters. Personally, I thought that I should have been transferred to the 5th Marine Sniper Platoon, with its legendary shooters like Sergeants Tom Casey of South Carolina, and Ron Willoughby, from Ohio. I was a "high expert" on the rifle range with the M-1 and the M-14 rifles. Tom Casey was a Marine Corps Team Shooter, like Carlos Hathcock and Jim Land.

I didn't know if I was in that league or not, but I didn't "shake up" when the lead came my way. Along with skilled Marine riflemen like John Lafley, Luther Hamilton, Manny Ybarra, Tim Kirby, Gary Woodruff, and my other Hotel Company "dingers" and friends, I felt like one deadly son of a bitch when we took the field. Snipers like Casey and Willoughby were the absolute cream of the crop, but they were also "grunts" and supported the infantry operations by shooting targets of opportunity such as enemy officers, medics, machine gunners, signalmen, or radiomen.

Once in a while they even shot at a civilian by mistake, if you can call anyone in Vietnam during the war a civilian. By that I mean the Vietnamese children planted booby traps and mines. Their mothers warned the enemy of our presence and hid the enemy from us. The men fought as guerrillas, especially at night, and aided the Viet Cong main forces units anytime they were ordered to do so. It readily became apparent that there were few friendly civilians in I Corps. The memoirs that talk about Marines who kept girlfriends in the local villages are fantasy. Any Vietnamese girl who fraternized with Marines openly in any small village near An Hoa would have wound up headless by morning. Americans were the invaders, pure and simple, though I'm not convinced that most Vietnamese differentiated between our predecessors—the French—and us.

At any rate, 1967 was the height of the Vietnam War with regard to pitched battles involving battalion-size units or greater, though there were slightly more American casualties the following year. During 1967, some 150 battles were fought in I Corps, and some four thousand combat patrols were fielded by the Marines to keep the enemy off balance and attempt to pacify the hinterland.

This book, the first in a series on the 5th Marine Snipers, begins in 1966 and leads into the full combat cycle of 1967. The second book will continue the story, ending in the apocalypse that was Hue City in the first months of 1968. The Marines of the 5th Regiment were the most highly decorated combat veterans in Marine Corps history. Vietnam proved once again that the 5th Marines, along with their 3rd Division brothers fighting along the DMZ, were truly worthy of the title United States Marine. And the 5th Marine Regiment Sniper Platoon exemplified itself by recording the highest number of kills and the highest kill ratio of any sniper unit during the Vietnam War. I know from articles in *Stars and Stripes* and *Sea Tiger* that the 11th Marine Regiment's artillery gunners stated that when they shot for the 2nd Battalion, 5th Marines, they felt they fired for the finest infantry battalion in the Marine Corps.

This compilation of stories is a true firsthand rendition of the experiences of the snipers who carried the bolt rifles, and the thousand-dollar Viet Cong bounties on their heads. This is a true story of Marine "grunts" in the thick of combat and how our sniper teams' rifles put the cutting edge on the art of jungle warfare. You'll read about courageous snipers like Corporal Ron Willoughby, for instance, whom I fought with on the sandbar of death during the initial assault of Operation Tuscaloosa. It took me decades to search for the men behind the scoped rifles, Loren Kleppe and Vaughn Nickell, who made long shots killing Viet Cong mortar men and allowing Foxtrot's riflemen to advance and ultimately crush the enemy. You'll read about Sergeant Tom Casey who rode an M-48 tank from Phu Loc 6 to the rescue of Hotel Company as we lay pinned down by machine-gun and mortar fire, but arrived too late to save any of Hotel's dead.

And you'll read of other sniper exploits. I am filled with pride and respect for having served with these great marksmen. Even though the years have put gray whiskers where our youthful cheeks used to shine, we still all take strength in the knowledge that we were brothers in that faraway war, and that long ago we were very special.

CHAPTER ONE

Opening Shots, 1966

In 1966 the Marines were landing in ever greater numbers and establishing the giant supply and marshaling yards in Da Nang, Chu Lai, and to the north in Phu Bai, with firebases spread along the Demilitarized Zone at Camp Carrol, Con Thien, the Rockpile, and Gio Linh. South of the DMZ, combat bases had been built out of ARVN camps at An Hoa and Hoi An, southwest and south of Da Nang, respectively. The combat patrols and major offensive operations were fielded against the Viet Cong's guerrilla units and their main forces. The North Vietnamese Army had yet to make any significant presence in the rice basins of the south, but as 1967 approached, the NVA began a major push into South Vietnam across the DMZ from inside Cambodia and Laos through the meandering roads and trails along the Ho Chi Minh Trail.

Several major infantry battles had been fought with the Communist forces, such as Operation Starlight and Operation Prairie, and they dealt the Viet Cong and NVA forces severe defeats. However, by 1967 the Communists were learning better techniques to fight their American nemesis.

The Viet Cong main force units blended into the surrounding Vietnamese population by day. By night, the Viet Cong became active, setting booby traps and mines and employing set ambushes with hit-and-run tactics against the stronger and better-armed American forces. The villagers, whether willingly or by coercive intimidation and torture, gave the Viet Cong and the North Vietnamese accurate intelligence about U.S. Marine troop movements and patrols. The Viet Cong main forces made detailed plans to ambush and destroy U.S. units that were patrolling hostile regions of I Corps and had no clue as to VC movements or intentions. Most Marine intelligence from its reconnaissance units was "stale" by the time it was analyzed and interpreted. The Viet Cong units fought the Americans by hitting hard and fast and melting back into the jungle with no sign or trace of their whereabouts.

American command philosophy was never centralized or executed with enough Marine units trying to pacify the Vietnamese people in their village environs through the fielding of Combined Action Platoons. These platoons consisted of ARVN or Vietnamese Army squads teamed with U.S. Marines to guard the sanctity of the hamlets out in the hinterland. The CAP concept was working despite the fact that an insufficient number of Marine units were available to properly blanket the countryside. The rice-growing regions of I Corps, particularly in Quang Tri and Quang Nam Provinces, were inhabited by South Vietnamese villagers in myriad small hamlets, each with its own specific rice fields to cultivate and harvest. These hamlets, with their peaceful villagers, were the targets of assaults by brutal Viet Cong and North Vietnamese troops intent upon refurbishing their exhausted rice supplies to continue the Communist push into free South Vietnam.

The American command was sharply divided as to operational strategy in dealing with the Communist invaders. General Westmoreland believed in fighting large conventional battles against strong Viet Cong and NVA forces, while Marine Generals Victor Krulak, Herman

Nickerson, and Robert Cushman preferred to attempt to win the hearts and minds of the local populace by denying the Viet Cong and the NVA the hospitality and active support of the villagers. When and if the main forces of the Viet Cong and North Vietnamese Army showed their heads, the Marines would be all too eager to join them in battle. Pitched battles were hard-fought affairs in which the Marines often had to overcome a well-prepared ambush and overrun the Communist forces to prevail, and often, the cost of victory was very high in friendly casualties, as was the case on Operation Tuscaloosa.

This is really where the story of the 5th Marine Regiment Sniper Platoon begins.

In late 1966, Ron Willoughby and Sergeant Tom Casey were transferred from the giant Marine base on Okinawa to report to the 5th Marines for duty. Both were expert riflemen and were later chosen as NCOIC and assistant NCOIC for the newly organized sniper program.

This regimental sniper platoon became the foundation of the first divisional sniper school officially established in Vietnam. Other sniper activity had been unofficially conducted by Captain Jim Land and a group of former Marine Corps Rifle Team members. One distinguished member of Land's group was Carlos Hathcock, who had helped create genuine interest in the development of combat sniping among the Marine leaders in the United States. In late 1966 the decision was made to bring an accomplished World War II and Korean War veteran out of retirement. At the request of the Commandant of the Marine Corps, Gunnery Sergeant Vernon D. Mitchell dusted off his herringbone utility uniform and reported to Camp Pendleton in February 1967 for direct transfer to Vietnam to head the newly founded 1st Marine Division Sniper School at the Happy Valley range outside Da Nang.

This true story will be composed of vignettes of each sniper's training and actual combat experiences. Since these Marines worked with different partners as both shooter and spotter, and with the many different rifle companies of the three battalions of the 5th Marine Regiment on operations all over I Corps, the experiences reported may at times overlap. It is a valid combat reality, however, that the events experienced by two men in the same combat action never completely dovetail. Given the understanding that much time has passed since we faced the enemy bullets, our brotherhood has continued mostly unchanged. We are still the patriots and Marines of times gone by and offer these tales of heroism, death, fear, and loyalty from the most decorated Sniper Unit in the Vietnam War. The 5th Marine Snipers set the records for the most kills, most combat operations, and lastly became the most feared adversaries that the Viet Cong and North Vietnamese would face during the height of the bloody Vietnam War.

The period from December 1966 through the final battle for Hue City in February 1968, comprised the most ferocious combat of the Vietnam War. The men that I have cameoed in this true story are real and will forever remain my friends and brothers. There are no finer Marines and certainly no finer snipers that ever tasted battle than these men. Each has his story to tell and hopefully the truth will finally come out about whom the real heroes behind the bolt rifles really were.

CHAPTER TWO

1st Division
Sniper School
Gunnery Sergeant
Vernon D. Mitchell

Since the Korean War, the Marine Corps has changed in organization, tactics, and weaponry. The one thing that will never change about the Marines, however, is marksmanship. There are legendary names in the Corps, like Captain Jim Land and Carlos Hathcock, but few people have been privileged to shoot with and be instructed by riflemen as distinguished as Gunny Mitchell.

Vernon Mitchell of Vista, California, was born in 1925 and served in World War II, as a teenager. As a rifleman and sniper, he was such an outstanding shot that he later became a sniper in Korea during the Chosin Reservoir breakout, when the Allied Forces were outnumbered and outgunned.

A famous story about then Sergeant Mitchell involved the young Marine and his shooting partner, who were sent to rescue a pinned-down U.S. Army outfit that was trying to advance past the MLR. The young Sergeant Mitchell and his partner arrived in a Willys jeep covered with snow, only to find the Army lieutenant hunkered down behind a stone wall under intense fire from a North Korean machine-gun emplacement. It seemed to Sergeant Mitchell that there were sufficient Army troops on hand to take out the machine-gun team, but as the gun ripped the flinty top of the stone wall into chips, the fearful troopers only curled lower into their holes and bunkers.

Sergeant Mitchell and his partner took their rifles out of the jeep and unzipped padded leather cases holding their match grade M1-D sniper rifles. Mitchell yelled to the Army platoon leader that he would just take a minute to get on target and this cluster fuck would be over.

Sergeant Mitchell strapped into his sling in a tight-legged sitting position that has become the Gunny's trademark. The Army lieutenant jumped to his feet and yelled that the Korean machine gun was positioned at least six hundred yards away, up the hill overlooking the Army bunkers.

The officer blurted, "Hey, you can't hit them from here." The rifle slammed into Sergeant Mitchell's shoulder. Sergeant Mitchell's partner watched a North Korean soldier get to his feet and point in their direction.

Mitchell squeezed the hair trigger on his Garand and the cold, icy air split with a resounding "Kapoow!"

The shot had broken, and the 173 grain match bullet sliced up the hill and through the chest of the standing Korean, who fell into the blood and gore spewing from his giant chest wound. The remaining Koreans looked at each other in awe and let logic run its course. All three machine gunners abandoned their weapon and ran straight up the hill, framed in the vast blanket of snow and ice. Sergeant Mitchell sighted in on the lead Korean and held a yard over his head, figuring for the bullet drop at seven hundred yards. As he squeezed the trigger again, Mitchell burned the crosshairs into the back of the running, terrified soldier. The Garand discharged, and the Korean pitched forward as if poleaxed, then lay motionless in the crimson-splattered snow bank.

The Marines got to their feet, and Sergeant Mitchell watched as the two remaining Koreans topped the hill at a dead run. He looked at the Army officer and commented, "I guess we'll be on our way, Lieutenant. Those boys won't bother you for a while yet! Call us if they do."

Sergeant Mitchell and his spotter placed their rifles carefully back into the snow-covered jeep and, with a final wave to the astonished Army lieutenant, drove bouncing along the trail's ruts, headed back to 1st Division Headquarters.

That story has been told to every Marine sniper candidate at the Happy Valley school, and it's not the most fantastic story told about Gunny Mitchell's shooting skills either.

After Korea, Mitchell was chosen to shoot on the Marine Corps Rifle Team at San Diego in 1952. He exhibited his outstanding shooting skills and in 1955 won the National Service Rifle Championship at Camp Perry, Ohio. In 1958, Sergeant Mitchell won the championship again, shooting a rapid-fire record with fifteen of his twenty bull's-eyes in the smaller V ring. These two National Rifle Championships, coupled with his combat experience and teaching ability, made Mitchell a natural for selection as NCOIC and head of the new sniper school at the Sea Bees rock quarry at Happy Valley, on the periphery of the Marine Base at Da Nang.

In February 1967, Mitchell opened the new sniper school to shooters from the 1st Marine Division. He chose as his second in command Sergeant Douglas M. DeHaas, a gifted instructor as well as a class A marksman who had shot competitively on East Coast Marine Corps teams. Gunny Mitchell and DeHaas tailored a three week course, later condensed into two weeks, that covered all phases of marksmanship, map and compass reading, terrain analysis, and the effects of wind and weather on live firing. There was also a course in camouflage, silent tactical movement, and sniper employment that utilized former Viet Cong soldiers who had shown the good sense to "Chieu Hoi" and join the American forces. These former enemy instructors knew a hell of a lot about American naiveté in the bush, and they painstakingly tried to demonstrate the boo-boos not to make when fighting the Communists if we wanted to stay alive. (My previous book, *A Sniper in the Arizona*, gives a thorough account of the 1st Division Sniper School.)

Sergeant DeHaas took us from the classroom to the Happy Valley rifle range before the first week of classes was entirely completed. The range was built on a hillside overlooking a deep cut in the terrain. The firing lines were at the top of the hill and the butts were in the cut or valley. Targets were set at 300, 600, and 1000 meters, and firing was generally from the prone position, although some Marines, like Gunny Mitchell, often shot from the sitting position.

I once watched Mitchell in late March 1967 when I attended 1st Marine Division Sniper School shoot a clip of eight rounds of 30.06 from an M1-D he kept at the school. From a tight-legged sitting position, he put all eight rounds into four inches at six hundred meters in a rapid-fire string that didn't take twenty seconds to fire. I think the Gunny was a great shot mostly because he could adapt himself to any terrain and shoot accurately from practically any distance. He would fire a round and watch the bullet strike, then hold off putting the second shot on target with no sight adjustment. He said that no one ever adjusted their sights during a firefight, and if we couldn't use Kentucky windage, then we might learn to shoot paper, but not actual people. The M-1 Garand rifle will kill an enemy soldier at over five hundred meters if the battle dope, or sights, are set at three hundred. A head shot at five hundred will hit the enemy in the guts, and a chest hold at three hundred meters will tear the man's nuts off! In combat you must set your battle sights at two or three hundred meters and adjust accordingly to the bullet strike for a second shot by holding off high, low, left, or right.

Even though I had qualified as an expert with the M-1 Garand and as high expert with the M-14, I was nowhere near the class of most Marine Team Shooters. However, I could make some very salty snap shots and clean kills on running enemy soldiers by applying tracking and the hold-off techniques taught by Gunny Mitchell. Most snipers have also made themselves aware of good instinctive shot placement by avid hunting. I had tried to kill everything that lived in the wheat fields of Oklahoma as a youngster. My father was a skeet champion, and I loved shotguns, rifles, or damn near anything that got me out of the house and away from Mother.

Gunny Mitchell and Sergeant DeHaas had a world of shooting experience under their belts, and they tried to give us pointers that would make us more effective marksmen and snipers. Small tips like working closer to the enemy before taking a shot made good sense to me. I had heard stories about snipers shooting enemy troops a mile away. At a mile, no one can possibly tell whether the target is a man or woman or a child, and I'll stake my life on that. And I could easily walk a half mile closer and then crawl another quarter mile closer before taking the shot.

Gunny Mitchell told us to always identify the quarry because when you shoot the enemy "point element" in a rifle platoon or company and you end up surrounded and trapped, you shouldn't feel sorry for yourself because you were stupid enough to take a shot when you didn't know what was facing you. My shooting partner at sniper school, Dennis O. Bolton, would get killed taking a shot exactly like that in blind terrain.

Sergeant DeHaas and Gunny Mitchell wanted to take as much of the guesswork as possible out of the situations we would face in combat. Reading the wind in terms of quarter, half, and full effects or values was critical. The instructors also went through the litany on wind speed, where grass blades bend at three to five miles per hour wind force, bushes and small trees bend and sway at eight to ten mph, larger trees and limbs at twelve to fifteen mph, and a small pennant or flag will stand straight out and flutter wildly at twenty to twenty-five mph. All these signs are indications that help the sniper adjust his windage or "hold-off" into the wind, whether its direction is from the right or left flank and is of quarter, half, or full force. Gunny emphasized that the best way to learn to shoot into the wind was to practice on windy days.

The Marine Corps has always emphasized "hands on" training, and the true test is as close to real life as possible practical training. In combat, as my distinguished company commander, Captain Jerry Doherty, once said, "Culbertson, remember in combat on operations like Tuscaloosa there are no do-overs. You got to live with your mistakes and pray like hell you have some good luck along the way." Captain Doherty was forced into a practically unavoidable situation during the river crossing on Operation Tuscaloosa, but his cool head, and timely help from his NCOs—Gunny Huzak, Manny Ybarra, Luther Hamilton, Roberto Gutierrez—as well as Ron Willoughby and Vaughn Nickell, saved the day if not every man.

I mention many of the Marines' names because they were all so unselfish in risking their lives to save their friends, and to convey the message that team effort and brotherhood in combat, make the Marines special. No Marine is greater than another, and a rifle company or team of snipers lives or dies as one unit. Operation

Tuscaloosa taught me that. Common valor is indeed a common virtue in the Marines, and never in my experience was that more so than among the men pinned down on the sandbar at the river crossing the morning of January 26, 1967, which we'll get to later.

Anyway, it's an honor to write about the heroism and dedication of great marksmen like Mitchell, DeHaas, and Sergeant Thomas Casey, who have become legends in their own time among the snipers of the 5th Marine Regiment. As I chronicled the missions, operations, and deeds of these great shooters, I feel that part of these men has filtered into my psyche and my soul. It's not easy to stay alive with a thousand-dollar bounty on your head and every enemy sniper aching to get a shot off in your direction. Training can only teach a sniper so much, but without it, very few Marines would have had the overall effectiveness and knowledge to make the 5th Marines Snipers the number one killers in the jungle war that pitted their elite hunters against ours.

For the record, the Viet Cong and NVA fielded some of the finest sniper teams in history. When it came to field craft, silent movement, camouflage, noise discipline, and tactics, the Communist snipers were superior to anyone on the battlefield. The Marines combatted the VC and NVA jungle skills with accurate and deadly marksmanship, courage, better weaponry, and the quick ability to learn how to play the game.

One final point before I plunge you into the paddies and drag you up elephant-grass-studded slopes in search of Charlie: There is no second place in this game of cat and mouse. There is only life and death and the opportunity to continue playing!

CHAPTER THREE

5th Marine Snipers Chu Lai, Vietnam Corporal Ronald R. Willoughby

Ron Willoughby was born after World War II ended and his father returned to Cleveland, Ohio, after serving in the U.S. Army. The environment in postwar Cleveland was one of fast-growing factories and plants producing the niceties of peacetime for a growing population of baby boomers, and Ron's upbringing valued hard work, devotion to God, and, most of all, a strong sense of patriotic duty. Academic subjects were not difficult for the intelligent and eager boy who was tall, straight, and strong, hinting at the athletic prowess he would soon enjoy as quarterback for the West High School football team. Ron learned that hard play and faith in his teammates translated into victory on the gridiron. Later, in Vietnam, Ron Willoughby would trust his closest Marine brothers to back his play when the 5th Marines went into action.

To a lot of American teenagers who knew about World War II, the U.S. Marines exemplified the epitome of bravery in combat. And as a kid who went to the movies, Ron watched John Wayne hit the beach in *Sands of Iwo Jima* until he knew every scene by heart. When his time came to serve his country, he did not hesitate to join. It was 1966, and he'd been out of high school for one year.

Ron reported to the Marine Corps Recruit Depot (MCRD) in San Diego, California, in the spring of 1966. After twelve weeks of grueling training, he graduated and entered the Infantry Training Regiment at Camp Pendleton, also in California. The high note of his boot camp experience was his three weeks of marksmanship training at the Edson Rifle Range north of the MCRD. Ron took to the instruction naturally, and became an expert rifleman with the battle-proven M-14.

The history and traditions of Marine riflemen in America's wars had sparked PFC Willoughby's imagination, and he increasingly longed for a chance to prove his mettle in the growing conflict of the Vietnam War. The first combat Marines were already returning to the United States with stories of hard-fought battles like Harvest Moon near the Da Nang Marine complex in I Corps. Ron visited the library and read about the ancient cities that had become the battlegrounds for the Chinese, Japanese, French, and finally the Americans as they invaded Vietnam to destroy the spread of Communism. The invaders also introduced the Vietnamese to Coca-Cola and McDonald's hamburgers.

It seemed to Ron that the South Vietnamese had been victimized by every foreign power that had set foot in the country, which had once been an ancient kingdom. Most foreigners had come in search of silk, rubber, oil, rice, and, above all, cheap and plentiful labor. It seemed that the hardworking peasants always got the short end of the stick when the fruits of their labors were apportioned.

Now, the Communist forces were descending upon the peasant villages to rescue them from their misery. The rub was that the peaceful agrarian villagers were the hardest hit by the Communist programs designed to purge the old capitalist regime from control of the rice production and its distribution in South Vietnam. Fueled by the vast rice harvest in the south, the North Vietnamese planned to invade through the Demilitarized Zone and from roads and footpaths leading off the Ho Chi Minh Trail, which slashed across the Vietnamese countryside. Villages and peasants who stood in the way of the North Vietnamese Army's juggernaut were terrorized and brought under the yoke of virtual slavery. South Vietnam's intellectual leaders and politicians were exterminated, along with the educated classes of military commanders, which desperately needed leadership and training support from the Americans. This situation was perfect for a leader like Ron Willoughby, who believed, like many present-day Vietnam veterans, that "goodness and right prevails."

After infantry training at Pendleton, Ron was given orders to the Marine Corps Sea School, where he would be trained in the traditions and etiquette of the U.S. Navy, allowing him to serve in a Marine detachment aboard a naval aircraft carrier or perhaps a battleship like the newly recommissioned USS *New Jersey*. His duties would be to provide ship's security and guard the captain and staff officers. Few young gung-ho Marines would choose to ride the waves in undress blues and polished brass when they could serve in combat with a rifle company, and fortunately for Ron, his orders were cancelled as the troop requirements for the growing shooting war in Vietnam took precedence over all Marine Corps troop deployments. As a result, Ron soon found himself back at Camp Pendleton with an 0311 military occupational specialty (Infantry—Rifleman). He was immediately transferred to Staging Battalion, where new personnel underwent a month-long crash course in jungle warfare.

The school emphasized weapons familiarization and

tactics used by the Viet Cong and NVA. Specific exercises included recognizing booby traps, punji pits, and other dangers that Marines would encounter in jungle warfare against the most experienced jungle fighters on earth. The North Vietnamese and the Viet Cong—under the name Viet Minh—had been almost constantly at war since 1946, more than twenty years, with the Japanese, Chinese, and French. The Communist officers and squad leaders would labor to teach the Americans and their allies how to fight a guerrilla war for the next ten years. For their part, the American command and junior officers and staff NCOs would give the Communists a lesson in courage, the tactical use of artillery, and airpower.

Ron Willoughby wanted to demonstrate the old school marksmanship techniques and close combat fighting skills that had made the United States Marines the most feared assault infantry in the world. He thought of the old 5th Marines of Belleau Wood and Chateau-Thierry fame, who had brought seasoned German troops to their knees with cries of "Die Teufelhoundes." He desperately wanted some of the "Honeur de la Guerre" that had stamped the veteran Marines of Guadalcanal and Okinawa with their brash demeanor and haughty stares, which told the world that other soldiers might indeed be heroes in many wars long forgotten. Simply, that the Leathernecks were at the top of their class. Their swagger and confidence was born of sweat and blood, shed on the most hard-fought, desperate battlefields in the world. They were America's "Old Guard," and they were confident of advancing into the smoke and chaos of Vietnam just as they had always gone marching to the sounds of the guns.

Snapping out of his momentary daydream, Ron Willoughby heard his name called as his orders were read by the company gunnery sergeant. Along with ninety percent of his buddies, Ron was headed for

WESTPAC (Western Pacific Command), or in the local gyrene jargon, "Nam."

Ron returned to his barracks and called his family. He packed his seabag and, wearing all-leather stateside boots, waited for the shuttle to Los Angeles for his flight to Vietnam—the land of the rice paddy daddy and Victor Charlie, and his cousins from the North Vietnamese Army. By early October the California skies were gray and rain was forecast. Ten thousand miles away in Da Nang the temperature was 95 degrees and there wasn't a cloud in the sky. The chartered Boeing 707 refueled in Guam, where the winter winds had yet to arrive. Then they were back into the clouds for a few precious hours of meditation before Pandora's box would fly open, casting more American souls onto the hot black tarmac at the Da Nang Airfield to face the killing fields of Vietnam.

Ron Willoughby deplaned and formed up in loose ranks where a welcoming officer with a clipboard in hand addressed the faithful who were craning their heads forward in anticipation of hearing their newly assigned units for the next thirteen months. As an 0311, Ron would be going to a combat unit, perhaps along the shell-pocked slopes south of the DMZ. Marines even now were slugging it out toe-to-toe with the NVA, which was pushing hardcore combat units farther southward for an eventual attempt at the encirclement of Saigon and ultimate victory.

The major reached for a megaphone and offered any Marines who had been designated as expert on the rifle range back in the States the opportunity to volunteer for the newly established Scout-Sniper Program. He explained that top shooters were being selected for the 5th Marine Regiment Sniper Platoon headquartered in Chu Lai, forty-five miles south of Da Nang down Highway 1. Ron knew this was his chance. Instinctively, as he'd faced every challenge in his young life, he raised his hand and shouted out his name and rank to the major. Only two other Marines volunteered. One man wore glasses, which was an instant disqualification, and the other Marine changed his mind when his buddies told him that the odds of getting wounded or killed were almost a certainty in the Fightin' 5th Marines. Ron Willoughby stood by his seabag as sweat ran down his face and soaked the heavy dungaree utilities that stateside Marines wore to Vietnam.

"Son, are you sure you want to volunteer for the snipers?" the major asked. "You know what Chesty Puller taught you men about volunteering." All the troopers looked at Ron as if he were nuts and shook their heads, inching away from their demented brother.

Ron spoke up as they awaited his response, "Sure enough, Major. I set my sights on being a sniper in ITR. Hell yes, sir. I volunteer!"

CHAPTER FOUR

VC Sapper Attack Marine Corps Base, Chu Lai Sergeant Tom Casey

The major finished reading the lists of Marines and their assigned units. The FNGs (fucking new guys) were parceled out to all the line companies in the 1st Marine Division. Marines were posted to the 1st, 2nd, and 3rd Battalions of the 1st Marine Regiment north of Da Nang, the 5th Marine Regiment at Chu Lai, and the 7th Marine Regiment at Da Nang. Each of these three regiments were hungry for new recruits as they pushed their Tactical Area of Responsibility ever farther into Communist-held territory.

Ron received his official orders to 5th Marine Snipers, grabbed his gear, and headed to the air traffic control shack to await his hop to Chu Lai, directly to the south. An hour later he boarded a hard-ridden C-130 transport flown by a couple of Air Force captains. He stowed his gear along the plane's cavernous bulkhead and parked his butt in the nylon mesh troop seats hung off the fuselage's interior. The rear loading ramp closed as the Hercules taxied to the north-south auxiliary strip, throttled up, and lifted off into the pale sky. In twenty minutes the plane sliced down and bounced onto the tarmac at Chu Lai. Ron deplaned into the afternoon heat and walked to a waiting six-by-six transport truck for the short run north up Highway 1 to Tam Ky.

The trip was hot, and a red mud mask covered Willoughby as he jumped from the truck bed and stared at the sign that pointed to the 5th Marine Headquarters on Hill 35. He learned that the small Marine base had been attacked the previous night, and that a small Viet Cong sapper unit had been caught in the defensive concertina wire and slaughtered by concentrated machine-gun and rifle fire. Ron and the few Marines who had made the trip to Tam Ky were jarred by the harsh reality and instant brutality of the war, which was breathing a cold, sobering blast against their exposed necks. He would never forget the horrid spectacle of the death-tossed enemy corpses, which shocked him out of his youthful naiveté.

The next day, at regimental headquarters, Willoughby was confirmed in his future role as a member of 5th Marine Regiment Snipers. His buddy who had trained with him since ITR (Infantry Training Regiment) was Bob Przybysz, who received orders to the 5th Marine Regimental Security Platoon. Over the next seven months Bob Przybysz would keep Willoughby tuned in on the regiment's future operational plans, and in particular those tasks involving sniper deployment.

Willoughby also met up with the senior sergeant, who was NCOIC of the 5th Marines Sniper Platoon. Tom Casey hailed from South Carolina and had attended the Citadel as a cadet prior to joining the Marines, in a rush to see action in the fast-developing Vietnam War. Both Willoughby and Casey were high expert shooters in boot camp. Casey had also spent a tour on the U.S. Marine Service Rifle Team with Gunnery Sergeant Mitchell before they transferred overseas to WESTPAC. He would become Willoughby's mentor and set the example for combat marksmanship and raw courage under fire for the remainder of their time in Vietnam.

Willoughby considered Sergeant Casey the finest combat sniper he had seen operate during the war, but it was the southerner's natural leadership and constant watchfulness that Willoughby employed to fine-tune his own sniper techniques. These character traits made Casey the ideal sniper commander. Willoughby recalls that out of the approximate forty ambushes he participated in, most of them were led by Casey personally.

Actual in-the-field presence and leadership by the officer in charge is the leadership trait that most impresses the troops under an NCO's command. When an officer sends his troops into harm's way without being present in a leadership capacity, with the personal risk that entails, the troops sense a vacuum in the command leader's slot and immediately lose confidence in him. When Ron Willoughby or Tom Casey led the sniper platoon's Marines into combat on major operations or on patrols, they joined their men and accepted the risks of death or injury with them. Sometimes Casey and Willoughby would carry the M-14 rifle and binoculars of the sniper team spotter to coach young shooters in the field on their first ambushes or stalks against bunkered weapons crews or enemy snipers. The snipers also joined most major operations with the line companies whose grunts did most of the close combat fighting and dying in Vietnam.

Willoughby's first combat mission with Tom Casey took place in early November 1966. Casey had been working with him on marksmanship skills and ambush techniques and felt that it was time to take their classroom training to the field. Orders came to take command of an infantry outpost and sentinel security bunker half a kilometer in front of the 11th Marines artillery pits. The snipers were ordered to screen the artillery crews from exposure to sniper fire and the ever-present possibility of being overrun during a nighttime sapper attack.

A combat regiment's artillery is always a primary target for attack by sappers. Marine rifle companies cannot patrol without protection from the artillery fan because of their inability to avoid ambush or enemy attack, which was disguised by the Viet Cong's natural blending with the village populations and careful night deployment using tunnels, riverbeds, and the cloaking anonymity of the jungle itself. The Viet Cong commanders also feared the Marines' skill and deadly accuracy with their artillery component. Many VC units had felt the Leathernecks fall under the hammer of their well-conceived ambushes and minefield traps, only to witness the horrifying deadly power of crushing high-explosive artillery shells falling on their men.

Marine artillery counterfire freed the Marine infantry to close to hand-to-hand fighting range, where no army could face that surge of death and destruction and survive. As a result, the Marine artillery batteries were always the main target for the Viet Cong, and the new emplacements at Chu Lai were especially vulnerable to the stealth and swiftness of a sapper attack. The sapper team's high explosive charges could be set off under the guns, and the destruction would be total. The sappers themselves were always drugged and willing to give their lives away in a successful attack that promised to vanquish these new American enemies from their homeland. In the People's Army of Vietnam, the Communists only dared to embrace total victory, and the cost of that effort in manpower was considered inconsequential, if the price in human lives was considered at all.

Tom Casey asked for "volunteers" to man the ambush outpost. Ron Willoughby and Denny Toncar were "volunteered" and reported directly to the Regimental

Security Platoon. The outpost was cut into the side of a small hill that sloped away from the artillery emplacements. The hillside gradually fanned out like a giant mushroom, facing the rice paddies and treelines that made a checkerboard quilt and blanketed the approaches to the Marine positions as far as the eye could see. There were five two-man bunkers dug into the hillside about fifteen meters apart, with each Marine armed with an M-14 rifle and a shit pot full of M-26 grenades. There was a hard-line communication system and comm phone that connected directly back to the command bunker in the center of the defensive fan.

The standard operation procedure (SOP) was for each Marine to stand two-hour watches until relieved by his partner, and so on through the night. Every quarter hour each individual bunker would report its situation report, giving an "All clear," or if something unusual was sighted, "Bunker Three reports noise and movement at eight o'clock." The outpost command would immediately relay the status of the entire perimeter on the Regimental Security Command Radio Net. Falling asleep at your post during wartime is considered a court-martial offense punishable by death, but in the Marine Corps, unit leaders usually improvise and concoct a punishment that is worse than death.

The following night brought one of the typical early monsoon deluges so despised by Marine sentries and loved by the Viet Cong, who used the torrential sheets of gray, freezing rain to shield their stealthy advances into American perimeters to wreak havoc. Sergeant Casey monitored the radio closely at Security Platoon Headquarters, and by 0200 hours all posts had reported all clear, except post five on the right-hand finger of the slope. Casey grabbed his helmet, an M-14, and shoved a fresh magazine into the magwell, slipping his red-clay-encrusted flak jacket over his shoulders.

Casey glanced at his bunker mate's astonishment and said, "Listen to the radio closely while I'm checking out post number five on the forward outpost. We got no radio communication from the security team. I pray to God that their dead dyin' asses got a busted phone and they ain't sleepin'." With long, forceful strides Casey slammed past the screen door to the duty hut and disappeared into the sheets of rain that fell like stinging pellets into the red clay mud.

After walking almost blindly down the company road past the artillery pits and out into the field surrounding the base outside the perimeter wire, Casey approached the bunkers of the security force from their rear. Unchallenged, he sought out the farthest bunker on the slope of the hill's starboard periphery. As he approached, he could see only one helmet visible in the hole, with a glistening rain-covered poncho over bent shoulders. Casey threw caution to the wind and jumped into the hole, knocking the sleeping Marine into the mud. He stared into the man's frightened eyes, grabbed his poncho and started strangling him. The sentry's buddy awoke and jumped on Casey until the livid sergeant turned his head and bore down with red-hot coals for eyes.

"Private, why is this asshole asleep on watch? Is he trying to kill my Marines because he is a lazy shithead and cannot keep awake!" Casey had alerted the other bunkers, and a corporal came over with Ron Willoughby and gazed in disbelief at the Marine who lay in the muddy wash at the bottom of bunker number five.

The next night saw Sergeant Tom Casey stake the offending private out on a listening post a hundred meters in front of the security outpost. When the sleepyhead Marine asked Casey how he was to report his sitrep since he was not to carry a radio, Casey told him to yell loud and clear, otherwise the VC would get him and carve his young ass up. When the Marine asked Casey what he was supposed to yell if the Viet Cong attacked him, Casey just smiled and said, "Yell a little bit louder and we'll come get your worthless ass if we ain't got anything better to do."

Sergeant Tom Casey always found a way to get the message across to his Marines that certain "fuck-ups" could cost more than your life. Sleeping on watch in the field or at base perimeter guard duty could cost everyone their lives. Needless to say, the message was received loud and clear, and the Marines of the 5th Marine Sniper Platoon learned that the stocky sergeant from the Citadel was all business when it meant success or failure in battle.

CHAPTER FIVE

Night Ambush, Chu Lai
Tom Casey and
Vaughn Nickell

In December the 5th Regiment Snipers moved north from Chu Lai to positions around An Hoa. Tom Casey had teams of snipers running ambush missions to harass the Viet Cong from the Marine firebase at Phu Loc 6, north of An Hoa. Marine patrols had taken increasing casualties in the Arizona Territory north of Liberty Bridge. The enemy was utilizing small patrols of infantry, with three-man sniper cells attached, to await the daily Marine sweeps in concealed ambush sites along the river. The hilly landscape of the Arizona Territory that jutted up from the terraced rice fields and treelines surrounding the myriad villages provided perfectly camouflaged ambush positions. These warrens and caves were unrecognizable from the approach trails until the Marines stumbled into the kill zones laid out by the VC.

The Viet Cong would usually initiate an attack first with deadly sniper fire at chosen patrol members. The VC were skilled at targeting and wounding or killing the patrol radioman who stood out with the tall radio antenna jutting from the AN/PRC10 radio on his backpack. The radioman was almost always followed by the NCOIC (noncommissioned officer in charge), or when the patrol was platoon-size, an officer (the platoon commander) would walk behind the radioman.

Viet Cong snipers fielded the antiquated but highly accurate 1940s-era Moishin-Nagant bolt action rifle in 7.62 × 54 millimeter Russian caliber. The Moishin-Nagant fired a 175-grain spitzer bullet that left the muzzle at over 2,600 feet per second and would still carry accurately downrange to three hundred meters at two thousand feet per second. The VC sniper techniques always utilized static positions, or hides where a known distance was already dialed into their 3.5 power PU scopes. They were patient and resourceful.

After a Marine patrol was sighted walking through a village or along a trail bordering a rice paddy, the peasants passed the word along to the Viet Cong, who were most likely their sons, brothers, or cousins. Once the patrol was identified as to the number of Marines, the type of weapons, the direction of march, and any other pertinent information like unit identity and experience in the field, the VC selected a prepared ambush site down the trail. They fortified their position with fresh cover and concealed their numbers skillfully while taking advantage of observation points and fields of fire.

When the Marine patrol arrived at the ambush point, the Viet Cong remained silent and motionless while the Marines crossed the kill zone. The VC snipers would be the first to fire, sometimes after a command-detonated mine or booby trap was set off to confuse the patrol members. The Viet Cong snipers would target the point scout first, to confuse and deflect the order of march, causing panic and confusion farther down the column. Next, the radioman and patrol commander would be targeted, to disrupt command and control within the patrol and cut off communication to the nearest Marine base and artillery or air support. This support was the VC's main fear, since the killing radius of An Hoa's

105mm and 155mm guns was wide enough and powerful enough to penetrate the strongest bunkers.

Once the Viet Cong had fired their individual targeting sniper weapons, they would rake the kill zone with automatic rifle fire from their AK-47 rifles. Sometimes they carried stolen American weapons, like Browning Automatic Rifles and M-14s. Some of these weapons were even likely former U.S.-provided weapons that had been given to the Nationalist Chinese under Chiang Kai-shek during World War II and resurfaced to torment the Marines. After trying to wound or kill Marines who were still crawling to cover and trying to get their bearings, the VC would break off the engagement before American firepower was returned.

The Viet Cong preparation and strategy required careful planning and immediate action on the part of the Marines, to provide a deterrent that would be effective and could be implemented in time to break up the ambush. The officers of the 5th Marines had concluded that the best way to fight these ambushes set by the VC was with Marine countersniper teams that would be attached to as many patrols as possible. When the patrols came under fire, the snipers marching in the middle of the column could deploy to return accurate fire upon the Viet Cong marksmen. Sometimes the Marine sniper team would drop off from the patrol's main body as a rice paddy was crossed or an open trail taken up. The snipers would scan the treelines and hillsides that lay ahead with their binoculars and rifle scopes, hoping to pick up movement in the deep jungle where no human eye could discern it but high-powered optics could pierce the shadows.

Sergeant Tom Casey was ordered to the duty hut and received his new patrol orders. He was to handpick teams of two Marines—one shooter with the scoped M1-D sniper rifle and one spotter with an M-14 and binoculars—to accompany patrols and provide counter-sniper protection. Casey had never operated from the rear, and like all great combat Marines, he preferred to lead his men on patrols until their skills and experience level allowed them the confidence to take on the Viet Cong man-to-man.

Tom Casey had received advanced marksmanship training after firing "high shooter" on the A course at Parris Island in 1964. He had joined L Company, 3rd Battalion, 2nd Marine Regiment, at Camp Lejune, North Carolina. He shot on the rifle team with the 2nd Marines at the Eastern Division matches, and later the National Rifle Association matches at the North Carolina State Championships. He finally went to school and was trained as a unit Marksmanship Instructor with a Military Occupational Specialty (MOS) of 8531. Later, in 1965, Casey attended and graduated from Battalion Sniper School. Due to the buildup in Vietnam, many of the 0311 (Infantry) Marines from the 2nd Marine Division were trained intensely in all phases of infantry operations and jungle survival. The result was that Casey was transferred to Camp Pendleton, California, for combat duty in Vietnam. After arriving at Pendleton, he underwent forty-five days of jungle training at Camp Pulgas, where he learned the basics of the unorthodox but battle-proven tactics that the Viet Cong were using against the small contingent of Marines near Da Nang.

On June 10, 1966, Sergeant Casey and 170 Marines who had flown from San Francisco to Okinawa changed planes and made the two-hour hop to Vietnam. By July the 5th Marine Sniper Platoon was being formed on Hill 35 south of Chu Lai.

Casey first tested the basic tactics of countersniper warfare near Chu Lai when he was dropped off as his patrol was rounding a jungle-cloaked hillside. Casey took up a camouflaged hide under the shadows of the thick overgrowth alongside the main trail. The Marines of the squad-size patrol strode along the upper reaches of the trail toward a village veiled in the hazy afternoon light. Casey waited, his rifle sweeping the open fields as the patrol ran across a series of paddy dikes into a treeline five hundred meters away. When the first shots from the Viet Cong sniper cell exploded in the afternoon silence, one of the Marines was wounded and crumpled by the trail.

Casey snugged his M1-D into his shoulder, focusing his sights on the general area of jungle where the muzzle blast had flared. As the sniper came up for a second shot, Casey held a yard high and squeezed the trigger. The powerful 30.06 shell tore from the muzzle and slammed through foliage and bamboo into the sniper lair. Casey's trusty old Garand sniper rifle bucked and then settled back on target for his second shot. Casey fired a third time, and the whack of the bullet was audible as the Viet Cong sniper was snatched from his hole's parapet and dashed against his partner in a torrent of blood from the gaping hole through the center of his chest. The VC fire lifted immediately and the paddies grew still again, except for the humming of dragonflies, while the hot glare of the sun broke through the light clouds and haze.

The wounded Marine had only been scratched and would hump into camp with his buddies. Tom Casey and his spotter, Lance Corporal Vaughn Nickell, rose up with wide grins from their leafy hide and quick-time marched up the trail to rejoin their patrol members. Casey thought to himself that the game of countersniping might just work out in the Marines' favor after all. Casey knew the Marines shot straighter and had more courage than the Viet Cong, but he also felt deep down inside that there could have been two Viet Cong sniper teams out in that far treeline, and likely that he and Vaughn Nickell might very well be dead by now. Little did Casey and Nickell realize how prophetic those feelings were until later in the war, when they would face off against the much better trained and deliberate Viet Cong main force snipers and their cold-blooded cousins from the Gulf of Tonkin, the North Vietnamese.

Casey and Nickell worked the next few days with Alpha and then Bravo Companies of the 1st Battalion, 5th Marines. They recorded one kill on a Viet Cong soldier who had exposed more of his upper torso than was prudent after his ambush team had fired upon Casey's patrol. Nickell had shot the VC from two hundred meters offhand (standing) after the first flight of enemy bullets had flown harmlessly overhead.

The ease with which Tom Casey and his spotter had broken the back of a half-dozen ambushes could have created overconfidence, which would have proved reckless and dangerous in a younger Marine. Casey had always believed that underestimating your enemy could prove fatal, and while at the Citadel he had studied the many blunders by the Union Army in the Civil War where tattered Confederate forces had used stealth and surprise to overwhelm and decimate their better-equipped foe. Sergeant Tom Casey was a true soldier, bred and schooled, and if he was dead set on anything, it was getting his men and himself back home alive.

Casey was also given a new responsibility due to his southern conservatism and his ability to adapt and improvise. He would be tasked with taking one or two sniper teams out on roving ambushes to counter Viet Cong attacks against the base at Chu Lai. His ambush forays would continue later at An Hoa and in the Arizona Territory.

In November 1966 the gun pits of the 11th Marines 155mm howitzer battery had been attacked by Viet Cong suicide troops called sappers. The enemy soldiers had crawled up to the wire of the camp at Chu Lai through the paddies and muddy clay. Using box mines and crude bamboo bangalore torpedoes, which they had shoved under the Marine wire obstructions, the sappers had blown a jeep-size hole through the double apron of concertina wire. The sapper commander had then rushed his demolition teams directly at the artillery pieces and set off several charges, trying to destroy or disable the big guns. Several of the giant howitzers were extensively damaged.

Afterward, Sergeant Casey deployed his teams to act as outpost sentinels and ambush teams. A few nights later, he and Vaughn Nickell crept out through the wire around 2200 hours and along the trail, negotiating the short dikes of the rice paddies leading north of the camp and out toward the first villages a klick into the countryside. The trail was muddy under their Vibram-soled jungle boots, and they cradled their rifles carefully in the crooks of their arms, ready to go into action if compromised.

After two hundred meters of slow crouching and stumbling in the inky darkness, they reached a long rise of foothills that lay like a giant mushroom dividing the main section of rice paddies. A third of the way up the plant-encrusted slope, Casey found what he was looking for—a small crevasselike fold in the earth. The sniper team blended into the hillside, and to any outside observer would have disappeared completely. Casey and Nickell both stayed wide-awake and divided the sector of the camp wire into a left and right section, which each man scanned back and forth, never focusing too long on any one place. When the eyes lock on a single spot in intense darkness, a sniper can conjure all sorts of things, like nonexistent enemy sappers and patrols. Casey looked for movement and restrained himself from fantasizing.

In a short while his night vision improved and the lights of the camp sparkled, casting an eerie glow over the hooches and coils of barbed wire along the base's lines. It seemed as if hours had passed, but it was just fifteen minutes later when a scratching sound reached Casey's tuned-in ears. It sounded like something was being dragged or pulled through the dirt toward the lines. Casey and Nickell strained their eyes harder and saw the rough shapes of men crawling toward the wire and the artillery gun pits. The dark shapes moved for a short distance in a smooth crawl and then lay silent. The scratching sounds became more audible as Casey focused on the packs or bags that the men were pulling.

Then it hit him like a hammer. It wasn't imaginings or blurred vision from watching the wire too closely or too long. He was watching Viet Cong sappers headed for the gunpits—and they were close. Too close for comfort!

Casey grabbed his rifle, realizing that if he fired, he'd be caught in the teeth of the Marine counterfire from the security bunkers, which were armed with M-60 machine guns and M-79 grenade launchers. Recognizing that it was a desperately fragile situation, he wracked his brain to come up with a solution.

Sergeant Casey looked at Vaughn Nickell and back at the sappers. Jesus, they were at the wire now! Casey whispered to Nickell, cupping his mouth—knowing that if they were discovered, they were both dead men. He whispered, "Please tell me you still got those two willy-pete grenades you carry on you?"

Vaughn Nickell felt along his cartridge belt in the fear-soaked darkness. Under the sheets of perspiration running down his sides from under his arms, he felt the lumps of the grenades he always wore inside an old canteen cover fastened to his utility belt.

Casey coughed and sputtered against Nickell's face, "Well dammit, Vaughn give me one of 'em, for chrissake!"

Nickell fumbled with the snap to the canteen pouch

and finally produced the grenades, slipping one into Casey's tense hand.

Casey brushed the sweat from his eyes with the sleeve of his jungle jacket and looked at Nickell's boyish face dimly lit in the camp's glow. "Okay, man," he said, "here's what we do. We pull the pins together and heave the fucking grenades as far down the hill as we can. When they blow, the grunts on the lines will see the gooks and hopefully kill the bastards. If the gooks run our way, we can shoot them or just lay dog and hope they miss us. What do you think?"

Nickell took another look at the slithery forms converging on the wire. "We got to throw the grenades now!" he said. "I don't know what the hell to do after that! Maybe pray."

Tom Casey thought that perhaps Vaughn Nickell was a touch smarter than the average trooper after all. Both men pulled the grenades and readied to throw. Then, as one man, they let fly. The two grenades bounced and hopped for what seemed an eternity down the small rise of the hill until they exploded in the most brilliant flash of white light imaginable.

The grunts' eyes must have been blinded by the bursting shards of phosphorous that cut eerie trails of platinum light into the dark sky. The Viet Cong sappers were exposed and blew their initial charges, only to shoulder their weapons and try to fight their way into the perimeter. The Marine machine guns coughed and spit fiery bands of tracers into the Viet Cong sapper platoon. Bullets and the bursts of HE grenades (high explosive) from the M-79 grenade launchers made the miniature battlefield a smoke-filled hell. After five chaotic, bloody minutes the Viet Cong withdrew under the firepower of their AK-47 rifles and the curtain of smoke and confusion from the explosives and grenades.

Casey and Nickell watched the spectacle of fire and

death from their earthen perch above the danger. It seemed their quick thinking had saved the day when a pair of VC soldiers stumbled by their haven on the hillside. The Viet Cong were running so fast they never saw Casey or Nickell, but the two Marines saw them. Together, they raised their rifles and sighted in on the Viet Cong soldiers' backs as they ran and fired a point-blank group of rounds into each man. Sergeant Casey whistled under his breath as the two flights of bullets tore through the VC and tossed their broken bodies like rag dolls along the trail.

Then Casey and Nickell looked at each other and rose, quick-timing it back toward the Marine lines and safety. When Casey yelled out, "Marine patrol coming in," he was so high on adrenaline that he couldn't have remembered the password even if it would have kept girls out of the Citadel.

CHAPTER SIX

Sniper Operation at An Hoa
Sergeants Tom Casey and Ron Willoughby

By November the 5th Marine Snipers were fielding eleven two-man teams. For the most part, they stood security for the 11th Marine Artillery Camp and ran night ambushes and some day patrols, with the grunts trying to interdict Viet Cong troop movements and stop sapper attacks. Sergeant Casey had proved his worth sending his teams in and out of the bush. His snipers were gaining confidence and jungle instincts that would serve his Marines well when they were asked to provide the "long rifle" support to the infantry during the regimental-size battles that were inevitable in 1967.

A new commanding officer ordered Sergeant Casey into the duty hut, and on November 13, 1966, the Security Platoon was secured. Sergeant Casey was given command of the 5th Marine Regimental Snipers Platoon on a permanent basis, and was tasked with training all new sniper recruits, keeping the teams fit for combat, and rotating ambush teams and patrols. He used the military experience he'd gained at the Citadel as a cadet and led as many ambushes as he could, instilling proper techniques of night movement, noise discipline, and above all, the common sense to know when to fire at the enemy or when silence and caution were necessary.

One instant result of Casey's leadership was that young snipers like Vaughn Nickell and Ron Willoughby realized their leader knew his business. Further, no one doubted Casey's bravery or his dedication and ability to lead their troops on major operations when the opportunities for combat distinction or death were equally obvious. However, few if any combat officers led the daily procession of "win the hearts and minds" patrols into the hamlets and through the rice fields past workers bent over their mud-laced labors, where the booby traps and the quick-kill ambushes were the daily practice of the Viet Cong. Tom Casey felt that the Officer Corps was obfuscating its duty by failing to observe firsthand how effective sniping could protect a patrol by eliminating or harassing the enemy sniper's ambush threat, which was a constant worry to the NCOs who led the great majority of combat patrols.

Tom Casey's men were akin to the Old West gunfighters who carved notches on the butts of their rifle stocks everytime a desperado fell to their blazing gunfire. Casey had started the makings of a Marine Corps legend. He knew that the move north to An Hoa would make or break the sniper platoon as an effective combat force operating with already combat-proven infantry units.

On January 3, 1967, Casey, Willoughby, Nickell, and Jim Flynn from Utica, Illinois—who alternated with Nickell as Casey's spotter when the platoon sergeant went on a combat patrol—boarded a C-130 to Da Nang before straightening out their itinerary to An Hoa. The old regional village of An Hoa was home to an Army of South Vietnam (ARVN) company, but was relatively unknown and new to the Marines. An Hoa was approximately twenty-five miles southwest of Da Nang and served as the westernmost Marine combat headquarters in I Corps. To the northeast were the Song Thu Bon and Song Vu Gia rivers, which were main Viet Cong arteries for infiltration of both men and supplies into the An Hoa Basin. Tom Casey's 5th Marine Snipers would team up with the battle-hardened 2nd Battalion, 5th Marines, which was pulling out of the DMZ at Con Thien to establish a new base of operations at An Hoa, in the center of Quang Nam Province.

When the C-130 flared its flaps and descended into An Hoa, the short landing strip was slicked down by recent rainfall. The Air Force transport skidded to a stop and the snipers deplaned and stood staring at the jungle-cloaked hillsides of the Que Son Mountains ringing the southern boundary of the base. The northern vista was a sloping plain that wove itself into a quilt of rice fields that flanked the main highway, which jutted out of the base's perimeter wire apron and snaked far away toward Da Nang. The day was gray and cold, with mists hanging in the trees that tilted away toward the rice fields on the edge of the airstrip. A sharp wind blew across the tarmac from the northeast and spread an icy warning of unseen dangers to be found across the river in the Arizona Territory.

Tom Casey pulled the collar of his dirt-streaked utility jacket up snugly around his neck. He looked back into the plane's open hatch and motioned to Ron Willoughby to get the men off the plane and fall in on the runway for a quick weapon and gear inspection. Rumor had it that the snipers would be surveying (turning in) their old reliable M1-D sniper rifles, to be rearmed with the new Remington bolt action rifles. It would just be his luck, Casey thought, if someone forgot their cleaning gear or side-mounted scopes. The Marine Corps was hell on troops who failed to survey the exact equipment they had drawn from supply. Tom Casey laughed in the easy southern manner that could confuse a new sniper about his legendary toughness and discipline. He thought about the story he had heard in boot camp about the combat Marine who returned from Guadalcanal or some bloody World War II battle without his M-1 rifle. The platoon sergeant had asked Private "Numbnuts" how he had lost his rifle, and the private said a Japanese artillery shell had hit his position and when he raised his head his rifle was gone. "Just blown up, I guess!" The platoon sergeant told him that he was issued that rifle, and by God, that rifle was a part of him. That rifle was his life! "The next beach landing that the company makes," the old platoon sergeant continued to bark, "you will attack the Japanese holding on to only your pecker. I don't imagine you'll find a way to lose that!"

Sometimes the Marine Corps was hilarious. Tom Casey grinned about all the crazy stuff that happened in combat and how his snipers would make a joke out of the situation. Maybe they laughed just to keep from crying. If the rumors were anything near accurate, the sniper platoon's new adventures with some of the blood and guts commanders of the 2nd Battalion, 5th Marines, wouldn't generate much humor.

Casey gazed out into the gray and misty clouds that blanketed the river as the platoon fell into formation for a brief inspection. Later in the day after being assigned two hooches near the Headquarters section of the 2/5, he led his men to the battalion mess hall for a welcome meal of fried chicken and real mashed potatoes with brown gravy. A gunnery sergeant met Casey as the snipers were leaving chow and gave him orders to turn in the old Garand sniper rifles at battalion supply. Tom Casey, Vaughn Nickell, Ron Willoughby, and Jim Flynn plucked their M1-Ds from their cases for a last farewell to the rifles that had made the Marines invincible from

Guadalcanal, Iwo Jima, Saipan, and Pelileu to the Chosin Reservoir in Korea. This rifle was the old warhorse that had been adopted in 1936 and had served America well against all comers for thirty years. The new Remington Model 700s would have slick bolt actions honed by Marine armorers. The medium-heavy barrels were made by Douglas and were air gauged for accuracy. The barrels were free floated in walnut stocks with Monte Carlo cheek pieces. The trigger was a match Canjar setup that broke crisply at three pounds. Atop the receiver rested a new Redfield variable 3 × 9 power telescopic sight with coated lenses that prevented fogging and housed an internal range-finding grid. All in all, the Remington Sniper rifle in caliber .308 NATO was the finest weapon the Marine Corps had ever fielded in Vietnam.

But Casey wasn't entirely convinced that the rifle would outshoot a 1903 Springfield A-4 Sniper rifle—the kind the Marines had used to pick off Japs on Okinawa, and North Koreans along the frozen mountain passes of the Chosin Reservoir. A tuned-up 1903 A-4 Springfield in the hands of a proven combat sniper—not some Marine Corps paper target puncher—was accurate out to eight hundred yards, and maybe past a thousand if Gunnery Sergeant Mitchell was the shooter.

Casey wondered why all the clamor about target shooters was such a big deal anyway. It was a fact that a combat sniper had to understand much more about terrain, winds, weather characteristics, and the enemy than someone shooting a fixed course with a previously sighted-in weapon. After some of the havoc he'd seen caused by the veteran Viet Cong snipers, it was evident that knowledge and experience in actual combat situations was much more critical than the type of rifle employed. To date, the Viet Cong had killed far more Americans with sniper fire than the reverse. This was mainly a result of knowing the terrain and maximizing the element of surprise. The Viet Cong were masters of camouflage, and deceptive in constructing ambush sites and killing zones. They were also renowned for their patience and their stealth. Their equipment was decidedly inferior to American weaponry, ammunition quality, and ballistics, yet they were dominating the ambush opportunities probably ten to one.

Tom Casey was a brave, proud, and careful man, but above all, he and Willoughby were hunters and wouldn't settle for second place. On their first patrol in the Arizona, Casey took Willoughby along as spotter with a reinforced squad from Hotel Company. The patrol leader was Sergeant Manual Ybarra from Hotel's 3rd platoon.

A hard charging Mexican-American from southern New Mexico, Ybarra worked five hundred acres of wheat fields with his father, who farmed the old-fashioned way—with a pitchfork and plenty of sweat. Manny had grown up tough as shoe leather and wasn't bothered by the heat or the cold in Vietnam. Sergeant Ybarra struck out from An Hoa down the runway and through the sentry bunkers on the edge of the strip. He led his Marines through the double apron of concertina and down the muddy, red clay slope that served as the main artery tying An Hoa's supply lines to the distant Marine base at Da Nang. After two hours they passed the Marine outpost at Phu Loc 6, which held the high ground two hundred meters above the stretch of rice paddies that ran a kilometer or so to the east. At the end of the paddies the Song Thu Bon ran in a giant loop, starting south of An Hoa and extending north of Phu Loc 6. The river turned eastward less than half a kilometer from the back side of the northern perimeter of Phu Loc 6. Across the Song Thu Bon lay the expanse of the "Arizona Territory," or simply the "Arizona." In the Arizona Territory all men were assumed to be gunfighters, and the area had always been a "free-fire" zone, meaning anyone with a weapon was fair game. Snipers instinctively liked this type of setting since it readily lent itself to "beaucoup" (many) opportunities to smoke Charlie's ass.

Tom Casey and Willoughby knew that the combat in the Arizona Territory would bring an entirely new level of ferocity, compared to the ambushes and short, savage firefights experienced at Hill 35 near Chu Lai. The Marines forded the river on an old rope bridge and, watching carefully for mines and booby traps that could be uncovered by the monsoon rains, the snipers felt their way deeper into the jungled hills. Sergeant Ybarra stopped the column a klick farther up the rough village trail and told Casey and Willoughby to drop out of the column before they broke out into the next section of rice fields. Casey nodded and clutched the forearm of his Remington bolt gun, an olive drab green towel draped over the scope to keep the moisture at bay.

He had three-hundred-meter dope etched on the scope, marked by one clearly recognizable knife scratch into the metal surrounding the elevation knob. Two scratches cut into the black anodized aluminum identified the six-hundred-meter-elevation dope. If Casey got a chance to make a quick kill at five hundred meters, he would leave the three-hundred-meter dope on the scope, "hold off" above the target a yard, and still get a torso hit. The match grade 7.62mm bullets for the Remingtons had a heavy bullet weight of 168 grains and would readily carry the distance up to a thousand meters, with sufficient energy to kill the enemy. The sniper had to plan his shots, and Casey knew the cold weather would make the bullets drop in their trajectory faster than on hot summer days. A yard of elevation hold-off should be plenty out to five hundred meters, and the close-lying hillside and interspersed paddies wouldn't allow much more than five hundred for any shot.

Ron Willoughby led Casey off the trail through a small clearing and up a tight trail that wound up the hillside to their right. Looking back, Casey and Willoughby could see the patrol from Hotel Company winding its way across muddy rice paddy dikes into the heart of the Arizona Territory. A large village loomed across the distant paddies, and Casey tucked his sniper team into a leafy hide about two hundred feet up the hillside. His gaze swept across the paddies and noted the long treeline that had been planted to shield the rice fields from wind. The treeline was cloaked in a thick mist, and further exploration wasn't possible as the sniper's eyes ran along the paddies' edges, seeking movement. Ron Willoughby caressed the cold stock of his M-14 rifle and felt comfort in the knowledge that his rifle could also reach any enemy threat that presented itself in the valley below.

Abruptly, Casey glanced far away toward the village and realized that the patrol from Hotel was gone, winding its way somewhere into the hostile jungle too far away to help. Casey and Willoughby felt alone, and took comfort in each other's company and their proficiency with their weapons. Casey reflected a minute and smiled, recalling the stateside bullshit he'd heard about lone sharpshooters who had gone out alone for days on end and killed a multitude of enemy soldiers while escaping without a scratch on themselves or their rifle. Every war fostered such legends, both true and fictional. Vietnam was no different, but Casey felt sure that no single man could ever come into or out of the Arizona Territory alive after killing an enemy soldier and revealing his position. No siree, that kind of crap was best kept to comic books for little kids. This kind of sniper business was the no bullshit variety, and the tension and fear made his muscles tighten and ache. Failure to move and shoot or get busy with something was the real enemy that created the fear before action. Once the bullets started flying, both Casey and Willoughby would forget their instinctive survival urge to flee and immerse themselves in the equally strong desire to kill.

Willoughby's elbow nudged Casey out of his moment of reflection as a file of soldiers stepped out of the treeline and turned away from the snipers' hillside lookout to follow the Marines of Sergeant Ybarra's patrol. Casey whispered, "Man, those men are armed, and I can see weapons even at this distance. We got to warn the patrol or those bastards will sneak up on their rear and cut them off from us."

Willoughby had his binoculars clasped tightly in his fists, and he stared along the edge of the rice fields at the column of Viet Cong. He put his glasses down and spoke in a muted tone. "I make them about five hundred meters at the rear and six hundred meters when their point man crosses that big dike trail up ahead. See if you can target the length of their column, and you'll hit somebody and then Sergeant Ybarra will be forewarned. What do you think?"

Casey looked at Willoughby like he'd just farted and replied, "I think it's a great fucking idea. What did you think I'd think?"

Willoughby, who was just getting to know Casey pretty well, looked hurt. "I think you better shoot now, Sergeant Casey, 'cause those bastards are moving up pretty fast and in another minute there ain't gonna be nothin' left to shoot at!"

Sergeant Tom Casey didn't look at Ron Willoughby. He took the towel off the scope, raised the Remington to his shoulder, and laid the barrel across a thick branch of a cedar tree to his front. The Viet Cong column was well past the six-hundred-meter dike marker that Willoughby had earlier range estimated. Casey took the rifle off his shoulder and dialed in six hundred meters of elevation. The wind was in his face and negligible. He held dead on the lead VC, figuring the bullet drop would take out the second man in the file. At seven hundred meters the bullet would fall maybe forty-five inches, but he was shooting down slope, so the target would appear closer than it actually was, perhaps as far away as eight hundred meters. The column had seven soldiers and a black-clad person who might have been a female Viet Cong nurse. Casey figured that it didn't matter because they were all armed and the woman was a combatant and subject to the same harsh rules of survival that applied to everyone else in this crazy fucking war.

The crosshairs settled on the point man's tunic, and Casey took up the trigger slack until the rifle discharged. Willoughby thought the blast and concussion from the rifle was so loud in the eerie silence of the rice paddies that everyone in the world would know where he and Casey were emplaced.

When the rifle barrel settled again onto the point man, there was a gap behind his position and a soldier lay sprawled on the trail. The other members of the Viet Cong patrol scattered into the treeline. The recoil of the rifle had lifted the scope off the target, and Casey never saw the bullet strike. But there was no denying that the body of a Viet Cong soldier still lay immobile next to the paddies, while his comrades made a quick exit into the nearest cover. Casey smiled and thought about carving a notch in the stock of his new Remington. No, on second thought he had to admit that it was a hell of a lucky shot in this kind of weather. He smiled, thinking about all the talk about checking out kills for documents and stupid stuff like that, and looked toward the treeline where the Viet Cong soldiers no doubt still waited for some dumbass Marine to confirm the kill. As far as Willoughby and Casey were concerned, the kill was plenty confirmed, and if the son of a bitch had any documents, he could damn well keep 'em.

An hour later Manny Ybarra and the patrol from Hotel Company came toward the hill and waved for the snipers to join up. Casey noticed that Ybarra had approached the sniper hide from the other side of the rice valley. Later, Ybarra would point out that the surest way to get ambushed is to come in from patrol using the same trails you went out on.

Manny Ybarra just smiled when Casey and Willoughby joined the patrol. "You guys saved our chili when you shot that gook," he said. "I owe you boys a couple of Schlitz beers when we get back to An Hoa. Remember, don't never come back in the same way you go out. I didn't make it through the DMZ by being a dumb fuckin' Mexican. We got smart Mexicans too. *Vamonos muchachos!*"

Tom Casey looked at Ron Willoughby and nodded toward Sergeant Ybarra, who had tucked into the column behind John Lafley as the point stepped on the gas back to An Hoa. "I think if we stick with these guys, we might just stay alive. What do you think?"

Willoughby looked Casey over and delivered his best John Wayne impersonation: "I think this Sergeant Ybarra is no dumb enchilada. What do you think, you big fuckin' gyrhead?"

Laughing, Casey and Willoughby humped home to An Hoa from their first patrol in the Arizona Territory, happy to still be alive.

CHAPTER SEVEN

Operation Tuscaloosa Ron Willoughby and Vaughn Nickell

Ron Willoughby was selected by Sergeant Casey to join Hotel Company for an upcoming operation against strong enemy forces across the Song Thu Bon near Go Noi Island. The operation was to kick off on January 24, 1967. Two reinforced rifle companies from the 2nd Battalion, 5th Marines, were chosen to penetrate the heart of the Arizona Territory and search out and destroy the veteran R-20th Main Force Battalion of the Viet Cong with all means necessary.

The battalion commander of 2/5 had first ordered Foxtrot and Golf Companies to provide the main body of the light battalion that would spearhead the assault into the enemy's most heavily defended sanctuary. Golf Company, however, had many new personnel and had just come back to An Hoa from a month of heavy patrolling where they'd taken high casualties, so they were not campaign ready. Lieutenant Colonel Airheart leaned on his most experienced company commander, Captain Jerome Doherty of Hotel Company, who'd proven his ability to command a unit in combat the previous fall up on the DMZ at the Con Thien firebase. Hotel Company and the rest of the battalion had taken heavy casualties in four months on the "Z," fighting tooth and nail with the hardcore NVA regiments that asked and gave no quarter in that bloody series of battles during 1966.

At the time, Hotel was completing its month-long tour of duty at the river outpost called Phu Loc 6, some six miles northeast of An Hoa and just south of the wide bend in the Song Thu Bon at Liberty Bridge. Doherty and his Marines had been running daily combat patrols into the Arizona Territory's hamlets, making the Marine presence known and trying to win the hearts and minds of the local Vietnamese villagers. The local villagers, meanwhile, were desperately trying to harvest their rice and stay alive, and the Viet Cong were interrogating their leaders and torturing and killing any teacher, doctor, lawyer, or person sympathetic to the Americans. Needless to say, the Marines had a hard time trying to win the people's trust during daily sweeps into the villages. The Viet Cong, on the other hand, merely waited patiently until Marine patrols swept back to An Hoa before entering the same villages and hearing the inside story firsthand from the terrified villagers. To deal with this losing proposition, the standard Marine solution was to try to force the VC main force into a conventional battle and decimate their numbers, allowing the small Marine patrols to return unhindered to the villages for pacification duty.

The regular Communist forces were very elusive, with a strategy of bleeding the American Marine and Army patrols just enough to wear out the resolve of the American public. The Viet Cong and North Vietnamese officials, and generals like Vo Nugyen Giap, knew full well that the Vietnam conflict was misunderstood in the United States. The war was becoming unpopular with an increasingly misinformed citizenry that had long forgotten the heroism and sacrifice for God and Country exhibited in the Second World War and on the frozen battlefields in Korea. The Communists' counted on the remote location and the obscure recent history of Vietnam to foster disinterest and annoyance among myopic Americans, who believed that nothing that occurred outside the continental U.S. was important. College students of all ages and genders were especially vocal in denouncing America's participation in the hostilities. The Vietnamese high command were no doubt gleeful when they read the U.S. newspapers with their daily features on rioting and unrest among the antiwar protesters on nearly every college campus in America. If the American military could be bled enough to create distrust for the American president and his generals among the fathers and mothers of the killed and wounded GIs, perhaps the U.S. would grow tired and pull out. This was the only hope for real victory the Communists had although they maintained the lie about a "united Vietnam" and promoted the idea that the conflict was a civil war and not a Communist-inspired territorial expansion.

In Vietnam itself, General Giap and his aides-de-camp were deeply impressed with the fighting spirit and resourcefulness of the American military machine, particularly the 1st and 3rd Marine Divisions in the northern sector of South Vietnam along the DMZ, which were rapidly learning jungle warfare. The aggressive Marine infantry assaults, combined with overwhelming air and artillery support, had begun to cut deeply into the enemy's manpower. Giap did not think the Viet Cong main forces could continue to resist the American Marines in battle and survive as an effective fighting force through the end of 1967.

General Giap was a shrewd and brutal tactician. American planners had evidently not bothered to properly analyze his military operations against the French which culminated in their total rout and destruction at the river fortress of Dien Bien Phu in 1954. Giap had also handily defeated the occupational Japanese armies left in Vietnam after World War II. Later, his Viet Minh, forerunner to the Viet Cong, had cut off the French and destroyed their elite airborne and Foreign Legion units piecemeal. This obscure North Vietnamese general was a tactical genius, and he proved to be politically astute and patient as a fox.

The Viet Cong would be used by the North Vietnamese in 1967 to spearhead major pitched battles against the Americans. Giap would learn the fine points of his enemy's battle strategy and finally defeat the American will to continue the hostilities by driving fresh North Vietnamese Army divisions into South Vietnam across the DMZ and down the Ho Chi Minh Trail complex in Laos and Cambodia, which cut east into the heartland of Vietnam. Giap expected the Army of the Republic of Vietnam to fold by the early 1970s without aid from their better-trained and -equipped American allies. Sacrificing the Viet Cong to soften up the Americans would also have a secondary benefit to the North Vietnamese. When the Viet Cong were finally destroyed in offensive attacks on American patrols and bases, the North would face no idealistic local challenge when all of Vietnam fell under the heavy yoke of Communism after the American president and Congress threw in the towel.

General Giap and his military staff, during their exhaustive hours of planning, did not want the Americans to unleash their famous 101st Airborne Division's battle-hardened paratroopers against Hanoi itself. The most brilliant North Vietnamese planners had speculated that if General Westmoreland ordered his crack paratroopers into Hanoi in an airborne assault from the west, and the American Marines were to attack simultaneously from the sea westward, cutting off the port facilities at Haiphong, then the North would strangle without resupply from China or the Soviet Union. The American divisions could then move in on the Communist flanks with their tanks, jet bombers, overwhelming artillery, and naval gunfire. Giap was also cautious about underestimating the U.S. Army's use of large helicopter assaults, which had been developing well-coordinated hit-and-run attacks against Viet Cong and NVA units in South Vietnam with destructive and demoralizing results. The American intelligence community envisioned a likely conversation between Ho Chi Minh and General Giap as they were formulating a plan to win the war and crush the South Vietnamese.

The question the North Vietnamese leaders had was whether to pour the bulk of NVA elite troops into the south and bleed the Americans, or to play it safe and hold back the best divisions to protect the capital. General Giap, like all great leaders, understood human nature, although he was a born gambler. He would bet the fate of the North that the Americans were too bogged down in their huge supply bases to ever seriously consider a lightning strike into North Vietnam. But it was possible that the speed of maneuver of the famed 101st coupled with the ruthless and diehard reputation of the U.S. Marines might overrun Hanoi and win the war in one bold stroke.

Giap had talked for hours late one balmy evening on the terrace of Ho Chi Minh's Hanoi residence about the temperament of the American body politic and its timidity and the lack of faith and patriotism expressed by American college students. Ho Chi Minh had massaged his ample white beard while answering General Giap's questions. Smiling, Uncle Ho, as he was called, rested his porcelain teacup on the ornate wrought-iron table, looked deeply into his favorite general's eyes and told him to put his fears away.

"The Americans are only interested in the 'commerciality' of their venture," he said. "They lie to their soldiers about our intentions and say that all Southeast Asia will fall to Communism. That may ultimately be true, and we may control the rice belt, rubber plantations, and oil fields from here to Thailand some day. When we take control, we will move like the spider that spins his web slowly, and when the trap is complete, nothing can escape its embrace. The American industrialists grow fat like the greedy blood-bloated louses they are. We will let them feed, and when they have had their fill, they will go away and gloat over their profits. The American public is slow to learn, but not stupid. The cowards in their universities and the news media will infect the people with hopelessness and panic. You must give the Americans many casualties to unsettle their determination. Our people will suffer greatly, but we will hide the losses and the enemy must never discover how close to victory he is even now. Our soldiers are being beaten in every battle, but they understand the hardships and will do their duty. Yet the Americans, for all their reckless bravery, forget their duty. Hold the course and we shall prevail. I am certain of it!"

General Giap rose to leave, always overwhelmed by the brilliant mind and stolid heart of this small old man who was the soul of Vietnam. His soldiers would pay for this victory with their lives, but no one had ever promised them anything better, and they harbored a strong contempt for the American bed wetters back in the States who couldn't sustain the will to fight on to victory.

Giap recognized that the American soldiers and Marines had shown implacable bravery time and again against the best troops he could muster. Giap scratched his chin and wondered how a country that produced such deadly Marines and Rangers who seemed to fight his soldiers for the mere sport of warfare could also produce the spoiled brats and crybabies that filled the halls of America's colleges and universities. Giap finally decided that there was little moral conscience or patriotic leadership at hand. After all, the intelligence reports had revealed that the American President Johnson and his wife owned the company that manufactured the helicopters his men were shooting down like ducks over the river. For a people with no faith and little courage, personal greed and the love of money would always dominate the requirement for self-sacrifice and loyalty. Yet many Marines and paratroopers from the famed 101st Airborne Division were putting their lives on the line in daily skirmishes with his elite troops along the DMZ and throughout I Corps, as the Americans called the northern sector of South Vietnam. He admired these young fighters and had privately told his most trusted aides that he longed to command men who were willing to fight and die with such disregard for their own safety. General Giap paused in his thoughts and stared long and hard into the southern sky. The general prayed that Lord Buddha would guard his soldiers from the terrible American offensive that was coming in 1967. How long could his divisions hold out in their tunnels full of disease and snakes, stalked by constant shortages of supplies while the Americans continued to build up their ground forces each day?

Back at An Hoa the word came to the sniper platoon that two teams of snipers would be attached to the maneuver companies: Foxtrot, commanded by Captain George Burgett; and Hotel, commanded by Captain Jerry Doherty. Ron Willoughby would be teamed up with Vaughn Nickell as his spotter, with the M-14 rifle. Willoughby would carry his old but deadly M1-D sniper rifle. Although it was rumored that the snipers would be receiving a new Remington bolt-action rifle with advanced optics, no one knew the actual date of the weapon's introduction. Willoughby didn't really think about a new rifle, since the Garand M1-D had more than proven its capabilities from Okinawa to the Chosin Reservoir. If it was good enough for Sergeant Casey and Gunny Mitchell, he thought, it was plenty good enough for any Marine.

Casey, meanwhile, had flown off the handle when the colonel refused to allow him to accompany his snipers into the field. Tom Casey was a Marine's Marine, and he never shirked the responsibility to be with his shooters when the sniper teams deployed for some trigger time. Colonel Airheart, on the other hand, would coordinate the rifle companies in the field from his command bunker at Phu Loc 6. Airheart respected the opinions of a seasoned veteran like Sergeant Casey, and he ordered him to monitor the sniper teams on the closed radio net from the command bunker. Airheart had been a trooper himself once and participated in some of the most brutal beach landings in the Pacific during World War II as a sergeant with the 1st Marine Division. In his estimation, his staff officers had plenty of gray matter between their ears, but when the lead started cutting into his Marines, he wanted the opinion of a bush-smart NCO who'd been in the shit before and crawled out of it alive.

As January 20 came and went, nerves grew tight among the officers and staff NCOs of the 2/5. Captain Doherty wanted no part of a river crossing attack with his weary patrolled-out Marines. Colonel Airheart consoled his two captains, who had strong reservations about Operation Tuscaloosa, which had the main body of Foxtrot going into battle by helicopter. Captain Doherty was aware of the high concentration of enemy .51 caliber heavy antiaircraft machine guns, which had just recently shot down a Marine A-4 attack jet two miles north of An Hoa. Airheart, always the practical commander, finally relented and told Jerry Doherty and

George Burgett that their troops would advance to the river from An Hoa, with Foxtrot taking the main highway north to the river. Hotel would march off the west side of Phu Loc 6 and, skirting the river, cross at Liberty Bridge. Then Hotel would join up with Foxtrot and the light mortar and communications sections from Headquarters Company from the firebase at My Loc 2. Two 105mm guns would be helilifted to My Loc 2 with two thousand rounds of ammunition to provide close artillery support for the maneuver companies. The main artillery battery of two self-propelled eight-inch guns and four 155mm guns would be able to provide artillery support out to 16,000 meters. The operational plans did not anticipate either rifle company going farther north of the Thu Bon River into the Arizona Territory than the artillery fan would cover.

Colonel Airheart also told his company commanders that air support would be on standby from the 1st Marine Air Wing at Da Nang, with two flights of F-4 attack aircraft ready to roll. The call sign for the air strikes, if needed, would be on Button Crimson FM. Artillery would be the arm of choice, because fire could be maintained for a longer period of time and a greater variety of warheads were available. Artillery support would be available on Button Gold FM. Both supporting arms were over the closed radio net to Phu Loc 6, with a relay to An Hoa for artillery and Da Nang for air. Airheart also tried to comfort the two young captains, neither of whom was over twenty-five years old, by telling them that special flights of Sikorsky Sea Knight helicopters with extra corpsmen would be standing by to retrieve casualties at the helicopter pad at An Hoa. The big Sikorsky CH-46s could carry a platoon of men loading through their rear hatch ramp, which meant that the colonel was expecting casualties to be high.

Back at the sniper hut, Casey ordered Willoughby and

Nickell to pack their seabags with enough utilities, socks, and green T-shirts to last a month at Phu Loc 6. Later that afternoon the six snipers and Sergeant Casey jumped aboard a six-by-six cargo truck for the six-mile ride up Highway 1 to Phu Loc 6 firebase. The diesels churned out bursts of black smoke, and the motor transport Marines swung their .50 caliber M-2 Browning heavy machine guns on their pylons behind the truck's canvas cab cover, fitting the heavy belts of gun ammo into the breeches of their weapons. As the trucks sped out the gate and picked up the rutted road north, the dual rear wheels slashed muddy red gouges into the clay road bed. The air was crisp, and low clouds loomed fat and rain-swollen over the river. It didn't seem like this would be another routine walk in the park for the snipers as they squinted across the wide paddies while thousands of rice sheaves flashed by. In twenty minutes the truck chugged up the shallow rise and entered the double apron of concertina wire that surrounded the sparsest, most forlorn firebase in Vietnam—Phu Loc 6.

The diesel truck pulled to a halt with squealing brakes and a shudder. Ron Willoughby looked at the sandbagged bunkers with several M-60 machine-gun muzzles sticking out the gun slits and tattered, grimy Marine grunts staring at them as if the visitors were alien creatures just arrived on the planet. The top of Phu Loc 6 was a bald, muddy knob surrounded by decaying bunkers with ripped-open sandbags dribbling sand down the sides. They were covered by angle iron and tin sheet roofs piled high with filthy, discolored sandbags, which were pocked with bullet holes and black-charred stains from the fiery bursts of nighttime mortar attacks. Willoughby looked at Vaughn Nickell, who looked at Tom Casey, who just hung his head and muttered under his breath, "Sorriest damn outpost I ever laid eyes on."

Vaughn Nickell was always ready for some humor at

Casey's expense. He looked serious and poked Casey between his humped-over shoulders. "You know, Sergeant Casey, me and Willoughby are sure gonna miss your company while we're out on operation dinging some gooks. I guess the best sergeants like you get all the perks and can stay in a great camp like this. You know, Willoughby, this place seems just like home."

Willoughby and Nickell had been together long enough not to miss a chance to piss Casey off. Ron looked out at the filthy camp and smiled at Sergeant Casey. "You know, Sergeant Tom," he said, "this place is probably just like home to a good ole' southern boy like you. I think it looks like . . . well, Uncle Tom's cabin."

Vaughn Nickell let out a yell as he and Willoughby jumped down off the back of the six-by-six truck bed.

"Yes siree, old Sergeant Casey has really gone and bought the big one on this trip. You really know how to screw the pooch, Sarge!" With a last quick glance at the South's greatest rifleman, who would be stranded for the entire operation at the Marine Corps' shittiest outpost—which even smelled like a cesspool—Vaughn Nickell and Ron Willoughby held their strapless helmets onto their heads as they ran laughing toward their fighting hole atop the firebase.

Two hours passed as Willoughby and Nickell settled into their dilapidated bunker. The night before, a Marine sentry had woken to find three fat paddy rats munching on his mint patty and cheese spread through a roughly gnawed hole in his box of C-rations. The startled grunt retrieved his .45 pistol and fired several rounds at the rats in the corner of his hole. The bullets tore through the bags and ricocheted through the camp, awakening the officer of the guard. The Marine would have stood a court-martial at any stateside base, but duty in Vietnam was so full of surprises that a certain amount of mischief had to be tolerated.

Promptly at six P.M., or 1800 hours, two individual rifle shots rang out from the back side of Phu Loc 6. The bullets spanked the sandbags surrounding the command post bunker at the top of the hill. The only visible damage was two .30 caliber holes a foot apart, just inches to the left of the bunker's entrance. Sand still oozed out of the rents in the weather-beaten canvas, but no one was hit, although the Hotel 3rd platoon leader, 2nd Lieutenant Smith, was highly pissed off.

"Dammit, it's that maladjusted VC son of a bitch Six O'clock Charlie taking target practice at my hooch again," Smith said. "Captain Doherty wants this pint-size asshole put to sleep. Where is my shooter? Culbertson, you psycho Okie bastard! Where are you when I need you?"

Someone yelled my name down the hill just as Six O'clock Charlie fired another wild shot through the camp. The bullet just grazed my shoulder as I sat facing away from our tormentor. The round continued unimpeded past my torso and sliced into and through Charlie Mexico's left buttock as Mexico stood three feet in front of me telling war stories about 2/5 on the DMZ. Charlie Mexico was an ex-Army paratrooper, and he was tougher than boot leather, but when the Viet Cong sniper's bullet whacked through the smooth flesh of his sweet butt, he screamed like someone had chopped off his Johnson or crushed his balls in a set of vice grips. Well, you get the picture. Mexico went down on his side and moaned about dying, or at least getting to go home. Everything had happened so fast that I never really put all the events together as I bent over Charlie Mexico, trying to pull down his utility trousers to check for damage. Checking for damage was purely SOP (standard operating procedure) since our young bodies were technically U.S. government property.

A medevac chopper was called by radio, and as soon as Mexico realized his wound was not only noncritical but quite humorous to his buddies, he grabbed his gear and ran up the hill to the waiting H-34 chopper. The medevac sat like a giant beetle, its engine throttled back awaiting its passenger and the conclusion of another chapter in combat lifesaving. Charlie Mexico, who at twenty-eight years of age looked like a Mexican Charles Bronson, waved his fist in the air and yelled good-bye to the *"pendejos y cabrones"* who had been his most trusted comrades.

A corpsman threw a stretcher out the cargo door of the H-34, which Mexico hefted with renewed vigor, only to toss the stretcher back into the chopper. Defiantly, he yelled that he was still a fightin' Marine, and "I don't need no sissy fuckin' stretcher. Mexico will return, my compadres!"

With that flourish of border-town Spanish, he disappeared into the chopper, which spun up and nosed down off our firebase, gathering airspeed for the quick hop to An Hoa. We never saw Mexico again since he was "too short"—insufficient time in-country remaining—to return to Hotel Company. All of us could imagine Charlie sitting in some border-town cantina lying to a young girl about his "near fatal" wound.

Lieutenant Smith ran toward my bunker after the helicopter shrunk to a speck in the distance. "PFC Culbertson, you are an expert rifleman, are you not?" he said. "You will position yourself each evening beside my bunker in a camouflaged fighting hole and kill that Commie sniper the next time he dares to shoot at the command post. Do you read me?"

I liked Lieutenant Smith, who had just come in-country and was our official 3rd platoon commander after 1st Lieutenant Jim Kirsche was grievously injured in both legs by a command-detonated mine just outside the perimeter of Phu Loc 6 earlier in the month. Kirsche was a professional officer and Captain Doherty's most trusted platoon leader. Doherty and Lieutenant Kirsche had teamed up to turn Hotel Company into 2/5's most combat-seasoned rifle company. Along with Foxtrot, Echo, and Golf Companies, the riflemen of 2/5 would rewrite the Vietnam legends of valor in combat against the Viet Cong main force and later the North Vietnamese Army. Battles like Tuscaloosa, Newcastle, De Soto, Independence, Union I, Union II, Swift, Essex, and the hell of nineteen days of street fighting in Hue City would make the 2nd Battalion, 5th Marines, the most decorated and feared Marine battalion in Vietnam.

I looked into the young eyes of Lieutenant Ed Smith, who hailed from Oregon and couldn't have been over twenty-five or -six. He looked intelligent, but he had that officer disease we all knew as the Chesty Puller syndrome. After Basic School, most young lieutenants didn't know shit, but the Corps had brainwashed them into thinking they were bulletproof. The real Chesty Puller had won five Navy Crosses during forty years of service and evidently really was bulletproof. For some reason, nearly every cocky young second lieutenant thought he was a reincarnation of old hardcore bulldog Chesty Puller, and would occasionally take irresponsible risks with their own lives in their first combat. That was fine with me, but when the young shavetails took undue chances with my ass, I objected strenuously. Well, maybe Lieutenant Smith wouldn't risk getting all of us killed just to earn a fucking medal, I thought, which almost any officer who led combat troops could count on eventually anyway.

I rose to my feet in respect to Lieutenant Smith's rank. "Sir, I'd be glad to take a shot at Six O'clock Charlie for you. But sir, this M-14's got no scope and the stock is wet and swelled up to beat hell. Sir, I don't know if I can hit the little bastard with one shot, and he may disappear if I miss. I hate to miss, sir!"

All my adolescent life in the wheat fields of Oklahoma, I had hunted everything from rabbits to white-tailed deer. My father was a World War II hardass and a truly mean drinker. Dad always jumped right in the middle of my chest if I didn't shoot straight and true like he'd taught me. Anyway, I had killed plenty of game and was very eager to kill my share of Viet Cong "scumbags" before I rotated home. I just hated to fuck up an opportunity to kill our six o'clock nuisance, especially with everyone watching me. Hell, a missed shot could have ruined my reputation, and any Marine who couldn't shoot accurately was no Marine at all. I looked past Lieutenant Smith into the gray misty clouds that fanned out over Phu Loc 6 and prayed that Chesty Puller was watching and would help me out!

Just after my short prayer ended, Lieutenant Smith ordered me to fetch my weapon and report to the command bunker tomorrow afternoon promptly at 1500 hours. "Culbertson, you will dig in, and when Charlie fires at me you will return fire, killing him," he said. "I have the utmost confidence in my Marines. Do not disappoint me, or the company. Chesty Puller will be watching. That is all!"

Just then, two Marines walked past Lieutenant Smith and did not salute, but gave the proper greeting, "Good afternoon, sir!"

As they walked past, Lieutenant Smith ordered them to halt. He looked the older Marine up and down. "What's your name and unit, Marine?" he asked.

Tom Casey stood to attention and answered, "Sergeant Thomas Casey, sir. I'm platoon sergeant of the

5th Marine Regiment Sniper Platoon that will be joining your company on operation."

The other Marine, strongly built and handsome, spoke up. "Sir, I'm Corporal Ronald Willoughby, the assistant platoon sergeant with the 5th Marine Snipers. We have four other Marines on board Phu Loc 6, here for the operation across the river."

"I have noticed Marines wandering about my firebase that are not part of Hotel Company," intoned the young lieutenant, scratching two days of stubble on his chin. "Where are the other snipers, may I ask?"

Sergeant Casey pointed up the hill where two bunkers faced the back side of Phu Loc 6, looking toward the Song Thu Bon, which slowly meandered in the distance. "Sir, I have Ulysses Black and Loren Kleppe in the left bunker and Vaughn Nickell and Ron Willoughby in the bunker to the right of the CP. Dennis Toncar is partnered up with Jim Flynn. Six snipers will form three two-man teams and be assigned to the headquarters sections of the maneuvering rifle companies."

Lieutenant Smith smiled at Casey, who looked like the perfect southern country boy, with deadly blue eyes that twinkled behind a boyish grin. Smith had seen the Tom Caseys and Ron Willoughbys of the Marine Corps before. Honest, straight-spoken youths who would swim the river's rapids back home to save a child or a drowning dog, but would also kill the Viet Cong with such brutal swiftness and reckless abandon that the platoon commander understood why these young men made the Marine Corps feared the world over. Willoughby was strong enough to beat a man to death with his fists, which hung like hams on a butcher's hooks. Both Casey and Willoughby had holstered .45 caliber pistols hanging from their sides.

Lieutenant Smith asked, "Where are your rifles? PFC Culbertson here is my best marksman, but he is bitching about the condition of his rifle in this wet weather. Perhaps you two snipers could join Culbertson and help him take Six O'clock Charlie out tomorrow night. Report to the command post at the top of the hill at 1500 hours with your weapons ready for action."

Casey and Willoughby looked at each other like two wolves salivating over a potential kill. Tom Casey muttered, looking off the back side of the firebase, where the latest shot from Charlie had emanated. "Tomorrow afternoon, Ron! This fuckin' gook sniper belongs to me!" he said. Then, with a last look scanning the rocks and hides off the Marine's hill, Casey slapped Willoughby on the back.

With gleeful grins on their hard faces, they trudged through the muck back to their fighting holes.

CHAPTER EIGHT

Six O'clock Charlie Gets Zapped

The day broke harder than an egg back on the mess griddle at An Hoa. The gray skies billowed and tilted against imaginary foes tossed on the whipping winter winds that cut across the rice fields. Tom Casey shivered in his bunker and sipped black coffee from a tin canteen mug. His poncho was tied snug at the neck, but the hood rattled against his utility cap, pulled down snugly over his brow. Casey held the weathered pair of government-issue binoculars to his eyes with both hands and scanned the paddies and dikes, trying to figure where a sniper would settle in to take his daily potshots at the uneasy souls nestled into the Marine perimeter.

Casey thought like a hunter, which harkened back to his early days of scouting the South Carolina woodlands for rabbits and squirrel. As he often remarked in his soft southern drawl, "Hell, it ain't no accident that southern boys can hunt and shoot. My pap had me weaned on a Winchester long time before I ever thought about giving up Mama's tits!" Casey was what the Marine snipers called a "dead ringer," and he could make shots that regular snipers thought were impossible.

He found a small group of rocks that jutted from a slanting mound about four hundred meters off the perimeter wire at about two o'clock. Casey mentally reversed the approach over broken terrain that was mostly hidden in the deep furrows of a potato field that lay barren above the long series of dike levees. Thinking like old Six O'clock Charlie, he mentally crawled inside the field's furrows, weaving with the natural contour of the mounds of dirt and steadily approaching the rock outcropping that he had first noticed to his front.

Casey pushed the stained bill of his Marine utility cover off his brow and let out a long sigh. "Well, that sneaky little son of a gun!" he said. "He's figured a practically invisible approach to crawl forward in them dirt pasture meanders until he reaches his rocky hide there along the base of that hillside. Smart little asshole can crawl up to his position while the dyin' sun blinds our eyes looking to the southwest around six o'clock. That's why the bastard is so damn punctual. He's got to come directly into his hole with the sunset or he'd be spotted."

Casey reflected a minute on all the tricks that he'd learned at sniper school in the 2nd Marine Division. Those PMIs (Primary Marksmanship Instructors) had never told the snipers about clever little Viet Cong who were so adept at traversing open ground that wind direction, sun glare, noise suppression, and extreme patience were natural habits of movement to them. The Viet Cong could crawl into and out of positions that compromised both mobile units (patrolling) and bunkered troops (perimeter lines), without so much as breaking a twig or making noticeable sound. These men were like ghosts, and no Marine was anywhere near being their tactical equal. Casey thought of all the shots that old Six O'clock Charlie had taken in vain at the grunts on Phu Loc 6. There had even been occasions when some of the craziest infantrymen had exposed their bodies to Charlie's gunfire out of boredom or maybe just to keep up their tradition of staring death in the eye. For whatever reason, Sergeant Casey had to giggle to himself, knowing if Willoughby, Nickell, or any of the others were in Charlie's shoes, the hillside would be littered with KIAs. Poor Six O'clock could traverse those paddies and pastures like a phantom, but he couldn't hit old "Maggie's drawers"—USMC lingo for a completely missed shot on target—to save his worthless soul.

Casey knew the Moishin-Nagant rifle Charlie carried was plenty accurate, and powerful enough to reach out four hundred meters with enough velocity left to kill a Marine. He didn't think it mattered a hell of a lot what weapon a man fired in combat, as long as the shooter had confidence in his rifle and knew how to read the wind, keeping his sights on target, and squeeze the trigger. Shooting schools back in the States stressed the benefits of American-made equipment maybe just to give Marine marksmen some extra confidence. The real world of combat marksmanship was decidedly more concerned with stalking, positioning, and mentally practicing every step leading to the final act of killing the enemy. The enemy snipers, whoever they were and regardless of who trained them, understood the techniques and tactics clearly. That is, if they planned on staying alive.

Sergeant Casey looked down at the dial on his wristwatch. The old Timex just kept on ticking, as the stateside ads used to proclaim. It was coming up on 5:45 P.M., or 1745 military time. Casey put down the binoculars and rubbed his eyes. He was tired of scanning the ridges for "salty dogs," as the prairie dog shooters in the Carolinas often said. He looked toward the bunker to his left flank and saw Ron Willoughby bent forward in a tight sitting position, glassing the fields with his rifle scope. Suddenly, Vaughn Nickell raised his head and waved at Casey, who was out of hearing range in the gusting wind that picked up across the hillside in the late afternoon.

Casey cupped his hands and yelled over to Willoughby, who had just taken his rifle off his shoulder. "Hey, Ron, what's Vaughn doin' hidin' in the bottom of your bunker? You got to learn to shoot in the wind, rain, and bright sunlight too! Don't be afraid of Charlie, he can't hit nothing, but he might just get lucky!" Casey threw back his head, cackling at his combat humor. His blond, close-cropped hair was sticking out from under his cap visor, looking a perfect double to Richie Cunningham giving some shit to Fonzie on the *Happy Days* television sitcom back home. Vaughn Nickell, as junior sniper, just blew the comment off as another tormenting remark from the *Beverly Hillbillies* section of the perimeter.

Suddenly, out of the blue, a shot reported and a bullet whined over Willoughby's fighting hole and whacked into the sandbagged command post. "Jesus." Willoughby thought he'd paint a bull's-eye on the bunker's side tomorrow. "What the hell was Charlie shootin' at now?"

Vaughn Nickell looked up from the bottom of the bunker at Willoughby and gasped, "The little rat bastard is shootin' at you for chrissake. Get down, man! There's only dead heroes."

Another shot rang out and a bullet sped inches over Nickell and Willoughby as they crouched ever lower against the mildew rot along the wall of sandbags. Casey had seen the Viet Cong's muzzle flash way off on the hillside about a thousand meters distant. Too far out to hit any Marines without greased luck, and too far for Casey's plan to return fire. He would give this VC rookie time and confidence to work himself closer, Casey thought, before he killed him. Casey eyeballed Nickell and saw him twisting into his sling, with Willoughby giving hand signals over the binoculars. God Almighty, they were waiting for Charlie to move closer or come out of his spider trap for another shot. Nickell held the

M1-D loose in his left hand along the fore end of the stock. His right hand pulled the metal butt plate tightly into his field-jacketed shoulder. The scope was fixed on 2.5 power, and he had chambered a 173-grain match boattail bullet from Lake City Arsenal.

Willoughby caught the slightest glimmer of movement over the paddy, along a ditch where the Viet Cong was working his way closer to the Marine lines. He pointed out the direction to Vaughn with his hand, making a chopping motion toward the ditch. Vaughn soon picked up the movement, although at that extreme distance he couldn't see a weapon or the sniper's face, even though he was looking dead on. He let the Vietnamese come directly on as he flicked off the safety inside the trigger housing and started taking up the trigger slack. Vaughn guessed the shot was over a thousand meters, but he figured that if Charlie got up and ran, he would only make a much bigger target. The aim point was definitely a guesstimate about six feet over a center mass hold, as if the target had been dead on at three hundred meters. The trigger broke cleanly and the rifle bucked, throwing the scope out of eye focus until the muzzle again found its aim point.

Dammit! Charlie was still there and crawling ahead undaunted. Willoughby had seen the round impact with his 7.5 × 50 power binoculars. The bullet had broken ground slightly left about one meter and another meter short and, ricocheting over the paddies, had splashed down a half mile farther down the valley. Ron spoke to Nickell as the M1-D came up into the shooter's shoulder for the second shot. "Your windage is a titch left, so come right a hair and hold about three feet higher or about two titches, whichever feels right. Okay, brother, let's kill this fucker."

Vaughn Nickell always played the game when Willoughby or Casey harassed him. Sometimes the snipers had extra time to bullshit around a bit when they weren't in the urgency of a sharp action in the field. The disciplined grunts thought the snipers were crazy, the way they joked with each other after every shot. But it was a fact that no one joked about the sixty plus kills the snipers had made so far since landing at Chu Lai. The joking and bullshit was just a tactic to cut through the stress of taking another man's life, and anyway, most of the snipers were just kids, except for Sergeant Casey, Ron Willoughby, and Gunny Mitchell.

Vaughn asked if he should add two titches, one hair, or maybe half a klick to the elevation. Finally he looked through the scope and said, "Hell, Willoughby, I almost hit him last time. I think I'll just wing it. If the winds gust up downrange, the bullet may head for Da Nang anyway!"

The rifle exploded, and Willoughby strained at the binoculars. Then he saw the Viet Cong's head burst like a split melon. The figure, way the hell out along the rice field, just lay motionless. Willoughby slowly put his binoculars down and turned his face toward Vaughn. Nickell still had the stock of the Garand rifle plastered to his cheek, and the leather cheek pad was covered with dark sweat stains. The two snipers finally locked eyeballs and speechlessly glanced over to the next bunker, where Casey sat holding his head in his hands as though he had seen a ghost or maybe a miracle. Vaughn looked back across the paddies and, grabbing the binoculars, ran his vision over the prostrate body of old, and now ex–Six O'clock Charlie.

"Holy shit, I did it! Criminy, Willoughby, it must have been one hair and two titches! Oh well, I forget which it was, but you shall not ever forget this 'Mother of Great Shots.' Holy Toledo, Thomas Casey stand aside! This may be the longest kill ever in Vietnam. Maybe on earth!

Is boy wonder Vaughn Nickell a genuine dinger or what?"

Vaughn yelled in Casey's direction just as Casey lifted his head from prayer or perhaps disbelief. "Goddang it, Nellie! That Vaughn Nickell can shoot, man! Yes siree, I don't guess nobody will be crackin' no more hillbilly jokes about me. Sergeant Casey, from here on out you best be callin' me 'sir'! Vaughn Nickell, sir! I like the ring of it, and it's fitting for the greatest shooter in the Marine Corps, maybe ever! Will Chesty Puller congratulate me in Heaven, or what? Sergeant Casey, this is a truly great day! The day the cream rose to the top."

Casey and Willoughby let Vaughn Nickell rave on. It had been a "Hong Kong" miraculous shot, and neither Willoughby or Casey had ever seen the likes of it before— not ever! Willoughby had one last little gag to pull on Vaughn, as he looked out into the rice fields through the binoculars. "Jesus, Vaughn, where did he go? He was there a minute ago, man. No shit, I thought you shot that gook dead to rights. But now as I peer through these glasses, he's fuckin' gone!"

Vaughn Nickell grabbed for the glasses while screaming, "No, no fuckin' way! He's dead as dirt, Ron. You saw the hit, partner."

Ron Willoughby gathered his boots under his legs and sprang from the bunker with a war whoop, running toward a hysterical Tom Casey, who still sat with the binoculars in his hand. Ron yelled out the second he slid into Casey's muddy hole. "Vaughn's gook has done rose from the dead and run away! I mean poof, vanished. I guess that will have to be scored as a hit and a wounding."

Both Casey and Willoughby smirked at Vaughn Nickell, who begged in tears for the binoculars to check out the world's longest kill. The two snipers then laughed at

Vaughn, who in truth was one of the nicest Marines in the sniper platoon.

Sergeant Casey had a stroke of mercy and spoke loudly into the gusting wind. "Hey, Vaughn, we're only bullshitting you, good buddy! That dude is already in gook Heaven. You made a great shot for a rookie! Someday you may just make a real Marine sniper!"

The tension was broken, and everyone leaned back and had a well-deserved laugh.

CHAPTER NINE

Casey's Shooters
Go into Battle

After Vaughn Nickell dispatched Six O'clock Charlie with one of the longest shots in the history of Vietnam sniping, the truth was laid out for the Marines in cold and hard fashion. The fact was, the Viet Cong, North Vietnamese, Chinese, Russians, and their Warsaw Pact sister nations could replace their battlefield casualties faster than the American forces could kill them. On the DMZ, the 2nd Battalion of the fabled 5th Marine Regiment had locked horns with the Communist hordes along the border with North Vietnam during the summer of 1966. The Communists had poured fresh North Vietnamese divisions into the Con Thien sector in an unending stream. Captain Doherty and his favorite battle chief, Lieutenant Jim Kirschke, had been up to their necks in casualties from each patrol fielded against the overwhelming number of NVA crack infantry soldiers slicing across the Demilitarized Zone with no sign of letting up.

After one fierce engagement, Sergeant Manual Ybarra, Luther Hamilton, John Lafley, Bert Romans, Dale Pappas, Charlie Lightfoot, and the usual gang of grunts from Hotel's 3rd platoon were checking the bodies after catching the "hardcore NVA" in a cross fire and annihilating a platoon crossing the Marine firing lines. The dead were clumped in the usual twisted splash of bloody, burst flesh, with no discernable identity until Lafley rolled one shot-up soldier onto his back.

"Jesus, Luther, take a look at this dude here. Either I'm goin' nuts or this big bastard here is way too tall to be North Vietnamese. Just look at his feet. Must be size fifteen or somethin'. It jus' don't add up."

Shortly, Sergeants Ybarra and Tim Hoole kicked the bent legs of another body straight enough to gasp at his six-foot length. The platoon members forgot the desperate urgency of the firefight as they bent over, laying out soldier after soldier, unfolding the limbs of the North Vietnamese Army's giants. After Sergeant Hoole looked over a few of the corpses' wide-browed faces with high prominent cheekbones, he gazed in disbelief at the enormous hands and equally imposing feet, clad in leather boots instead of rubber "Ho Chi Minh" sandals. The Marine platoon sergeant then voiced aloud every grunt's worst fears: "Boys, these troops are Chinese regulars, and from the size of 'em, I'd guess Manchurian infantry. These are the hardcore assholes we've faced for the last three months in this jungle nightmare they call Con Thien. No wonder they're so hard to kill. The bastards probably take thirty minutes apiece to bleed out!"

The grunts broke into laughter mixed with the harsh realization that it was no fantasy that these troops were indeed the first of countless soldiers standing ready to aid the North Vietnamese from the People's Republic of China.

The newspapers in the States had been warning against the U.S. bombing of the port facilities of Haiphong, the supply facility for offloading both Chinese and Russian war material. American senators and the press kept warning against excess aggression that could bring China or Russia into the war. The general public believed that the Chinese and Russians were basically neutral and would not intervene further unless the

Americans commenced "unconditional air warfare" on North Vietnam. Therefore, North Vietnamese targets were carefully chosen so the Russian Bear and the Red Chinese Dragon wouldn't get their feathers ruffled. In the meantime, the U.S. Army Airborne soldiers of the famous 101st Airborne Division and 173rd Airborne Brigade were fighting major battles to the death against the Viet Cong main forces, the local Vietnamese guerrillas, and their Chinese and Russian advisors and regular infantry units. It was even highly suspected by American aviators like crack F-4 pilot Captain Gary Bain, who regularly overflew Hanoi and other industrial targets in North Vietnam, that North Vietnamese MiG fighters were being flown by Russian and Chinese pilots. The Communist leaders needed to assess the fighting tactics and general capability of the American air armada. The American public was kept in the dark while our downed pilots were tortured, beaten, and tormented during ceaseless interrogations in the infamous Hanoi Hilton Hotel. College professors at home in the United States condemned the military for "war crimes and atrocities," while they smugly hid in their apartments and homes, cowering behind a thin veil of cowardice laced with marijuana and fear.

Luther Hamilton walked among the bodies of the dead Chinese. He was a red-haired country boy from Ponca City, Oklahoma. Luther's family had raised him to believe in fairness and decency. But Luther Hamilton's kind also had a deep and abiding love for America, and the "tough as a steel beam" redhead had seen enough of his buddies maimed and killed to last the rest of his life. Captain Doherty and Jim Kirschke had stayed awake nights on end planning patrols and defensive tactics to keep their men alive, and Doherty thought of the Marines under him as more like his sons and brothers than just his troopers.

Hamilton stared first at Lafley and then at Gary Woodruff, who was a burly warrior from Michigan and no stranger to death. "You know, Lafley, I'm sick to death of killing these bastards!" he said. "The sad part of it is that they probably don't even know what the hell they're doing down here. Hell, they're just takin' orders. The newspapers in the States talk about being afraid of pissin' off the Chinese. Well, from where I stand, it looks like we done pissed off a whole bunch of 'em."

John Lafley, the Montana Salish Indian who had become Hotel's ace point scout, spat a dark brown spray of tobacco juice into the dirt at his feet. He looked across the face of the jungled hillside from where the Chinese platoon had marched into his rifle sights. "Shit, Luther, it don't matter whether these boys are Chinese, Vietnamese, or from Berkeley, I'll keep killin' the fuckers until I run out of lead. You gotta know that ain't too damn likely!"

Hamilton smiled and picked up his position in the column as Lafley broke the underbrush out on point. The Marines headed back to their base secure in the knowledge that Chinese or not, the enemy they faced would have to do some serious dying before this war was over. Lafley glanced back at his squad leader, Hamilton. Then he gazed at the sprawl of dead Chinese infantry scattered in the open thicket to the rear of the column, which was rapidly moving due west into the splash of sunlight that bathed the deathly peaks of the far hills.

Back at Phu Loc 6, Tom Casey slipped into Vaughn Nickell's bunker. "Seen any more movement to your front?" he asked. "You know that there's more than one Six O'clock Charlie. Hell, every Marine outpost in Vietnam has some Viet Cong guerrilla trying to get famous by wasting one of our asses." Casey scanned the valley behind the firebase, looking from left to right and letting his vision focus only momentarily on terrain features that showed some promise of providing cover and concealment for another VC sniper.

After a half hour of painful observation, the sun was setting into the river. The dying globe still pulsed with energy that spread golden-purple fingers across the paddies and hills leading up to Phu Loc 6's western perimeter wire. The rice fields shimmered in the soft evening wind, bringing a cool chill to the equatorial panorama that spread out like a tourist's postcard picture. The scene was absent of peasants and water buffalo, which almost always trod the paddies in their never-ending daily toil.

Just as Tom Casey began to relax a bit and give up on Charlie, a shot rang out against the hillside and a bullet whined and cracked over their fighting hole. Casey felt his heart beat strongly in his chest. He squinted into the binoculars as he feverishly sought the enemy hideout. Another shot boomed, and the enemy bullet dug into the dirt and ricocheted, whining over the Marine bunkers on the other side of the firebase.

Tom Casey was a hunter by training and instinct. He picked out the first small mound of dirt and rocks about four hundred meters to his left front. His M1-D sniper rifle came up easily to his shoulder, and he let the barrel fall to its natural point of aim while he snugged his left arm into the hasty sling and brought his left hand back along the gunstock, steadying his aim. The scope came into focus, and Casey went into "killer mode," with his mind and trigger finger on autopilot while waiting for Charlie to show himself. As one of the Marine Corps' finest shooters, Casey didn't ask for much from Charlie. He'd even settle for a head shot at four hundred meters and bet the farm back home and the old brown cow on the outcome.

Vaughn Nickell gazed through the glasses as Six O'clock Charlie number two stuck his head out to the side of the dirt hide and shouldered his Moishin-Nagant sniper rifle. The Moishin-Nagant was an antiquated Word War II rifle, but it shot straight enough and had accounted for more Marine deaths than the Americans cared to admit to. Sergeant Casey's job, and only thought, was to even the score as the crosshairs settled on the Viet Cong's head—bisecting his face. He squeezed the trigger slowly and was as mechanical and smooth as the sunrise. The Garand coughed deafeningly and spat its match boattail bullet toward the lost soul still scanning the Marine lines, hoping for a clear shot. The .30 caliber bullet split the man's skull wide open, like a farmer chopping kindling back home, with the hatchet blade slicing effortlessly through the wood.

Casey and Vaughn Nickell watched as the enemy sniper's head seemed to expand as the force of the bullet slammed into the flesh and bone and the head—or what was left of it—exploded with a violent red spray of blood and tissue that never ceased to amaze the Marine snipers. The game of life-and-death combat along the river would be played out each day, with no return engagements for the vanquished.

Afterward, Casey stroked the forearm of his weapon, secure in the knowledge that his 5th Marine Snipers were gaining vital experience every day. Tomorrow morning the snipers would paint two more Viet Cong stick figures on the platoon killboard. At this rate, Sergeant Casey figured his snipers might just run out of room by summer.

CHAPTER TEN

Storm Clouds Gather over Go Noi Island

A tall, lean, and serious professional, Jerry Doherty had a rare combination of courage and compassion tempered by considerable combat experience. He had commanded Hotel Company for the first time in the spring of 1966, in the offensives around Chu Lai and Tam Ky. After his tour of three months on the DMZ as battalion logistics officer, he'd volunteered to guide Hotel Company's battered seasoned grunts once again in the Winter Offensive of 1967. The Third Marine Amphibious Force Command planned a series of thrusts aimed at dislodging the indigenous Viet Cong main force units that controlled the rice basin north of the new 5th Marine combat base at An Hoa.

As a preliminary action, Lieutenant Colonel W. C. Airheart, commander of the 2nd Battalion, 5th Marines, ordered Captain Doherty and the other line commanders to lead extensive regular patrols into the rice basin north of An Hoa. This area was to become infamous during 1967 as the staging area for some twenty-one enemy battalions. The Viet Cong used the An Hoa Basin to replenish their supplies of rice and munitions prior to pushing south to continue the Communist military onslaught on Saigon.

Captain Doherty personally led his Marines through

the rice paddies to search out and destroy the enemy combat units that harassed the civilian agrarian Vietnamese population. The Communists even murdered the village chiefs and teachers, doctors, and merchants, who showed any deference or cooperation toward American efforts to pacify the countryside. Doherty was above all things a realist, and he maintained a strong dependence on common sense and rational thought. After a series of patrols where the grunts of Hotel Company were ambushed after searching villages, the Hotel skipper had been ordered to utilize ARVN officers as advisors. Doherty got a hunch that wouldn't go away: Perhaps his ARVN friends weren't so loyal to the American war effort as the senior U.S. generals and their staff planners thought. As a result, on the next major sweep Doherty wisely left the ARVN soldiers behind at An Hoa, and glory be—there was no surprise ambush! After that incident Jerry Doherty relied on his own good judgment and looked after his own troops personally.

Sergeant Tom Casey was surrounded by officers of the 2nd Battalion, 5th Marine, line companies as Colonel Airheart carefully went over his operation plan. It called for a battalion-size assault into the deadly Arizona Territory, which was tentatively scheduled to jump off on January 24, 1967. Airheart addressed the assembled leaders of Echo, Foxtrot, Golf, and Hotel Companies, represented by their company commanders, platoon commanders, and company gunnery sergeants. Tom Casey would receive the marching orders for his sniper units, which would be OPCON (under operational control) of the rifle company commanders.

Colonel Airheart glanced up from the crude desk in his hooch, lit by a pair of naked lightbulbs with green shades suspended from the rafters. He looked at Jerry Doherty and George Burgett, his two most seasoned combat leaders. Doherty and Burgett had come over with 2/5 from Okinawa in 1966. After the brutal and heartbreaking combat along the DMZ at Con Thien that summer, both young captains were becoming short-timers and scheduled to return home within a few months. As a sergeant, Colonel Airheart had fought the desperate Japanese in World War II in the Pacific on some of the bloodiest island campaigns. He became a captain and combat leader years later in Korea during savage fighting, and his Marines were forged into out-standing fighters in the icy blizzards and rugged moun-tains. Airheart meant to put his veteran cold-hearted killers to work immediately. Communist military activity had grown by degrees in the An Hoa Basin, until almost every patrol or company-size sweep was ambushed in force and taken on in vicious, close-quarter firefights that tested the Marines to the maximum.

A man of action, the colonel had determined to strike with force directly into the Viet Cong's riverine sanctuary along the converging meanders of the Vu Gia and Thu Bon rivers in the Arizona Territory. Airheart had planned to send Foxtrot and Golf Companies, reinforced by Headquarters and Service Company, which would pro-vide 81mm mortar support and handle medevac and most signals operations. Captain Doherty's Hotel Company was perhaps the most seasoned veteran company in the battalion, but they had been constantly patrolling off the firebase at Phu Loc 6 for the last few weeks and needed rest. However, at the last minute Airheart changed his plans.

"Jerry, I know your Marines have run the paddies hard the last few weeks," he said to Doherty. "The brass has ordered a full-scale attack of Go Noi Island next week. This operation will be planned and implemented at the battalion level. You realize that the future reputa-tion of the battalion as well as my own career depends on the successful total destruction of the Viet Cong main forces and their North Vietnamese advisors.

"Intelligence advises that the R-20th Main Force Regiment is occupying Go Noi Island and launching harassment and interdiction operations against our patrols along the river. Intelligence further estimates that a full-strength Viet Cong main force division is operating in the area and receiving tactical aid and leadership from a company-size North Vietnamese advisory unit that is active in their combat planning and operational decisions. I feel I have no choice but to order Hotel Company to take the field again and spearhead the battalion into the attack."

Jerry Doherty had seen enough combat during two full tours of command. He had learned to place the security of his company and the lives of his Marine brothers ahead of his personal opportunities for combat distinction. As for the men of Hotel Company—they had a deep and abiding faith that their commander would do his utmost to see that they lived to see tomorrow.

Captain Doherty looked as lean as Abe Lincoln as he leaned over Colonel Airheart's desk and spoke slowly. "My men have run their legs off," he said. "It's our turn to guard the airstrip after coming off Phu Loc 6 and constant patrolling in the Arizona. I appreciate the honor of leading the operation, but my men are worn pretty thin, plus my best platoon commander, Jim Kirschke, has been crippled by that freak explosive device last week. Colonel, I don't know if we'd do the job you're expecting us to do! Lieutenant Kirschke is my right hand, and we don't have a seasoned replacement."

"Jerry, you and George Burgett are going to take your companies into Go Noi reinforced with extra corpsmen, S-2 scouts, K-9 dogs and their handlers, and Sergeant Casey's sniper teams," Airheart replied. "Sergeant Casey's boys have killed over sixty Viet Cong already at

Chu Lai and off Phu Loc 6. We'll have the 1st Marine Aircraft Wing on standby, with F-4s loaded with napalm. The artillery batteries of the 11th Marines here at An Hoa will be ready to support your attack. Hell, all we have to do now is rest the troops a couple of days and go kick Charlie's ass off that island and into the river. Jerry, you and George are my fighters! I wouldn't send you if I wasn't certain you could kick the shit out of these Viet Cong infiltrators. The Arizona Territory and the An Hoa Basin belong to the United States Marine Corps. By God, I'm ordering you to carry a message to our neighbors that Mother Green is serving their eviction notice."

Captain Doherty looked at his close friend, Captain George Burgett, and just shook his head, knowing further argument was a waste of effort. It would be just like up on the DMZ in 1966 again. Foxtrot and Hotel. Slaughter alley. Find the VC. Fire their sorry asses up. Bring up the heavy guns. Call in fast movers heavy-laden with the tanks of napalm-jelly-gasoline-death under their wings. Count the enemy dead. Call in the medevacs. Watch your men, your brothers, your sons, loaded like cordwood into the Sea Knights. March back to base with tears streaming down your cheeks. Enter the hooches and count the empty cots. Remember the faces of your boys. Nineteen, twenty. Cut down in their prime in a war no one understood. A war no one was allowed to win. Wake up late in the darkness of a sweat-laced night. Picture the faces of your Marines, and realize that part of you had died with them.

Captain Jerry Doherty and George Burgett saluted Colonel Airheart and left the duty hut knowing they would have to face the bullets again and write the letters to the parents after the battle: "Your son Thomas was a brave Marine. He willingly sacrificed his life for his friends on . . ." Anyone who thought being a combat leader didn't have a downside was smoking something strange. No amount of medals or heroic honors could outweigh the personal sense of responsibility and grief that plagued even the most successful Marine officers. Personally, I was proud to serve with Captain Doherty and be one of his deadliest riflemen. Then again, I couldn't even begin to comprehend the psychological and moral effects of our actions until I grew much older.

Sergeant Casey, on the other hand, was a true combat Marine. He believed that it was his solemn duty as an American to crush the ugly specter of Communism wherever it reared its head. Casey would be sending three sniper teams into harm's way on Operation Tuscaloosa. Ron Willoughby and Vaughn Nickell would team up with Ulysses Black and Loren Kleppe and be attached to Hotel Company. Jim Flynn and Denny Toncar would be attached to Headquarters Company. Sergeant Casey was ordered to man the radio at the battalion communication center where Colonel Airheart and his staff would monitor the maneuvering companies' progress as they crossed the river and went into the assault.

On January 24 the three sniper teams left An Hoa with Hotel and Headquarters and Service Companies, while Foxtrot filed off the west slope of Phu Loc 6 to join Hotel later that afternoon, when both companies would approach the river from the south. The snipers knew their main responsibility was to screen the grunts' front as they went into the attack. However, if any opportunities to shoot enemy patrols or break up a Viet Cong ambush presented themselves, the snipers would be ready for action. Ron Willoughby watched the red mud squish and cake around the leather uppers of his jungle boots. The sky was swollen with moisture, and gray clouds slowly scudded across the low-lying hills, threatening rain. Willoughby always kept a green towel draped over the scope of his M1-D sniper rifle. Vaughn

Nickell followed Willoughby's footprints, ever mindful of the need to watch out for mines and booby traps. Both Willoughby and Nickell had seen other point scouts with the grunt patrols trip explosive devices and get wounded by shrapnel, or even worse—get blown up by a command-detonated bomb or mortar round rigged with a fuse and electric wire. Some point scouts were instantly torn apart by the blasts, while others lived to tell their tales, showing off the tears and jagged lumps inside their wounds that still carried pieces of fractured steel.

The Hotel point scouts were reputed to be some of the finest in the 1st Marine Division and had earned their spurs along countless trails from Chu Lai to the DMZ during the summer of 1966. Willoughby watched John Lafley lead the column with a smooth gait and decisive judgment born of countless hours patrolling the heavily booby-trapped and mined jungle. John Lafley, part Salish Indian from the wilds of Montana, was Hotel's chief point scout and master of the "approach march." Today he was ushering a new apprentice, who walked "trace" or second scout position in the column. Lafley stopped periodically and pointed out earthen mounds, depressions, thickets, and cuts in the terrain that could harbor mines or an enemy sniper team poised to "fire up" the Marine column and then escape like drifting smoke into their spider holes.

PFC John Culbertson paid a hell of a lot more attention to Lance Corporal Lafley than he had at Oklahoma University, where he'd screwed off, drinking and carousing late with his buddies instead of studying. Culbertson had volunteered for Vietnam, and was overjoyed with being posted to the 5th Marines. After some half-dozen patrols in Arizona Territory, the new point scout trainee still thought Vietnam was one hell of an adventure for a young buck ready to sow his oats. The deeply cut lines around Lafley's hollow eyes promised the new Marine grunt a brand-new perspective on the war's brutality and the cost of "staying alive." Lafley's thousand-yard stare could chill a new Marine to the bone. When the veteran cast his cold, dead eyes into your soul, young riflemen like PFC Culbertson didn't need to ask how it all came to pass. The stare grew harder and more lifeless with every mutilated brother Marine and each touch of the Grim Reaper's icy embrace.

Ron Willoughby turned and looked down the column of green-clad warriors as Foxtrot's lead platoon swung into view and paralleled Hotel. Nearly five hundred Marine infantrymen headed for the Thu Bon River and their rendezvous with Victor Charlie and his bloody-minded cousins from the north—the NVA. Willoughby cursed quietly to himself and snugged his free thumb up under his pack straps, relieving the weight and pressure for a moment. The Garand sniper rifle was no lightweight either, and along with two C-ration meals, two bandoleers of match ammunition, an entrenching tool, poncho, and extra socks, Willoughby figured he was humping about fifty to sixty pounds of gear through six inches of the slipperiest mud and slimiest rice paddy shit ever known to man or beast.

After four hours of march the company commanders ordered the platoon commanders to form their respective platoons into defensive perimeters for the night. Foxholes were immediately dug and machine guns were set in with fields of fire, carefully interlocked. The commanders got on the secure net to battalion headquarters and laid out the friendly coordinates for their lines so defensive artillery fires could be registered in the event of an enemy attack. Company 60mm mortars were set in, with 81mm mortars commanded by Headquarters and Service Company providing nighttime illumination and protective fires for the perimeter. Ambushes were sent out in fire-team strength, and individual listening posts were established close to platoon lines to provide security along likely avenues of enemy approach.

Ron Willoughby and Vaughn Nickell went out with one ambush team to provide sniping cover as well as the ability to call in accurate artillery fire support. The snipers' duties were explicit, and no team was to engage an enemy force of platoon or company size by rifle fire. The snipers had been carefully picked, partly for their mathematical acumen, and were well-schooled in map reading and the techniques of calling in close artillery fire support against large enemy formations. Rumors floated around the grunt outfits about snipers who had shot up whole enemy rifle companies with bolt-action rifles. Anyone who had been in combat knew those rumors were the kind of bullshit that could get a sniper team killed if they were stupid enough to try something idiotic like that. In the Marine Corps, Ron Willoughby knew that killing Charlie was a team effort, and that a hell of a lot more VC got their passports to hell stamped courtesy of U.S. Marine artillery, the "King of Battle," than ever got shot to death by any sniper or grunt marksman.

As the ambush team moved out, Willoughby and Nickell felt reassured by the hard faces of Tim Kirby, John Jessmore, Luther Hamilton, John Lafley, and his rookie point scout apprentice, John Culbertson. An hour later the seven Marines scanned the fields leading toward the river, which lay a mile distant and wound through the jungle and rice fields like a giant green cobra. Each bend in the river offered sanctuary to the enemy. It was virtually impossible to predict when an enemy column might just march into view, only to disappear again into the protective cloak of the jungle. Willoughby reminded himself that this wild and dangerous country was Charlie's backyard, and Marines who made the mistake of taking extra chances went home early in a steel casket. This wasn't 1965, or even 1966, when small patrols could walk the countryside with relative safety. This was 1967, when more large engagements would be fought in I Corps than any other year of the Vietnam War. This was the year that the American Marine high command at III MAF would chase the Viet Cong regiments down in their own backyard and force them to stand and fight.

Willoughby tensed as the full realization of 2/5's mission hit home. This operation was the first round in a new campaign that would be fought tooth and nail to the bloody end against the Viet Cong and the new aggressors from North Vietnam. The first years of the war had just been a sideshow! This new offensive was for all the marbles. And it was a cold, hard fact that the professionals like Colonel William C. Airheart and his gunslingers, Captains Doherty and Burgett, would not come home without some serious enemy blood on their hands.

As the sun sank in a splash of golden fire into the river, a file of Vietnamese entered a long paddy dike system and walked at an angle toward the ambush site about a thousand meters to the west. Vaughn Nickell got his binoculars focused and glassed a group of farmers in black pajamas and white linen smocks. They looked like the local Viet Cong guerrillas who often guided main force and NVA ambush teams close to Marine perimeters. The grunts took up their rifles, waiting for the file of VC to come into range. Neither Willoughby or Nickell doubted that the hardcore grunt riflemen would kill the Vietnamese at the drop of a hat. Hell, no one doubted that any villagers along the bends of the river within the score of hostile villages like Cu Ban 4, La Bac 1 and 2, or La Thap 4, would gleefully aid the Communist effort to attack and destroy the Marine invaders. The grunts had seen so many of their brothers maimed and killed that they were pretty damn lax about who they shot, as long as they carried a weapon or threatened the security of the Marine positions.

Sergeant Casey came from a southern background where honor and fidelity were considered hallmarks of the warrior class. Obsolete in the vicious jungle war of Vietnam where the Geneva Convention was a joke, Casey had drilled his snipers on the value of what he called "righteous killing" as opposed to "wanton killing." Strong-minded as well as strong-armed, Casey had embedded his code of personal battlefield behavior in his snipers. Just like the personal ethos of Captains Doherty and Burgett, who never shrank from a fight but would never tolerate the killing of women or children. This war would be won by the Americans, Casey believed, because we fought harder and followed the rules of engagement, not because we were murderers like the Viet Cong and their henchmen, the North Vietnamese.

Vaughn Nickell spoke firmly as the grunts flipped off the safeties inside the trigger guards of their M-14 rifles: "Hold your fire, boys. That file of gooks is only farmers. They got no weapons and they're two women in the group. If they don't come any closer, then we got to let 'em go!"

Several of the grunts snapped their rifle safeties back on and looked at Vaughn like he was nuts. One hard Marine spoke for the grunts, saying, "You got the glasses, my man! But for fifteen cents I say we should waste these assholes. They spy on us and tell the Viet Cong the distances to our perimeters so they can mortar the shit out of us come nightfall. I hate all these fuckers and nobody can convince me that any of 'em are worth shit."

Well, so much for the proprieties of war in Vietnam! Vaughn Nickell had saved the lives of a bunch of villagers he would never get to know. But the raw truth of the matter was that it was an even bet that they were

Viet Cong, and that by nightfall the mortar rounds would come tearing into Marine lines with a deadly accuracy that only spies could provide.

Ron Willoughby looked at the grunts as they placed their rifles back into their holes. He had no doubt that when the chance came, these men would kill the enemy like the Tartars of olden times and never bother to blink as the gruesome piles of dead stacked up.

CHAPTER ELEVEN

Searching for the Enemy

Ron Willoughby and Vaughn Nickell blended into the green, mud-spattered column as the Marines left the hurtling blue meanders of the Thu Bon River behind and snaked ahead toward the glistening green mountains of the Arizona Territory. The elongated column combed the small hills that opened into large rice fields completely surrounded by jungled hillsides and thick treelines.

Willoughby and Nickell knew the column could be taken under fire at any time by Viet Cong sniper teams or machine gunners. It was that one dreaded moment that all snipers feared. The urgent call "Snipers up!" would ring out and the team would run through the incoming bullets to the point and take countersniper measures to destroy the enemy threat. John Lafley or another point scout would guide the snipers into a shallow defilade or irrigation ditch from where the position and range of the enemy sniper team could be identified. Then the point scouts would take over fire control of the platoon, allowing the snipers time to level their long rifles at individual enemy soldiers. The snipers' aimed shots would invariably dispatch them, not in a cloud of bullets, but in a spray of Viet Cong blood from one or two well-placed shots.

The Viet Cong snipers could also fire very accurate and deadly aimed shots. Sometimes VC sniper bullets would cut into a Marine column and several men would crumple dead in place. Or as my sniper school instructor, Gunnery Sergeant Vernon D. Mitchell, would later say to our class at the Happy Valley range in Da Nang, "When you boys place your shots and all your dope is right, the enemy ought to be what we used to call in Korea 'DRT.' You boys know what that means, don't you? *Dead right there!*"

Nobody doubted the ability of Casey's snipers to eliminate the Viet Cong ambushers, snipers, and back shooters in proper fashion—"DRT." Willoughby kept his eyes on the nearby hills and the narrow jungle-choked trails that could provide a sniper a perfect hideout from which to shoot. Hours passed as the Marines worked themselves away from the river and into the higher hills and mountain passes.

Hotel had remained in trace behind Foxtrot, which had point scout Vic Ditchkoff setting a furious pace into the heart of "Indian country." The grunts were more eager to surprise or catch a fleeting glimpse of the enemy so that the maneuver companies could surround and attack any force in its path. The infantry commanders didn't care much where Charlie was sighted so long as they could bring the awesome firepower of their grunt platoons to bear on the enemy forces. The infantry bristled with a variety of automatic weapons, machine guns, rockets, and grenade launchers, not to mention the 60mm mortars in Weapons Platoon and the 81mm mortar sections of Headquarters and Service Company.

The sniper teams were a very sophisticated weapon if properly employed. An experienced sniper and his spotter would primarily target the enemy officers and crew-served weapons like machine guns and mortars. A trained sniper was always ready to take extra risks to kill an enemy sniper who was harassing the grunts. In the 5th Marines, snipers operated as the long arm of protection for the infantry. No sniper ever left the column to venture into the Arizona Territory alone. If he did, he would be recognized, captured, and brutally tortured his first day in the bush since American boys didn't resemble Vietnamese.

Late in the afternoon, as the sun burned through the leafy boughs of the high canopy jungle, the Hotel point scout sighted some Viet Cong soldiers running through the treelines toward a distant village. The VC guerrillas often shadowed the Marine formations and reported the Americans' progress and position to their main force commanders. The Hotel platoon commander, Lieutenant Ed Smith, urgently called out "Snipers up!" Ron Willoughby and Vaughn Nickell ran as fast as their mud-crusted boots would carry them up to the point and slid into position along a shallow mound already manned by a squad of riflemen. Nickell got his glasses out and was able to see through the light haze along the treeline where the Viet Cong were slithering in and out of the patches of sunlight that broke through the roof of the forest canopy.

Nickell called out the range and direction of the enemy march to the Hotel squad leader. The riflemen were chafing at the bit to open fire on the Viet Cong. Their M-14 rifles could easily reach out six hundred meters or more with deadly results when the whole squad opened up in volley fire. Vaughn guessed this squad of VC were about nine hundred meters distant and moving rapidly away. It was too far for a shot, especially when most of the VC would escape by crawling into the jungle after the first bullet slammed into their patrol.

Willoughby scratched his chin, waiting patiently until he could stalk closer and hopefully take the whole enemy patrol under fire. He thought about Sergeant Casey's admonition before the operation: "Remember, Ron, we are out there to protect the Headquarters section and be a combat multiplier. Our job is to give the grunts a long-range tool to disrupt or kill Viet Cong or NVA officers, NCOs, and snipers. We must be patient and work closer to the enemy target to ensure the chances of delivering a fatal shot. We are not in the field to show off or try impossible shots! The fucking Communists can make new soldiers faster than we can kill 'em anyway. The only way we can dominate the battlefield is by overwhelming firepower and ruthless aggression. Learn to work with the grunt riflemen. You might find out some of 'em shoot better than you do!"

Every Marine wanted his first taste of enemy blood, but the Viet Cong were moving away rapidly to join their main force unit. If Hotel followed the trail of the enemy patrol, they would hopefully be led to the Viet Cong main force somewhere up ahead through the dark green shadows that closed in on the long column of Marines. Fearless in their pursuit, the Marines continued their forced march, looking for signs of elusive Charlie.

After another hour's march it was obvious that the slippery Communist troops were playing cat and mouse games with the Marines. Captain Doherty ordered his platoon commanders to fold their units into tight perimeters that interlocked in a circular defensive position, awaiting the fast-approaching night. Stalking the Viet Cong and their North Vietnamese advisors would be postponed until tomorrow. Hotel and Foxtrot would then force-march, completing a big loop north of the Song Thu Bon into the heart of the Arizona Territory. The Marines would search every village before swinging southeast back toward An Hoa. The enemy was out in the field, all right, but the Communist commanders kept to the hillsides and river channels where they could hide from American air power, which could not only alert the infantry units on the ground, but would likely conduct rocket and strafing attacks with devastating ferocity.

As the nighttime shadows grew, Hotel and Foxtrot's

commanders sent out listening posts and ambush teams as early warning measures against Viet Cong squads probing Marine lines to locate automatic weapons positions and to keep the Marines tense and on edge. If a full-size attack was launched, each Marine position would have to defend itself and provide covering fire for its neighbor without the benefit of immediate orders. In other words, it was every son of a bitch for himself, and if you weren't in a fighting hole when the shit broke loose, you might just end up a stiff, dead asshole come morning.

Ron Willoughby and Vaughn Nickell dug an extra-deep foxhole and constructed a parapet where Nickell could lay out his clutch of grenades—just in case. The M1-D sniper rifle was virtually worthless at night because of the scope, but Nickell had his venerable M-14, which the grunts revered as the finest battle rifle ever produced. As John Lafley always said while having a weapons discussion with Burns, Woodruff, or Hamilton, "This M-14 is a killing machine in my trusty hands, boys! When you hit a gooker with a .308 cal bullet, that bastard is a dead man. A fuckin' DRT, or maybe by the next day if you only wing one of the little fuckers. It always bothers Burns when one of the slopes gets gut shot and takes a day off before he dies. But you all know, my friends, that bloody slopehead is a Hong Kong corpse still walkin'."

Ron Willoughby, Vaughn Nickell, Denny Toncar, and Jim Flynn all knew that they had to pick out the enemy leaders and machine gunners during an attack and kill them quickly to give the grunts a chance to turn back the tide. No sniper ever bit off more than he could chew unless he wanted to go home early in a metal box. The grunts looked on the snipers with a kind of awe, mostly in respect for their shooting skills. One grunt told Willoughby, "I think you snipers got some pretty big balls runnin' up to the point under fire all the time. Most of us grunts think you're all crazy as hell."

Willoughby had put his hand on the infantryman's shoulder and looked into his combat-hardened eyes. "I'll tell you straight, my brother," he said. "All the snipers are scared shitless when the call 'Snipers up!' is yelled out. Sometimes I wake up at night in a cold sweat when some fucking officer yells 'Snipers up!' and we ain't even in the field yet."

Both Willoughby and his new grunt buddy broke up laughing.

In fact, nobody crawled through more blood, guts, mud, and shit than the grunts. The grunt machine gunners also had to bring their weapons up to the point when the column came under attack. One hard-ass officer had told his M-60 gunners that he wanted them to spring to the point a little faster each time the company was engaged. In the Marine Corps, when the enemy put the shit on you and the bullets coned in, shrieking like hornets, nobody retreated. Instead, the whole unit stiffened and the platoon or company retaliated like a cobra that was stepped on hard by an errant foot along a jungle trail. Snipers, mortarmen, machine gunners, and riflemen were all Marines, and when the shit hit the fan they reacted as one with a deadly and terrible resolve. Their counterattacks were physically and psychologically intimidating. This was of small consolation to Charlie, who was usually only moments from getting his ass totally annihilated.

For all the petty horseshit in the stateside Marine Corps, Ron Willoughby would choose no other group of men to serve with on the battlefield than the Leathernecks of the 5th Marine Regiment. Some of the officers were a bit overzealous and the veteran grunts were crazy as hell, but together they were the deadliest soldiers that ever faced constant suffering and death without so much as a "Thank you" or a casually spoken "Job well done." Like all the misunderstood and ill-used Nam veterans, Willoughby had learned that all Marines fought for each other. The 5th Marines constituted a very exclusive club and operated under a contract signed in hell by the Grim Reaper himself.

CHAPTER TWELVE

The Viet Cong Brace for Battle

As the early evening hours wore on into the black as pitch night, Vaughn Nickell and Ron Willoughby kept their eyes and ears open to the cadence of jungle sounds. Hordes of bats flapped through the night, seeking shelter in caves and tunnels that opened up from the hillsides where the plants under the flyways drooped, crusted with dung. Crickets hummed in nearby rice paddies swollen in the winter months. Monkey cries shrieked like lost souls high along the mountain slopes, and each Marine could hear the beating of his own heart as his eyes filtered over the dark landscape.

It was easy to deceive yourself if a sentry focused too hard on one object. In the thick darkness, trees, plants, boulders, and trails took on the images of Viet Cong sappers or some giant beast, like a water buffalo or perhaps even a dragon. Fear mixed with sweat, and the troopers' necks felt clammy and tight. Nervous trigger fingers clicked the safeties on and off of M-14 rifles when a grunt was "fucking positive" that he had seen Charlie "out there somewhere." As the night wore on, the troops became trigger-happy, and occasionally some position would open fire on a suspected infiltrator.

Willoughby and Nickell thought about Sergeant Tom Casey, who had been ordered to stay on duty at Phu Loc

6 to advise Colonel Airheart about the status and movement of his three sniper teams. They knew that Casey, the 1st Marine Division's best sniper, was no doubt chomping at the bit to escape down to the river and rejoin his snipers. But Willoughby and Nickell were confident in their abilities and excellent training and trusted in their instincts to shoot straight and ask questions later.

All of a sudden, automatic rifle fire impacted less than a hundred meters to the left of the company lines. The short bursts seemed to emanate from about two hundred meters out from the forward Marine lines. The green tracers flew into the dirt pasture on their left flank and ricocheted high into the sky over the snipers' foxholes. The sounds of clipped Vietnamese voices broke through the cover of night as more incoming green tracers mixed with the red bands of outgoing Marine machine-gun and rifle fire.

Willoughby strained his eyes toward the fields to his left and saw the silhouettes of a herd of cattle hiding several Viet Cong riflemen firing AK-47 assault rifles into a thicket of bamboo. Marines were running through the bamboo grove, and the chatter of friendly fire erupted into the field. A Marine stood in the open, exposed in the flashes of the rifle fire, and shot his M-79 grenade launcher out into the plowed field that seemed to undulate away a hundred meters or more into a treeline.

Willoughby wiped the sweat away that was cascading into his eyes from his helmet band. He held up his rifle trying to see the combat develop through the 2.5 power of his World War II vintage rifle scope. The night seemed endless, as if a giant daub of tar had been smeared across a picture's canvas, covering the landscape in dull tones of grayish black. Willoughby thrust the M1-D back against the bunker wall with a curse and told Nickell to be ready with the M-14 in case of attack.

The firing in the bamboo grove quit almost as quickly

as it started. The rifle fire was replaced by the furtive yells of Marine riflemen who called, "Corpsman up. We got a Marine wounded down here!" There was another commotion, and Willoughby could see the Leathernecks hauling something large and heavy between them from the bamboo stand toward the Marine lines. There were mumbled voices, and then Willoughby and Nickell heard someone curse, "God Almighty, put him down. Doc, it ain't no use. He's got himself plumb shot up to beat hell. Culbertson was on the listening post and he's okay. Jus' scared to fuckin' death is all! Someone help me turn him over. I can't see his face good in this shitty light."

The voices drifted away on the night winds that wafted in off the paddies laced with a night chill that seemed to assert the presence of the Grim Reaper. A chill ran up Willoughby's spine, and Vaughn Nickell looked scared enough to piss his britches. The snipers were almost always selected from the brightest infantrymen and best marksmen. On college campuses across the United States the Marines were being portrayed as cold-hearted, drug-addicted baby killers and murderers. A few might have fit that description, but Willoughby and Nickell were both the all-American boy-next-door type. It took time to mold the average patriotic American kid into any semblance of a hardened killer. The grunts had their mavericks, like John Lafley, who could walk any man alive to death, or Benny Burns, who had become a cold-blooded killer of startling violence. Then again, Burns's brother had been killed by the Viet Cong and Benny wanted some payback.

In the morning, when the first light brought the Marines stiff and tired out of their foxholes to crowd around in small groups over a steaming cup of joe (coffee) and a cigarette, Willoughby finally got to meet Burns, Lafley, Luther Hamilton, Manuel Ybarra, John

Jessmore, and Stephen Gedzyk. These grunts were the salty veterans of the DMZ and had fought under the able command of Lieutenant Kirschke and Captain Doherty from Chu Lai to Con Thien.

Hotel Company was made up of well-blooded veteran grunts who had faced the best the North Vietnamese had to throw at them and spat it back in their faces. If the Viet Cong were sighted today, at least Willoughby and Nickell and the other snipers would be in good company. There were no finer rifle companies in the Marine Corps than those fielding the veterans of the 2nd Battalion, 5th Marines. Captain Doherty and his Korean War veteran staff NCOs had seen enough combat to hold their own with any Communist regiment or division sent out to engage them. Willoughby thought, So, what's the worry? Vaughn and I can handle this deal, no problem! Except he had to admit that the action the night before had been shockingly sudden and furious, and a Marine was shot to pieces trying to protect the listening post.

Willoughby finally got the pleasure of meeting the young Marine who had been "fired up" on the LP. The Marine was introduced to the snipers as one PFC Culbertson, and he looked wired and still had sweat rings under his arms and down the front of his jungle utilities. His utility pants were soaked with bloodstains, and his face was covered in a fine layer of dirt from the plowed field. Culbertson took Willoughby's offered hand and smiled more from relief to still be alive than from the pleasure of the moment.

Ron Willoughby threw the remains of his coffee into the dirt and said, "Well, man, I guess that was a long hard night. I didn't sleep much myself."

Culbertson started to answer, but Lafley put an arm around his partner's shoulder, saying, "Naw, Oklahoma will be all right. He just learned to keep his young ass real still on that LP last night. It was probably VC guerrillas that shot his butt up. NVA troopers would've likely killed his sorry ass for sure. Shit, this ain't nothin'! Bad boy Burns didn't even hardly wake up when the shootin' started. Jus' maybe today we'll hit the Viet Cong main force. Then you boys gonna really see the fur fly. Yes siree!"

Lafley had been on several major operations and didn't get very excited unless the killing got messy. Then Burns, Hamilton, Gedzyk, Jessmore, Matarazzi, and Ybarra would show the snipers what combat was all about.

The platoon sergeant's voice rang out across the fighting holes: "Saddle up, men. Lafley and Burns, make trail for the river. We just might get lucky today!"

All the Marines hefted into their haversacks, which were stuffed with C-rations, cigarettes, socks, extra bullets, and canteens full of spare water. Mortar and machine-gun rounds were strapped high over their ponchos and blanket roll straps. The day looked cloudy and rain threatened from the northeast as the green columns of Foxtrot and Hotel snaked along in tandem heading for the northern banks of the Thu Bon River. It was January 26, 1967, the final day of Operation Tuscaloosa. If the enemy was not sighted, the operation would be scrubbed as a failure, and the Marine General Staff would hit the planning tables with renewed vigor, trying once again to pin down an elusive enemy and make him stand and fight.

Back at Phu Loc 6, Colonel Airheart had the 1st Marine Airwing ready to scramble two flights of F-4 Phantom fighter-bombers to provide close air support to his maneuvering companies once they approached the river. Intelligence reports had 1st Force Recon locating an entire division of Viet Cong main force troops, aided by an unknown number of North Vietnamese advisors, in the general area where the Thu Bon and the Vu Gia river branches converged in the midst of the deadly Arizona Territory. Artillery had been moved up to My Loc 2, where two 105mm howitzers had recently been emplaced. The remainder of the 105mm howitzer battery at An Hoa could still fire into the river valleys, but their fire missions would have to be more closely adjusted by the ground commanders. There were forward observers with each rifle company, although Captain Doherty of Hotel Company and Captain George Burgett of Foxtrot would have overall command control if any battle should ensue.

Colonel Airheart was patient, but understood that any extra time his rifle companies spent on the move, especially into the late evening hours, gave the Viet Cong commanders ample time to set up the Marines in a lethal ambush. The river channels and banks along the Song Thu Bon were laced with bunkers, tunnels, and trench lines where the Viet Minh of old Indochina fame had probably slugged it out with the French colonial troops or perhaps even the Japanese. This infamous Arizona Territory was a beehive of enemy traps and mines and a maze of tunnels that could hide a large battalion-size force from American airpower, or shelter an ambushing blocking force from American artillery. Airheart knew there were high risks in invading the Arizona Territory with some twenty-four enemy battalions active in the adjacent areas, but the colonel's mission was to search out and destroy the Viet Cong. If the VC and NVA refused to come to him and attack An Hoa, then he had no choice but to send his best combat units marching directly into their home bases.

The grunts moved quickly through the savanna and treeline-fenced rice paddies. By 0900, Hotel's point had halted the column at the banks of the Thu Bon tributary called the Quan Duy Xyem. Ron Willoughby and Vaughn Nickell stared through the small leafy trees and thick underbrush that lined the riverbank above the blue thread of the Thu Bon tributary that divided into two branches some four hundred meters apart, sweeping along the periphery of a huge sandbar island nicknamed "Football Island," because of its shape. It was part of the Go Noi Island area complex where the Viet Cong had their main headquarters to establish Communist control over the local river traffic, which filtered supplies from the Ho Chi Minh Trail all the way to the sea near Da Nang. The Viet Cong used the Song Thu Bon and Song Vu Gia as waterborne highways to bring heavy supplies of munitions and personnel into the Arizona Territory from Laos. From the Arizona, new battalions would be formed, trained, and provisioned for their push south to eventually strike the capital of South Vietnam, Saigon. The Marine Corps mission was to disrupt matériel and men flowing into the Arizona Territory by using airpower, artillery, and ground units. Since air and artillery could not bring Charlie to his knees by themselves, it required the careful insertion of Marine combat units to close with and destroy the Viet Cong in their home bases.

Captain Doherty had been on the secure radio net with Colonel Airheart, and received specific orders to cross the river to the friendly banks. There was a real concern of having to fight out of a trap by a Viet Cong regiment or perhaps even a division if the two rifle companies waited too long on the northern or enemy side of the river. Doherty huddled with Captain Burgett and they decided on running a left enveloping maneuver where Foxtrot would cross the river's single stream a thousand meters to Hotel's left flank. Then Foxtrot would be in position to cover Hotel, which would advance frontally by platoons directly across the open sandbar of Football Island. The first two sniper teams, with Willoughby and Nickell as team one, Jim Flynn and

Dennis Toncar as team two, would assault with the infantry through the first stream and set up on the sandbar. The third sniper team would assault with Foxtrot to provide covering fire while they crossed.

As Foxtrot moved down the riverbank and into position, Willoughby waved to Loren Kleppe as he faded into the green column whose point scouts had turned south, facing the single blue channel of fast-moving water. Foxtrot would cross their water obstacle at the far left extreme of the football-shaped sandbar island. After fording the four-foot-deep stream, the grunts would fan out into skirmish lines and assault into the high riverbanks. Once all the troops had crossed, the snipers would set up positions to provide covering fire for Hotel as they crossed the middle stretch of the sandbar.

As Willoughby and Nickell strained their eyes on the Foxtrot point scouts now splashing chest deep through the stream, they heard the loud reports of rifle fire. The Leathernecks of Foxtrot had no way to backtrack or deviate the direction of their advance, and in classic Marine Corps fashion the grunts hit the deck and returned fire at an almost invisible dug-in enemy. More Marines forded the stream and became pinned down under the withering fire of the Viet Cong's automatic weapons. The point fire team was well beyond the water and had started inching up the flanking banks when all hell broke loose. The gunmetal-gray cold sky was filled with the terrifying shrieks of 82mm mortar rounds as they arched downward into Foxtrot's column. The Marines formed a loose perimeter and got down along the sandbanks, trying to escape the deadly salvoes of high explosive.

The Viet Cong had fought on this very ground more often than their commanders could remember. Above the VC trenchline and far to the right flank of the sandbar island stood the mortar pits of the Communist People's Army's veteran gunners. These artillerymen had learned their trade from the Viet Minh gunners who had toppled the French army fortifications at Dien Bien Phu in 1954. They were perhaps the finest mortarmen in the world, though they had very little equipment in their artillery inventory except mortars and rockets with which to war against the American technocrats. The mortar had become an almost sacred weapon against imperialism since the days of the Japanese occupation during the final days of World War II.

The mortar rounds slammed with fiery vengeance into the Marine lines, where frightened young troopers held their helmets tight to their heads as they wriggled their bodies ever deeper into the sand dunes. An errant missile crashed into the unlucky command post group and severely wounded the company commander, Captain George Burgett, in the legs. Burgett's radio operator was cut into a bloody sack of mush by the direct hit and died instantly. Another rifleman felt the hot shards of shrapnel tear into his body as he tried to shoulder his weapon and return fire. The riflemen on the front edge of the perimeter kept shooting into the maze of tree-lined riverbank that stood a full thirty feet above their position just across the stream.

Targets were hard to find, but Loren Kleppe zeroed in on the muzzle flash of an enemy machine gunner. Kleppe's M1-D bucked as his heavy 173-grain match bullets tore into the Viet Cong gunners, flinging them back into their gun pit in a spray of blood flecks. Big pieces of flesh were sliced off their facial bones like the meat a butcher cleaves off a carcass when the blade nicks into a thick chunk of bone. The rhythm of the VC rifle and machine-gun fire picked up a nauseating cadence as the Marines were strafed time and again by devastating plunging fire.

Captain Doherty had tried several times to get the Foxtrot Six (commander) up on the battalion radio net, to no avail. Finally, a weak, panicky voice got on the horn and desperately begged for relief. The Foxtrot executive officer was now in the middle of the worst shitstorm imaginable, with not much in the way of tactical options left at his disposal.

Captain Doherty called in the 105mm howitzer fire from the forward-positioned guns at My Loc 2, some three miles to the southwest. As the howitzer shells from the two guns were adjusted onto the positions of the Viet Cong infantry, Jerry Doherty's quick mind realized that the Marine battery couldn't defend Foxtrot and silence the VC mortars at the other side of the Communist trenchlines some two thousand meters to the west. Doherty desperately tried again to raise the Foxtrot XO. No luck! The fire was too heavy, and it would be a miracle if the boys in Foxtrot survived the pounding from the mortar battery and the heavy small arms fire that sought out and found Marine after Marine huddled in their crude sandbox holes that were being sealed off like leadlaced caskets.

Dale Pappas of Reno, Nevada, had served as Captain Doherty's radioman since the bloody battles on the DMZ in 1966. Neither Pappas nor Doherty got shook up when Hotel went into battle, and together they made a reliable and efficient command center in combat. Pappas had learned to anticipate his commander's field instincts. When Captain Doherty yelled for Pappas to ring up the 11th Marines artillery fire pits back at An Hoa, Pappas had already dialed in the radio frequency for the battalion artillery net.

Doherty grabbed the radio mike and spoke urgently to the artillery relay operator at An Hoa. "Steel Curtain, this is Crimson Two Actual. Expedite Fire Mission, 155 mike mike spotting round, willy peter. Fire AT9552 across AT9652. Target is southern bank of Quan Duy Xyem. Crimson One is pinned down by hostile fire at eastern edge of sandbar. Casualties not estimated at this time. Alert medevac to stand by for mission after artillery fire lifted. Crimson Two Actual, over."

The artillery commander came back on the net and said the fire mission was being run. The Hotel commander (Crimson Two Actual) would have to adjust the artillery. Doherty would also have to take over command of Foxtrot and move his Marines into position to save whatever was left of the tattered remains of Foxtrot, which was now fighting for its life just past the first stream of the seemingly pleasant blue ribbons that tied the looming mass of the sandbar into an elongated ball.

Down on the sand banks, Loren Kleppe and Ulysses Black had dodged the shrapnel and bullets for about fifteen minutes. It seemed like hours, and every soul prayed for the Marines of Hotel to come recklessly assaulting across the sand dunes to their rescue. Kleppe and Black were just shy of twenty years old and used to taking chances. Kleppe, an Iowa farm boy who had worked his butt off in his family's wheat and corn fields since before he could remember, had already shot two machine gunners. The bullet strikes, although plenty fatal, had not been witnessed by the two snipers. After each shot, the spotter and his sniper would duck down into their shallow hole, which had been hastily dug by hand two feet deep into a sand dune. The artillery from the two 105mm guns at My Loc 2 didn't seem to do much damage except raise the dust to the choking level. A cloud of gray smoke hung over the trenchline, giving the Marines of Foxtrot more concealment than was apparent from Hotel's vantage point on the northern bank.

Each time the two howitzers ceased firing in order to reload, two Viet Cong snipers peered out through the smoke and dust, looking for targets. Loren Kleppe lay prone in his hole, scanning the bank some hundred meters away, knowing a quick head shot was all he would get. He saw a brave enemy sniper crawl over the lip of his trench and sight into his PU scope, mounted on an antiquated but deadly Moishin-Nagant sniper rifle. This was what Kleppe had trained for in the hot marshes and arid hills around Chu Lai. Few Marines ever experienced head-to-head duels with an enemy sniper, and even fewer ever actually killed one. Vaughn Nickell and Tom Casey had killed two enemy snipers off Phu Loc 6 back in December, but they were protected in their bunkers with a good field of fire off the hill. This shot would take an uphill angle into the foliage that covered the bank, with only the head and shoulders of the Viet Cong sniper visible from Kleppe's position.

The Viet Cong sniper's rifle barked, and a Marine who lay wounded on the flat ground above the stream twitched in agony as another enemy bullet burst through his leg. While the Marine yelled for help, Kleppe realized that he had to make the shot or the sniper would waste his buddies one at a time. The Viet Cong were masters at creating chaos and panic in the kill zones of their ambushes. They much preferred to wound a Marine than kill him outright, since the more casualties a sniper produced, the more Marines were required to tend his wounds. The Viet Cong also did not fail to understand the psychological damage to troop morale near a kill zone, when men had to endure the anguished moans and helpless agony of their wounded comrades.

The sniper's rifle spit leaden death into the Marine ranks again, and another youngster cried out in pain and mortal fear. Loren Kleppe raised his rifle above the bunker's lip and sighted in on a dark shadow that lay facing his bleeding brothers. The smoke and debris that had filtered over the battlefield made a clear sighting impossible. The Viet Cong sharpshooter no doubt felt a degree of safety, with the Marines bloodied and confused by mortar rounds still tearing into the sand dunes as they lay stunned and weary. Loren took up the trigger slack, and the M1-D bucked hard against his shoulder. The heavy match bullet tore through the short hundred-meter distance between friend and foe. Kleppe couldn't see clearly through the smoke as the Viet Cong sniper's head blew apart like a pumpkin smashed by a mallet during a Halloween prank back home. No more shots were fired from the enemy bank, and Kleppe slumped down like a drugged animal into the bottom of his bunker.

Captain Jerry Doherty took the radio mike from Dale Pappas and adjusted the heavy artillery barrage onto the enemy riverbank. Privately, Doherty was incensed that the battalion's executive officer, Major Cooper, or the battalion commander, Lieutenant Colonel Airheart, were not physically present to help move the troops and adjust the artillery fire. Captain Doherty rapidly calculated his predicament before making another SITREP to the battalion command post at Phu Loc 6, where Major Cooper and Colonel Airheart monitored the radios marking the rifle companies' progress on the situation map spread before them.

Doherty spoke into the radio mike: "Crimson Leader Actual. This is Crimson Two Actual. SITREP follows. Crimson One Actual WIA. Radioman KIA. Number KIAs and WIAs presumed high. Enemy automatic and rifle fire extremely heavy. Eighty-two mike mike mortar fire now lifted. Crimson One assault stalled fifty meters past north side of river. Crimson Two standing by with two assault platoons waiting for orders. Artillery prep only moderately effective. Recommend changing shells to delayed fuses. Enemy bunkered north bank of river. Crimson Two now receiving 82mm mortar attack and intense sniper fire. Awaiting orders, over."

The battalion commander had been in the midst of chaos during World War II beach landings in the

Japanese-held Solomon Islands. Colonel Airheart knew the battle had been joined and that the enemy was primarily the hardcore Viet Cong main forces backed by North Vietnamese Army advisors who surely knew their business. His Marines had received a bloody nose at the river crossing, and they would hemorrhage to death unless the two fresh platoons from Hotel Company were committed to the fray. He grasped the radio mike at once and rang up Hotel Company, which was now coming under heavy mortar and small arms fire from the Viet Cong positions on the far riverbank across the sandbar.

"Crimson Two Actual. This is Crimson Leader Actual. Your orders are to cross the river with platoons assaulting in column. Repeat: Cross the river with platoons setting up on sandbar until artillery can be shifted to your sector. When artillery is adjusted on enemy positions, form rifle platoons on line and conduct frontal assault enemy trenchline. Radio Crimson Leader Actual when trenchline penetrated and secure."

That was it. No turning back now. Foxtrot was in shambles, and more mortar rounds were slamming into Hotel's command post bunkers with horrible force.

Loren Kleppe and Ulysses Black swapped off the M1-D sniper rifle and kept up an accurate harassing fire on anything that moved inside the haze of smoke and gunfire that was now letting up in the enemy trenchline. The casualties were being treated by Navy corpsmen, while the rest of the company was pouring out return fire as the Marines got their bearings back after the initial shock of the enemy ambush. Kleppe and Black brushed the cold sweat laced with burned powder and fear from their faces and gazed into the sky with simple thanks for just being alive. At least they were still breathing this far into the battle, which hadn't slowed up in its fury but had merely shifted downriver to take on the new threat from Hotel Company.

The point Marines guided the 2nd platoon onto the steep trails cutting down the northern bank toward the first rapidly twisting branch of the river.

The platoon took the sniper team of Ron Willoughby and Vaughn Nickell with them. It was assumed that the sandbar crossing would be mostly unopposed, that Charlie had retreated after shellacking Foxtrot in the first ambush downriver. But unknown to Marine intelligence, the Viet Cong trenchline was actually over two thousand meters long, and it was a reinforced trench connecting all the enemy bunkers, including those that had opposed Foxtrot with the hardened bunkers that now opposed Hotel. The 2nd platoon of Hotel Company spread out after wading chest-deep through the river, continuing its advance across the sandbar and toward the enemy bank.

Now, Captain Doherty, following his "clear orders" from Battalion, ordered the 3rd platoon commander, Lieutenant Ed Smith, to lead his men across the river and hold position on the left flank of 2nd platoon. Third platoon was lead by point scouts John Lafley and John Culbertson, and backed by Gary Woodruff, Luther Hamilton, John Matarazzi, and his ammunition humper and assistant gunner, John Jessmore. Corporal Tim Kirby from Knoxville, Tennessee brought up his squad, with another sniper team in the center of the file.

The column of green-cloaked infantry slowly descended the steep northern riverbank, leaning back against the slanting, hard-packed clay walls that fed the Marines into the solitary trail twisting down to the sandbar. The sand itself stretched thirty meters or so before Lafley and his new apprentice scout, Culbertson, slipped into the four-foot-deep stream. The fast, twisting current made the going hard, and the grunts held their M-14 rifles over their helmets to protect the weapons from the crud and corruption of the river. One by one the Marines forded, while another fusillade of Viet Cong sniper bullets tore into the rippling current and cracked close over the struggling men.

The snipers had an even tougher time protecting their delicate scoped rifles. Willoughby and Nickell stepped out into the swirling tide and sloshed ahead, following the point element across the first stream. Willoughby crawled carefully up the sand dune obstacles of the island, pulling Nickell up behind him and using his rifle butt as a handhold for the water-sodden Marine. The terrain on the sandbar was varied and broken by grassy dunes and shallow depressions that had not been visible from the bank where the Hotel Company commander still huddled, watching the lethargic progress of his platoons as they fought the river's mighty force.

Willoughby passed the grunts who had stopped to unburden themselves of their mortar rounds and extra hundred-round canvas boxes of belted machine-gun ammunition. The point scouts had already moved fifty meters past the river, over the mounds and depressions of the sandbar. John Lafley finally halted the 3rd platoon another fifty meters up the sandbar island. He and Culbertson hastily began to dig into shallow fighting holes as the first bullets from the Viet Cong's southern bunkers slammed into the loose sand, throwing fistfuls into the air.

Willoughby looked back at Nickell and made an immediate decision: "Hey, man, let's hit the deck and dig a hole right here. These rounds are close! I can see the muzzle flashes along the far bank."

The Marines of 3rd platoon weren't in need of formal orders. It was all "assholes and elbows" as each man burrowed into the dunes with hands, helmets, and entrenching tools. In two minutes most of the platoon had crabbed into small burrows and pockets scooped out of the deep sand by any means possible. Urged into immediate frenzied action by the loud cracks of the enemy bullets that tore overhead, Willoughby and Nickell had lost sight of Jim Flynn and Dennis Toncar, who had buried themselves somewhere along the wavy stretches of sand. No doubt the snipers were frozen in their holes, trying to gauge the enemy strength and the direction of incoming fire. Willoughby looked sideways across the dunes and was shocked to see the 2nd platoon caught in the middle of a deadly close-quarter ambush.

The 2nd platoon had preceded the 3rd platoon onto the sandbar, heading toward the enemy trenchline atop the southern bank. The highly disciplined Viet Cong had allowed the Marines to come within fifty meters of their positions before opening fire with their AK-47 automatic assault rifles. Then the VC weapons crews began firing B-40 rockets point-blank into the startled mass of men.

The first assault line of Marines to approach the Viet Cong trenchline formed a skirmish line, but were instantly mowed down by an invisible wall of screaming automatic rifle fire. The Marines of 2nd platoon were twisted and lifted into the air, flailing and grasping for some margin of cover and concealment that wasn't available at that close range. Ducking and running, seemingly in slow motion, as if caught up in some horrible nightmare, the grunts struggled to escape the bullets that screamed toward them like swarming hornets.

Willoughby watched as the hard bodies of young, vibrant, and courageous American boys were sliced and diced in a two-minute orgy of blood-flecked death that made him retch with fear. What would become of the 3rd platoon when the angry guns of the Viet Cong's professional killers were turned on them? He glanced at Vaughn Nickell, who had covered his ears with his hands as he lay next to his rifle in their foxhole. Nickell was trying vainly to drown out the screams and forlorn moaning of the dying troopers of 2nd platoon.

Willoughby felt something rise up in his chest, hot warrior blood flooding his senses as he got to his knees and sighted his rifle, firing toward the muzzle flashes of the entrenched enemy. The veterans of the Viet Cong's bloody R-20th Main Force Regiment were having a heyday slaughtering the Marines. Willoughby stared through bloodshot eyes at them and methodically took his revenge, bullet after bullet from his M1-D streaking angrily into the enemy trenchline and through the docile bodies of the now dead Viet Cong gunners.

Nickell, meanwhile, fired a magazine of well-placed snap shots from his M-14 into the enemy bunkers. The snipers had temporarily forgotten their fears in the tortured spasm of retribution that drove their minds and bodies into a deadly rage. As primitive survival instincts took command of them, they forgot their own safety in the desperation of the moment and killed without conscious emotion. The two snipers killed with a primeval lust for vengeance that was so powerful it overwhelmed the instincts for self-preservation. Willoughby had the strangest thought as he squeezed the trigger of his Garand over and over. The fact was that his fear of dying had receded to be supplanted with an instinctive animal drive to kill and maim the enemy. Even at the cost of his own life, he would protect the lives of his 2nd platoon brothers who were being shot to death piecemeal. Marines, after all, were men who would routinely die for each other when the enemy they were facing spilled first blood. Marines had a special bond that was like no other, and it was because of this unwritten brotherhood that they had never been defeated on the battlefield in their two-hundred-year-old history of bloody victories around the globe.

As Willoughby's bullets crumpled the bodies of two

Viet Cong machine gunners, he smiled and knew he'd stared down the Grim Reaper and his cold, dead eyes. "Come on, you godless motherfuckers!" he shouted. "Come closer and die! You ain't killing any more Marines, because this M1-D bad boy ain't hearin' it!"

Willoughby's rifle fire was joined by sporadic bursts from other Marines, who desperately tried to throw off the Viet Cong ambush net that had eighty of them hemmed in and pinned down in a kill zone not a hundred meters wide. All along the firing lines, Marines risked getting their heads shot off as they lifted their torsos from their sandy graves to fire back at an almost invisible enemy. The mortar rounds tore across the Marine positions again and again as the Viet Cong gunners made certain that no escape path was available to them on the beach.

Farther up the sandbar, Luther Hamilton screamed for his squad members to stay down and stay alive. Lafley, Jessmore, and Culbertson crawled along the valleys between sand dunes and tried to dress the gaping bullet wounds of buddies who were slowly bleeding to death. Patches of sticky hot crimson were spreading out from the small clutch of Marines as 3rd platoon fought to keep calm in a hailstorm of death.

Ron Willoughby rolled onto his side and looked at Vaughn Nickell, whose face was white as a sheet. "Hang on, partner," he said. "The skipper will bring in the artillery soon, and we'll get off this fucking sandbar. Keep your head down, man. All the heroes out here are dead men!"

Up the sandbar, young scout John Culbertson's rifle had a spent round jammed in the chamber, rendering it useless. As Culbertson moved to aid another wounded man who cried out for his mother through bullet-shattered teeth, a volley of enemy fire cut the sling from his rifle and tore the canteen from his hip. Another flight of lead cut the tops off a grunt's buttocks, a man who'd been firing his weapon a few yards farther to the front. The bullets tore the utility trousers to shreds and flung pieces of the Marine's cheeks, saturated with blood like meat twisting out the mouth of a grinder. The mangled gore was flung into Culbertson's face, sticking to his sweaty skin in pulverized crimson chunks.

At that moment with death close by, the twenty-year-old Marine made his first urgent request to God. Culbertson closed his eyes tightly as the cracking and whining bullets transformed the bloody scene into an almost dreamlike state where every action transpired in slow motion. Like many others on the sandbar, Culbertson had a fleeting moment of insight. He earnestly pledged to God—and anyone else who would listen, for that matter—to serve the Lord and his fellow man if allowed to live. Then Culbertson pushed his head deeper into his blood-caked helmet and willed the swarm of bullets away.

Sometime later Culbertson heard the Marine artillery slam into the Viet Cong bunkers, and for the first time that morning he thought he just might stay alive.

CHAPTER THIRTEEN

The Snipers' Assault

After an hour of enduring the intense automatic rifle fire of the Viet Cong gunners, Ron Willoughby, Vaughn Nickell, Loren Kleppe, and Jim Flynn were still alive—barely. They huddled in their positions while the severely wounded Marines of Hotel Company yelled in vain for aid from their already dead and wounded corpsmen. The numbers of KIAs and WIAs had grown since the first VC bullet impacted the sand dunes and bunkers of the trapped Marine warriors around 0915 that morning. Now it was past 1030 hours, and the sun was vainly trying to break through the deathly gray haze that shrouded the river.

The first heavy 155mm artillery round spiraled down over the southern enemy bank and burst in a shower of fiery white phosphorous petals. The Hotel skipper in the command bunker was on the secure radio net, instantly adjusting the artillery fire. "Steel Curtain, this is Crimson Two Actual. Adjusting fire. One-five-five millimeter willy peter spotting round shot long. Drop 150 meters and repeat mission. Repeat, drop one-five-zero meters. Friendly troops engaged along sandbar at AT955534. Enemy target is southern bank of Song Thu Bon. Crimson Two Actual, over."

The artillery gunners at An Hoa immediately lowered their aim. After a short wait, the report sounded from the lone cannon belching the heavy round up through the gray mists and over the flush paddies. The shell fell with a horrid shriek onto the enemy-held bank along the Song Thu Bon. Captain Jerry Doherty nodded from his bunker atop the northern bank as the shell exploded in a flower pattern of burning metal. The white phosporous billowed into a black-and-white-spattered cloud that hung like the terrible spread wings of the mythical Angel of Death over the Communist positions. Doherty was on the radio requesting a "Fire for effect" mission, which ordered the gunners back at An Hoa to fire a full four-gun battery into the newly acquired target area armed with high explosive warheads. The harried troops could finally get some relief from the Viet Cong gunfire, and once the enemy trench was silenced by the artillery mission, Doherty could rally his Marines into the attack.

The snipers had provided a defensive miracle on the sandbar. Their skilled marksmanship had cut down many of the VC machine gunners and snipers who were raking the sandbar with relentless deadly fire. Ron Willoughby had considered how much more effective his sniper teammates could have been had they been allowed to dig in on the friendly riverbank, providing long-range covering fire for their Marine brothers on the sandbar. Then the mortar fire from the hidden Viet Cong battery found Captain Doherty and his command group and commenced blasting them from the northern bank's bunkers.

Hotel Company's gunnery sergeant, Huzak, had been shot through the left forearm by a VC sniper as he monitored the radios giving aid to Doherty. The Hotel skipper had eventually taken command of over 450 Marines, called in sixteen air strikes, and over a hundred artillery fire missions. Gunny Huzak helped manage platoon control and troop movement. Later, Jerry Doherty was also tasked with overseeing the precarious flights of medevac choppers that descended to the less than secure sandbar island where more than fifty Marines and corpsmen lay dead and gravely wounded.

Doherty had performed a coordinated series of attack maneuvers and rescue missions while calling in artillery and air strikes. He continued encouraging his troops under levels of stress and fatigue not experienced by Marine commanders since the days of the Chosin Reservoir in Korea and the beach assaults on Iwo Jima and Pelileu. Willoughby thought that the captain was handling this combat crisis with decisive resolve and that the situation was well in hand. Jerry Doherty was still a few months shy of his twenty-fifth birthday.

Down on the sandbar, sniper Loren Kleppe heard the last of the fire missions slam into the Communist trench-line with devastating force. Trees were shattered and hurled over the heads of prostrate Marines like tooth-picks thrown from a speeding car window. Dirt and plants brewed up into a salad mix that was flung into the air, and then drifted with the winter winds across the battlefield. It gave a tattered and torn appearance to the previously clean white sands of the river channel and the glistening green foliage of the curving riverbanks. Deep gouges and giant craters now appeared in the slick mud walls of the riverbank where the humongous artillery rounds had crunched deeply into dense, tree-rooted soil before detonating.

The whole river valley had been transformed in less than two hours from a pristine blue ribbon of life into a burned and blood-splattered field of death and chaos. Men moaned like lost and forgotten souls while their wounds were bandaged and the lifeblood continued slipping out of their crippled bodies. Ron Willoughby was a good Catholic. He closed his eyes a brief moment, invoking the grace of Mary and the love of Jesus Christ to save his friends from this terrible hellish evil. He knew that the images he had witnessed would never heal fully.

He would also adopt a new gentle humility and respect for life after seeing it snatched away from so many youngsters in such a ruthless display of ideological hatred and aggression. It was ironic that Willoughby realized clearly, for the first time, that he would never know or understand the true motives of his enemies. But he could well understand the greed of the politicians and business interests that never hesitated to commit young American boys of good conscience to the furnace of death so they could line their pockets with riches that would put the gold treasure of Nebuchadnezzar to shame. Along with Tom Casey, Loren Kleppe, and mild-mannered Vaughn Nickell, Willoughby thought that dying for your Marine brothers and your country was one thing, but dying so some corrupt, senile old pirates at the World Bank, Bell Helicopter, and at McDonnell Douglas Corporation could get filthy rich was quite another.

Little did Willoughby, Jim Flynn, or any of the others know that this moment in history was changing forever the way Americans would view their governmental leaders. In years to come, cynicism and doubt would creep into people's minds whenever American forces were ordered to take the battlefield during foreign wars, ethnic clashes, and police actions that would put American kids unnecessarily at risk. Dwight Eisenhower had said it best after the allied victory over Nazi Germany and Imperial Japan in Word War II: "My fellow Americans, we must never again fail to recognize the dangers of the Military Industrial Complex."

Keeping the Communists at bay along the Pacific Rim had been thought a necessary task, though one fraught with danger. In Vietnam by 1967, the American forces in I Corps, under brave combat leaders like Captains Jerry Doherty and George Burgett, had begun to break the back of the Viet Cong. Victory was definitely in sight, and the Marines were building the veteran battalions of experienced jungle fighters necessary to crush the invading Communist NVA divisions.

There was a problem, however, with turning the professional Marine commanders loose to pursue the North Vietnamese Army and destroy its legions at the gates of Hanoi if necessary. Many business leaders in the States had already sold their souls to raise profits at the expense of the lives of young American boys. These merchants of greed and death hid behind the old adage that "the business of America is business." They salted away their bloated profits in illicit foreign deals and turned their tuxedo-slick lies into polite conversation at cocktail parties. All the while, their sons and countrymen lay bleeding in the paddies, dying alone in sand-flecked graves along the Thu Bon River after obscure battles like Operation Tuscaloosa.

Lyndon Johnson, Dean Rusk, and Robert McNamara looked into the nightly news cameras and lied repeatedly to the American people, in effect saying that Marines like Ron Willoughby, Tom Casey, Loren Kleppe, and Vaughn Nickell weren't quite up to defeating the Viet Cong. Not quite yet! General Westmoreland called for more troops to invade North Vietnam and end the war. President Johnson and the resident managers at Bell Helicopter in Fort Worth, Texas, sent more helicopters instead.

A particular gripe of the Marine snipers was that Defense Secretary Robert McNamara saw to it that the battle-proven M-14 rifle was taken away from expert riflemen, only to be replaced by the noneffective, prone-to-jamming, and low-energy-impacting, plastic piece of crap then known as the M-16 rifle. The Marines had to wonder what kind of leaders their country tolerated, who would issue an untested rifle to its combat forces during the middle of the worst fighting of the Vietnam War. After hundreds of Marines had died because their untested rifles had jammed in the dirt, mud, and blood always present on any battleground, these same politicians made excuses for the shoddy quality control and cheap design of the weapon.

In contrast, the Viet Cong and the NVA had weapons made by nonindustrialized Communist China. Yet their weapons worked in the mud, rain, and grime of the rice paddies, firing every time. The VC and North Vietnamese ran over the American Marines, whose weapons failures led to their untimely combat deaths, while Robert McNamara and Colt Industries racked up record corporate profits. The heroes of those bloody battles would never forget what they saw as the betrayal by their own countrymen, which senselessly stole the lifeblood from their departed brother Marines.

Willoughby looked at the trenchline, covered in a pall of thick smoke that obscured the Viet Cong bunkers, as Gunnery Sergeant Huzak, a giant Marine, walked fearlessly across the sand dunes, rallying the troops. Huzak and Gunnery Sergeant Roberto Gutierrez of Hotel Company yelled for the infantrymen who were still alive to form an assault line preparatory to attacking the enemy trenchline.

Gunny Huzak's barrel-chested frame moved like an armored personnel carrier through the shot-up bunkers where youngsters lay prostrate splashed in blood. Only two hours earlier they had been breathing, fighting, and desperately hoping to survive the close-quarter melee that had engulfed their fighting holes.

Gutierrez, a small, hard Mexican-American from San Diego, California, hustled his troopers out of their dugouts and onto their feet. He held the pistol grip of his M-14 rifle, its stock chopped off for easy point shooting in the tight jungle trails along the river.

"The captain wants every Marine on line. Get off your asses and form up on Gunny Gutierrez," Huzak shouted, waving a muscled forearm at Ron Willoughby and Vaughn Nickell. Looking into the fear in rifleman John Culbertson's nineteen-year-old eyes, Huzak said, "Are you ready to go kill some gooks, son? We're counting on you! Let's go get after it!"

Culbertson looked at the bullet wound along Gunny Huzak's left forearm. A VC bullet had gouged out a canoe-shaped divot over a foot long that ran from his elbow to his wrist. The blood ran down Huzak's forearm to his fingers and splattered in the wet sand at his feet.

Jumping to his feet, Culbertson joined the already forming first assault line. His weapon was clogged with sand and he couldn't chamber another round, but he stepped ahead at a quick-time march holding the useless M-14 at his hip and mouthing the words *bang, bang, bang, bang*. Culbertson stepped gingerly into the second stream before the assault line reached the enemy banks. Looking over his shoulder, he saw Ron Willoughby shoulder his M1-D rifle and fire round after round into the enemy trenches. The artillery had already killed many of the Viet Cong defenders, but a squad of wounded soldiers had been left defending their bunkers to slow down the Marine advance.

The enemy troops suddenly appeared and kneeled, sighting along the Marine assault wave and firing point-blank into our wavering line. Several Marines fell wounded and lay immobile in the shallow water of the second stream. Willoughby and Nickell paused to fire their weapons into the smoke and chaos of the now rejuvenated trenchline. The heavy bullets from the M1-D and Vaughn's M-14 tore into the Viet Cong defenders' trenchline, knocking one of the enemy riflemen into the air and flipping him onto his back, leaving him "dead right there."

John Lafley strained his eagle eyes and, drawing on a decade of hunting and guiding experience in the mountains of Montana, expertly picked up the movement of a

Sniper Ken Barden off Phu Loc 6, March 1967.

A 5th Marine sniper sights his rifle at the Chu Lai sniper base, 1966.

Fifth Marine snipers at Chu Lai, 1966.

Ron Willoughby in a bunker at Phu Loc 6, January 1967

Vaughn Nickell scopes the approach to Phu Loc 6 from the north across the Thu Bon River.

Ron Willoughby fires an M1-D Garand off Phu Loc 6 during the rainy season of 1967.

Third Platoon, Hotel Company, 2nd Battalion, 5th Marines on bunkers atop Nong Son Mountain, overlooking Antenna Valley to the south. These Marines were the veteran grunts of the most decorated regiment in the Marine Corps. Author is second from right in profile.

Fifth Marine scout-sniper hootch at An Hoa, October 1967. Left to right: H. Moore, J. Hudson, D. Toncar, B. Milligan, B. Wills, E. Rackow, and Art Bean

Ron Willoughby (left) and Sgt. Tom Casey before Operation Union I, April 1967.

Fifth Marines after Operation Union II on Hill 29, June 1967. Kneeling, left to right: A. Bean and T. Spanopoulos. Standing: H. Moore, J. Carter, R. Milligan, D. Toncar, T. Elbert, R. Willoughby, F. Tuitele, and A. Draper.

Gunnery Sergeant Vernon D. Mitchell (left) coaches snipers at Happy Valley, 1967.

William S. Moore and Dennis Toncar after Operation Swift, September 1967.

A section of the 5th Marine Sniper Platoon at Hill 29, June 1967.

Kneeling, left to right: John Howell, Ken Barden, Art Bean, Al Levandoski, Fofo Tuitele, and Gunny Cummet

Standing: Tom Casey, Pat Montgomery, George Wilhite, Fred Sanders, Tom Elbert, Verne Smith, Vaughn Nickell, Ron Willoughby, Tony Spanopoulos, Bill Wills, Loren Kleppe, Dennis Toncar, Ricky Allison, and George Nash

Fifth Marine snipers at An Hoa, 1967

Sniper Ken Barden, 1967

The backside of Phu Loc 6, facing the Thu Bon River. Across the river is the Arizona Territory—the hottest combat area in Vietnam.

Sgt. John J. Culbertson in January 2001, posing for three articles about the combat exploits of 5th Marine snipers for *Soldier of Fortune* magazine. Age 55—once a Marine, always a Marine!

wheeled machine gun as the VC gunners rolled their antiquated 1908 Maxim water-cooled World War I vintage gun into position to strafe the assault wave. Lafley kneeled and fired slowly, taking out all three gunners, who were exposed while the gun was being unlimbered. Spitting tobacco juice into the muddy water, the Salish Indian smiled briefly before turning his attention back toward the front and the dozen Viet Cong suicide troops who huddled alone in their holes.

Ron Willoughby and Vaughn Nickell slipped and crawled up the wet clay mud of the Viet Cong's riverbank. Most Marines used their rifle butts and entrenching tools to claw their path up the bank. The VC survivors waited with only a handful of bullets each in their fortified bunkers, knowing that their commanders had abandoned them to create a last bloody obstacle for the attacking Marines. Many of the Viet Cong were too badly wounded to retreat when the main body of the main force fled to the Communist-dominated villages of La Bac 1 and La Bac 2 a mile west up the river.

These forgotten men would fight like devils, wounded or not. Their commanders and political cadre officers had convinced these poor souls that the Americans were in Vietnam to murder their women and children, and the Viet Cong had been taught that the Marines were mercenary troops released from American prisons and trained in fanatical military practices without any conscience or decency. The Marines would rather die in battle and would never run away, so the Viet Cong had been schooled to always prepare to fight the Marines to the death, since no mercy would be shown to any wounded combatants, much less to any prisoner of war. Pictures had been disseminated showing Americans pitching tied-up Vietnamese prisoners out of airborne helicopters. Every effort had been made to paint the Marines—and other allied troops, for that matter—as the very incarnation of evil and utter ruthlessness.

In some ways, when I considered the combat ferocity of Lafley, Gerald Burns, Hamilton, Ybarra, and some of my other fellow grunts, perhaps the Viet Cong were partially right about Marines being bloodthirsty and ruthless. It's a matter of exposure to the ugliness and barbarity of modern combat that I have always felt causes otherwise kind, gentle American boys to be transformed into the bloody killers they become in a war like Vietnam. As our Korean War hero Harold Wadley used to tell us, there was only one clear rule in Vietnam—that there were no clear rules. The winners lived and the losers died, and it really made no fucking difference whatever how the killing went down. The American press would continue to lie to the student agitators at Cal Berkeley, and the Viet Cong and North Vietnamese would continue to lie to their own soldiers and people. It's noteworthy that thousands of Communist Viet Cong and North Viets surrendered to American "Choi Hoi" programs and eventually fought against their own people, while American traitorism was pretty much nonexistent except for the "Traitor-Bitch" Jane Fonda who will hopefully rot in hell for eternity.

Ron Willoughby found his footing and jumped over the top of the riverbank to witness the shattered remains of the R-20th Main Force Battalion. The Viet Cong soldiers lay in piles, with disjointed limbs reaching every direction. Some bodies were searching for heads while others lay twisted and mauled by the cruel barrages of the heavy Marine artillery. There were rough drag marks cutting across the ground from bunkers where the dead bodies of VC soldiers had been pulled by ropes attached to crude wooden body hooks. The Viet Cong always buried or tried to hide any dead soldiers after a battle turned against them in order to confuse American body count statistics. The Communists were well aware of the power of propaganda, and tried desperately to deny the Americans any good news that would show progress on the war front at home.

After a short halt, the Hotel skipper ordered his platoons into the attack to trap and finish the Viet Cong survivors who had fled to the main force's secondary defensive positions in La Bac 1 and La Bac 2. As the grunts of Hotel formed a fast-moving column, with John Lafley and John Culbertson taking the point and cutting overland through the heavy fern and bamboo obstructed jungle, Willoughby and Nickell heard the call "Snipers up" and ran ahead to join the Marines of Foxtrot. The grunts were braced in an attempt to break the defensive threat of a Viet Cong mortar position that had been bunkered behind a shallow hill and well-camouflaged. A VC machine-gun squad covered the mortar position from the right flank, and several riflemen were in shallow spider holes, situated to cut down the double-timing point scouts as the long Marine column approached their kill zone.

Willoughby and Nickell were one of two sniper teams attached to Foxtrot, and they took their instructions directly from Captain James A. Graham. Initially attached to Captain Jerry Doherty's command group to assist and observe, and new to combat in Vietnam, Captain Graham had been forced into command when George Burgett was seriously wounded on the riverbank after crossing the Thu Bon River on Hotel's left flank. Now, Graham was faced with the problem of crossing a kill zone raked by machine-gun fire and covered by heavy mortar fire. A direct attack might work if it were rapid enough and the riflemen could find their targets in the dense jungle. It was considered a deadly risk, however, and after the longest one-day firefight in the history of the Vietnam War to that point, no one doubted the skill, toughness, or willingness of the VC to hold their positions at all cost.

Graham paused a minute and thought that perhaps the Viet Cong or North Vietnamese senior commanders had fought along this very river in the not too distant past against the French or even the Japanese. Whatever the case, the Viet Cong obviously knew every inch of the river and its banks, and their defenses were strong and well-prepared. The Viet Cong main forces had many veteran soldiers that senior American planners thought might be the finest jungle fighters on earth. Their U-shaped ambush at the river had been well-conceived, and the Marines had marched bravely through the flanking sniper fire into the heavy machine guns of the main blocking force, as planned. Many unlucky Marines had been shot to pieces. Captain Graham's basic school training and raw instinct told him to run over the enemy, but his common sense told him to draw them out first. He knew he had two sniper teams available to pick their defenses apart before he attacked en masse. He put his hand on Ron Willoughby's shoulder and gave him his attack orders.

"Willoughby," he said, "you and Nickell take the trail to the right and crawl in as close to that mortar position as you can—staying in cover. Hold your fire and wait for the other sniper team to crawl into position on the high ground to your left flank. When Kleppe and Flynn get into position, they will fire into the mortar bunker as accurately as possible. The VC machine gun should open fire at that moment to neutralize the threat to their mortar team, and your team will draw down on and kill the machine gunners. Then we can attack the mortar crew with riflemen and M-79 grenadiers. We have absolutely got to eliminate the machine-gun crew, or they will cut my scouts to pieces when they charge in on foot. Any questions? You boys are the best shots I've got, and you cannot miss your targets! Go now, and keep in cover."

Willoughby's throat tightened as he looked at Vaughn Nickell, who stood nodding at his side. The first sniper team took the narrow trail to the right, praying that it wasn't booby-trapped. Loren Kleppe took the left approach to the Viet Cong mortar site just as the enemy tube coughed somewhere nearby in the jungle. Another brace of shells headed toward Foxtrot's Marines, who knelt inside the deep shadows of the high jungle canopy, loading magazines and slaking their thirst from half-empty canteens.

Loren Kleppe crept rather than walked toward the sound of the mortar coughing in the near distance. After ten minutes of brushing aside limbs and plants and stepping over muddy holes in the trail, he saw the dark outline of the mound that hid the Viet Cong mortarmen. Taking a prone position, Ulysses Black focused his binoculars and glassed the slopes along the mortar position, looking for the guarding riflemen. Finally, he saw a bush move as a VC sniper crawled to a more forward position. Black motioned the direction toward the enemy rifleman, and Kleppe brought his rifle to bear and focused his scope on the still-moving bush tied to the Viet Cong's back. Black nodded as Kleppe took up the trigger slack and the M1-D bucked, throwing a heavy 173-grain .30–06 bullet shrieking toward the Viet Cong. The bullet slammed through flesh and bone and kicked the enemy sniper's body over on his side, where he lay motionless. Another Viet Cong came up for a look, and Kleppe fired a snap shot that tore directly through the VC's face, exploding his head in a torrent of blood-caked hair and chunks of jagged skull that embedded themselves into the sniper's leafy camouflaged pith helmet.

Willoughby and Nickell lay prone and well-camouflaged a hundred meters to Loren Kleppe's right flank when the shooting started. After two shots from the heavy-hitting M1-D, Willoughby heard the first burst of the Viet Cong's RPD light machine gun cutting into the jungle foliage, searching for the Marine sniper team. Willoughby and Nickell went into a low crawl and closed in on the VC machine gun that coughed away in short, disciplined bursts. About forty meters ahead, Willoughby stood up in a low crouch to eyeball the machine gunners, while Nickell stayed back with his index finger on the trigger of his M-14, ready to back up his partner's play in case they were spotted. Willoughby was kneeling and rapidly scanning the left flank, wondering why Kleppe had ceased firing and hoping to hell that he wasn't already dead.

Just as Ron Willoughby brought his rifle around in an arc to scan the battlefield, a VC rifleman appeared from nowhere. He was dressed in khaki trousers and wore a dark green shirt and a pith helmet covered in foliage. Another large mass of foliage was fastened to his backpack and extended out to his sides, making him nearly invisible when he went to ground. He held an SKS rifle at high port arms with the spike bayonet menacingly extended. As he brought the rifle butt up to his shoulder, Willoughby lifted the heavy M1-D sniper rifle up in self-defense, although he knew he was likely a dead man. As he closed his eyes, bracing against the Viet Cong bullet that would surely come tearing into his chest and end his young life, the terrific blast of a rifle sounded to his rear. Vaughn Nickell had reacted as he was trained, and shot the Viet Cong through the chest from less than thirty meters away. Nickell hadn't had time to aim, so he'd brought up the M-14 and snapped off the shot, looking only at the front sight of his rifle, down the long flat of the barrel.

The 7.62mm bullet lifted the pint-size VC warrior

into the air and unceremoniously flung him onto his backside. Willoughby blinked as a river of sweat coursed off his brow from under his helmet band. He stared at the Viet Cong rifleman who was now just another DRT. Then he glanced back at Nickell, who knelt down with a somber look on his face. Vaughn Nickell, a kind and religious person, was weeping and deeply troubled after killing his first enemy soldier. Sergeant Tom Casey, who was legendary for his guts and glory in combat, finally had to take Nickell back to the rear for some counseling so his young shooter could understand that the Boy Scouts part of his life was definitely over.

Satisfied that the mortar crew was trapped without supporting arms, Captain Graham radioed battalion headquarters at Phu Loc 6 for an air strike. Ten minutes later a pair of camouflaged Marine F-4 Phantom jets rolled in and bombed the mortar team into oblivion. Once again James Graham proved his combat instincts were sound, if highly dangerous. The savvy use of skilled Marine air power had saved many grunts' lives, while the Viet Cong were eliminated as they bravely stood and fought desperately to the last.

Willoughby and Nickell pulled back into the safety of the jungle as the Phantoms rolled in for the kill. Loren Kleppe had done some fantastically accurate shooting, and Sergeant Tom Casey would be very pleased with the performance of his "13 Cent Killers" in their first pitched battle. Thirteen cents was the cost of one round of match ammo used by USMC snipers.

Upriver in La Bac 1, Lafley led Culbertson and Burns along with the remainder of 3rd platoon into the hedgerows of the sprawling rubber plantation that dominated the high ground above the river. Several bunkers were encountered and reduced to burial plots for dead Viet Cong. The grunts of Hotel Company 2nd Battalion,

5th Marines, had no reservations about killing the enemy. After the shellacking the grunts had taken on the sandbar, everyone wanted some payback. Private Burns lit up a cigarette and blew the smoke in a jet out his tight lips over his upturned helmet. He looked at Lafley and Culbertson before he tried to add up the situation.

"Lafley, the way I got it figured," he said, "there must be at least a hundred gooks alive up the trail in that village. I say we call in some artillery, and the minute the last rounds come in, we follow-up before the little bastards can get out of their holes. What do you think?"

Burns always plotted a way to maximize his chances of getting even with Charlie for killing his younger brother. No amount of death and mayhem could satisfy the big redhead. Burns had become a cold and calculating killer of startling proportions. Lafley and Culbertson thought his cold brutality was the perfect counterweapon to the utterly ruthless butchery of the Viet Cong. Finally, the artillery was directed in on the remaining soldiers of the Viet Cong main forces, who chose to die bravely fighting to the last, rather than submit to the overwhelmingly destructive machine that the 2/5 Marines had become.

Ron Willoughby, Vaughn Nickell, Loren Kleppe, and Jim Flynn had performed admirably as a "combat multiplier" and had helped to ease Hotel out of a death trap on the sandbar island. The snipers had taken out the security for the Viet Cong mortar crew pinning Foxtrot down. Then, they helped ease pressure on the battalion's finest point scouts, Vic Ditchkoff from Foxtrot Company and John Lafley from Hotel.

Sergeant Tom Casey had finally hitched a ride down to the river aboard an M-48 tank. When he saw the carnage and destruction left in the battle's aftermath, Casey found a new respect for the courageous efficiency and dedication of his sharpshooters. In a battle of this scope, it was always hard to assess enemy casualties, but in his heart Sergeant Tom Casey knew his snipers had done an outstanding job in supporting the grunts and "taking out the garbage" during the fiercest fighting ever along the river.

CHAPTER FOURTEEN

Snipers Invade Antenna Valley Fred Sanders and Dennis Toncar

January 1967 had brought four new replacements to the 5th Marine Snipers and assurance to Sergeant Tom Casey that the informal training of his shooters was being noticed at 1st Marine Division in Da Nang. Casey had taken his three sniper teams of six Marines to An Hoa to accompany the increased combat patrols in the deadly Arizona Territory when the new sniper candidates settled into the old sniper billets at Hill 35 outside Chu Lai. He was informed of the arrival of his new charges, but with the preparations for Operation Tuscaloosa in their final phase, he was consumed with his operational orders.

Tuscaloosa jumped off with little enemy contact, but the river crossing presented the Leathernecks of 2/5 with one of their greatest battlefield challenges in the Vietnam War. Casey had to give hard-earned credit to his three sniper teams. They had eliminated over a dozen Viet Cong and North Viets while removing enemy snipers and heavy weapons that threatened the grunts trapped on the sandbar and later along the jungle trails to La Bac 1 and La Bac 2.

By now, the 5th Marine Sniper Platoon had racked up

over sixty confirmed enemy kills. Generally, it was assumed that ten to twenty percent of all wounded Communist combatants would eventually die of their wounds due to lack of proper medical aid and the high incidence of infection. The actual contribution to the official "body count" figures amassed by the 1st Marine Division after each patrol skirmish or battle probably would have more accurately shown over a hundred kills by the snipers. During 1967 in particular, the high number of large-scale battles made the tally of official enemy battle deaths very sketchy indeed. The Communist forces always removed any dead or badly wounded soldiers during chaotic battles, often dumping their bodies into previously dug holes or tunnels to deceive American officials.

The grunts and sniper teams both expressed little concern about the body count figures. They knew when they were kicking Charlie's ass. They also knew when the enemy got an ambush to click just right and chewed up an American patrol. The distinct advantage in surprise and stealth went to the Viet Cong, who never tried to completely annihilate the Marine forces, but instead settled on giving the Americans a good bloody nose now and then which was sure to make headlines with the anti-war press back home in the United States. Tom Casey thought his Marines would win the war if they could make the Viet Cong and the recent North Vietnamese infiltrators stand and fight.

The average American military thinker could not accurately fathom the planning and political objectives of their Communist counterparts. This period of large-scale, relatively static conventional battles would eventually convince the more flexible Communist high command that it was impossible for them to win against the powerful American military's vast advantages in firepower, mobility, airpower, and fighting spirit. The early years of the war pitted the Marine's finest all-volunteer units, with extremely high morale, against Viet Cong soldiers who were growing weary of dying and living like sightless moles inside the tunnels that undercut the countryside.

The only major obstacle that the Marines had to get a handle on was the Viet Cong's absolute mastery of the terrain. During the river crossing on Tuscaloosa, the Viet Cong set up and executed a masterful U-shaped ambush of startling proportions. If the Communists had possessed the same level of offensive firepower as the American Marines, they might well have won the battle. The Marine generals in Da Nang knew they had Charlie on the ropes, and they pressed their battalions ever more aggressively into the hostile paddies, praying for another decisive fixed engagement. Meanwhile, Sergeant Casey represented the ideal aggressive warrior spirit that had made the Marines masters of every battlefield and foe for over two hundred years. He constantly worked on increasing his snipers' proficiency by providing ambush and highly accurate supporting fire for the large number of squad and platoon-size patrols now crisscrossing the Arizona Territory daily. The success of the snipers' supporting efforts on Tuscaloosa also reached the ears of other Marine battalions in the regiment.

The 1st Battalion, 5th Marines, at Hill 51 just south of Tam Ky requested the services of Casey's sniper teams to run ambushes and night patrols in their TAOR in the rice fields twenty-five miles south of Da Nang. Casey was starting to chafe at the bit to get back to Hill 35 while his new snipers had been going out on patrols, but the youngsters had not received any of his personal attention. The late December group of newly arriving sniper candidates included Ramon Mendoza, Martin Berry, Charles Monroe, Dennis Bolton, Calvin Brown, and Jimmy Hudson. The monsoon rains were falling in increasingly heavier torrents, and most patrols experienced scant success in cornering the enemy, who was consumed with hit-and-run ambushes and the nightly mining of the major roads, thwarting Marine supply efforts.

Casey was finally relieved and ordered back to Chu Lai. His three sniper teams based in An Hoa were left in the capable hands of Corporal Ron Willoughby, who'd distinguished himself on Operation Tuscaloosa along with his young, heroic partner, Vaughn Nickell. The two men had made a name for the sniper platoon as fearless and deadly marksmen. All the platoon leaders in 2/5 started requesting the services of the "Grim Reaper's" younger brothers from the 5th Marine Sniper Platoon. Ulysses S. Black and Loren Kleppe were sent out on daily road sweeps to guard the engineers on their regular mine-removal tasks over six miles up the main road from An Hoa to Liberty Bridge. Black and Kleppe also put in their share of night patrols and ambushes.

The Marines of 2/5 were commanded by Lieutenant Colonel William E. Airheart, who had seen the benefits of night patrolling in providing security to the home base by interdicting enemy patrols. The Viet Cong were especially active during the winter season when long dark nights prevailed over the An Hoa Basin. The Viet Cong had never been timid about probing Marine lines at night. Once the veteran VC commanders found a weak spot in the perimeter defenses, a suicide team of sappers would be sent in to infiltrate by surprise and set off high-explosive charges. The explosives carried by the practically naked VC suicide soldiers were bourne in knapsacklike satchels and were either time or command detonated. The Viet Cong targeted Marine ammunition dumps, artillery emplacements, helicopter parks, and any command communication centers. They would often soften up An Hoa with a short mortar attack and then employ infantry small-arms-probing fire before running their sappers through a breech in the Marines' defenses. An Hoa had never been successfully penetrated before, although the Viet Cong had mortared and probed the security guard's bunkers along the airstrip on many occasions. The giant Marine base at Da Nang had been successfully attacked, and the ammunition and aviation fuel dumps blown up.

Chu Lai had been attacked on several occasions in late 1966, and the snipers provided the ambush deterrent and the vigilant observation missions that had saved the 11th Marines artillery batteries from total destruction.

Sergeant Tom Casey had devised a regular schedule of night ambushes, daylight patrols, and defensive bunker placements that had made the vital artillery positions safe from continued sapper infiltration. He had finally received the credit he was due for planning and executing a solid defense strategy protecting the artillerymen on Hill 35. The commanding officer of the 11th Marines, Maj. I. L. Carver, in a memorandum dated December 21, 1966, recommended Casey for the Bronze Star with Combat V Device for outstanding combat performance in keeping with the highest traditions of the U.S. Naval Service.

Casey was courageous, skillful, and completely devoted to his men, but naturally, since he was only a sergeant, he never received his medal. As Captain Doherty, perhaps the most honest and forthcoming officer I ever served under, said: "Culbertson, if the Marines gave medals to every man who performed a courageous act on the battlefield or risked his life for his buddies—well, I'd need an army of clerks to type out all the awards. I can tell you this one fact, though—on Operation Tuscaloosa during the fight on the sandbar, all my boys were *men* that day!"

Sergeant Thomas G. Casey, 2110719/0311/8541 USMC, can forever be remembered here, at least, as a true and proud combat leader whose snipers would follow him anywhere. There was perhaps no finer combat leader serving in the Marines during 1966 and 1967 than Sgt. Tom Casey. With or without his Bronze Star, he will forever serve as an example of strength, honor, and leadership to his snipers.

In keeping with this little excursion into the realm of battlefield glory, let me also say that Luther Hamilton, John Lafley, John Jessmore, the big redhead Benny Burns, and I would also have followed Captain Jerry Doherty into the flames of hell. And we felt more confident when battle-proven NCOs Gunny Huzak, Gunny Jones, Gunny Gutierrez, or the battlefield's premier combat NCO, Sergeant Harold Wadley, were present to back up the officers with experienced counsel and a steady hand.

The first major operation scheduled after Tuscaloosa was Independence. Sergeant Casey selected Dennis Toncar and Fred Sanders to accompany the Golf Company warriors of the 2nd Battalion, 5th Marines. The Golf Company Marines were raring to see some combat after providing a platoon-blocking force on Tuscaloosa that finally halted the Viet Cong's escape and forced their fleeing commander and his remaining troops into La Bac 1 and La Bac 2. The Golf Company Marines had proven their toughness and resiliency by patrolling the An Hoa Basin month in and month out. Now the razor-sharp Marines were gung-ho as they boarded choppers to commence their assault on Viet Cong strongholds to the south in the Que Son Valley.

On February 1, 1967, Sanders and Toncar heaved their gear up the slanting ramp of a CH-46 Sea Knight helicopter. The entire assemblage of Golf Company was transported in four helicopters over the Que Son Mountains directly south of An Hoa. The rice fields swam like sunfish under the helicopter's belly as the double-propped troop transport cleared the mountains. The paddies ran into a series of small, jungle-infested hills that grew smaller until they disappeared under the lazy blue ribbon of the Thu Bon River as it wound past An Hoa to the extreme west.

The green buglike choppers came in low in single file, and the rear cargo ramps hydraulically lowered as swarms of green-clad Marines jumped off into the dirt pastures of the valley. The Marines deployed without incident and formed up into platoons marching in columns abreast and fanning out across the flat landscape. The officers and NCOs moved their troops about a thousand meters through light brush toward a shallow series of dark hills.

Almost at once, small arms fire cracked into the Golf point unit, and the Marines went to ground, seeking a clear direction to return fire. Sanders and Toncar, in the middle of the column, tugged at their equipment, trying to break out their binoculars to get a fix on the enemy fire team. The first shots were followed by a long burst of automatic fire while more Viet Cong reinforced their ambush team and directed heavy, accurate, plunging fire onto the Marine point. Fred Sanders shouldered his M1-D and peered through the scope, trying desperately to pick out the muzzle flashes of the enemy gunners. Just as he and Toncar located the dust kicking up from the enemy muzzle blast, an accurate burst of fire tore into the point man's chest and he fell dead on the spot. Two other point fire-team members took glancing hits that were not fatal, but the effect of having three point scouts down in the first minutes of the firefight was unnerving as hell. Fortunately, the Viet Cong were satisfied with their initial success and immediately broke off the encounter.

Golf Company got its composure back and hurriedly

formed a loose perimeter while the skipper radioed An Hoa for medevac. After ten minutes elapsed, the trusty old UH-34 slid out of the sun and bounced to a rest in a cloud of dust and turbulence. The Golf corpsman had raced to tie off the wounds of the two surviving grunts with battle dressings. One man was a serious bleeder, and the corpsman tied a tourniquet around his upper thigh to slow the bleeding. The Marines were tagged, and the KIA (Killed in Action) was lifted by his shoulders and boots by four other survivors and shoved into the helicopter's cargo bay. The chopper lifted off and headed north toward the battalion aid station at An Hoa, fifteen miles away.

The Golf Company commander gave the order to saddle up, and the new point scout broke trail, heading deeper into the Que Son Valley. Within ten minutes the Marine column was snaking over an incline of paddy dikes that rose toward treelines that shaded another of the many hamlets in the area.

Suddenly, another flight of incoming bullets ripped through the humid midday air and slammed into the point scout and his lead fire-team members. The deadly rounds cut clean through the protective Kevlar flak vests, then flesh and bone, killing the fourth replacement point scout where he stood. He never knew what had lanced into his tender body and ended his young life. Two more line grunts were hit along with the point scout and went down screaming in fear as the 7.62mm short, Chinese 123-grain full-metal-jacketed bullets with steel cores broke through bone and sinew, sending the rest of the point squad diving for cover.

The Golf Company gunnery sergeant glanced at Sanders and Toncar. They were still scoping the field, looking for enemy shooters. The Company gunny was another Korean War veteran, and he knew he had to get some accurate return fire on the Viet Cong position right away or there would be hell to pay. The Viet Cong gun-fire picked up a rhythm, and the deadly missiles from their SKS rifles and AK-47 assault rifles poured into the Marine lines. The gunny waved a massive hand toward the point and yelled at Fred Sanders, "You two snipers, get your weapons and take the point. We got to shoot our way out of here. There ain't enough fuckin' cover here to hide a damn rabbit."

Fred Sanders was a Tennessee boy. All "Sons of the Confederacy" take a certain pride in battlefield heroics, which no doubt emanates from the bygone fields of glory at Bull Run and the bitter defeats at Shiloh and Gettysburg. However, there was one thing Fred Sanders was not, and that was a dumb shit. Sanders looked at Toncar, who looked back at him in mortal dread of taking the point with a scoped sniper rifle that had no field of vision for close-quarter shooting. Sanders got up his nerve and explained to the gunny that he couldn't see the enemy well enough close up to keep on target. Every shot from the heavy recoiling M1-D Garand would throw the scope completely off target. By the time Fred Sanders could ride the recoil back to his natural point of aim and fire again, he might well be "dead right there."

"Gunny, I can't see shit through this here scope up close like that," Sanders said. "We ain't taught to take the point! We're supposed to cover your troops when they move, or shoot somebody way off yonder!"

The gunny looked around as the enemy fire stopped for a second time that afternoon. He rubbed the sweat off his face and looked into Sanders's eyes. "Well, dammit, if you two boys can't walk point or shoot that fuckin' rifle up close," he said, "what the hell are you snipers good for?"

The Golf Company gunny was expressing the same doubts that many old combat hands felt about the proper employment of Marine sniper teams. The infantry commanders and staff NCOs knew that their veteran point scouts and riflemen could shoot better than any soldiers on earth. The average Marine combat leader relied on company artillery, such as mortars and recoiless rifles, heavy artillery and air support, when their units got hit hard and couldn't advance. Most combat leaders considered snipers to be a pain in the butt. Many officers simply told the sniper teams to get in the column and become regular infantry.

On Tuscaloosa, of course, the 5th Marine Snipers had made a decisive contribution to the survival of the trapped Marines on the sandbar. Later in the battle, the snipers eliminated enemy mortar positions and machine-gun nests, allowing the infantry to advance and destroy the enemy. Carefully and wisely employed, the snipers of Tom Casey's growing detachment would prove that an accurate long-range weapon team could take out enemy leaders, crew-served weapons, medics, signalmen, and opposing menacing snipers.

Another medevac chopper was called in to remove the second group of dead and wounded. The Golf Company commander got on the radio to the 11th Marines artillery batteries at An Hoa and gave his company's position and azimuth of march. Artillery would stay on call with 8-inch howitzers that could reach the Marines position if they were ambushed again.

The column got to its feet and moved more warily toward the string of hamlets nestled along a grove of banana and date trees some five hundred meters to the southeast. The Marines were being sucked deeper into the Que Son Valley and were rapidly extending the limits of their protective artillery fan. Finally, the third Golf point scout broke through light brush that skirted the second village. The point fire team went to ground as the gunny called Fred Sanders and Dennis Toncar forward to scope out the ville with their binoculars.

Toncar observed about a dozen small hooches and as many men grouped around a fire in the middle of a small clearing. One Vietnamese was holding a Chi-Com automatic rifle as he stood watch at the front of a hut. The others bullshitted and smoked long Vietnamese pipes. Another two Viet Cong porters strode past the gathered soldiers, hefting large bundles of rice or some other foodstuff over their shoulders.

The gunny got on the radio and made a Situation Report (SITREP) to battalion headquarters at An Hoa. The artillery battery at the 11th Marines Headquarters looked over their plotting boards and realized that the Golf Company patrol was at the far limit of the big guns' range—out to almost 17,000 meters. Finally realizing that his company was getting into some deep shit, the gunny ordered Sanders to take out the Viet Cong sentry. Two squads of Golf Company grunts edged forward, low-crawling with M-14 rifles cradled in their elbows.

Fred Sanders spread his legs into a comfortable prone position and pulled his left wrist back, tightening up the slack in his hasty sling. The M1-D was heavy but the weight steadied the shot. The side-mounted, 2.5 power scope came up into his eye, and the focus was bright as the crosshairs centered on the sentry's chest. Sanders had time, and watched his sights bore into the Viet Cong. The air filled his chest, and he slowly exhaled most of it until the rifle's sights fell back on the sentry, who looked bored and relaxed. The trigger slack took up until the two-stage pull stopped. Sanders squeezed ever so gently until the trigger broke, sending the heavy .30-06 match bullet smashing cleanly through the Viet Cong's sternum— exploding his heart as if it had been cleaved by an axe. The sentry was lifted off his feet and flung against the nearby hut, where he lay limp—DRT.

Never underestimate the Marine Corps' ability to achieve the proper degree of destruction when there are villages to be burned and Viet Cong to be violently dispatched.

As Fred Sanders took his sniper rifle down from his shoulder and gave a self-assured smile to his buddy Dennis Toncar, the two squads of Golf Company grunts opened fire with everything they had in the general direction of the unlucky Viet Cong village. M-14s blasted away, tearing the thatch in chunks from the walls of previously pristine huts. M-79s lobbed 40mm high explosive grenades by the dozen through the roofing and interiors of now burning hooches. A young Golf Company grunt stood stiffly aiming his M-72 LAAW (Light Antitank Assault Weapon) into the center of the ville's main street, where the prostrate bodies of Viet Cong who had not escaped into spider holes or tunnels under the huts still lay. The rocket-propelled warhead sped behind a stream of propellant gases into a large outbuilding, blowing the thatch and lodge poles high into the gray sky in a fiery orange ball of death. M-60 machinegun crews traversed their weapons from one side of the village to the other. Their bullets lifted thatch and hundreds of wood splinters that brewed up into a storm of chaos spreading across the village.

The grunts finally got their fill of death and disaster, and their adrenal glands could finally rest for another tortured day. A perimeter was set up around the village, and the fallen Viet Cong were left lying where they had died. Some lucky few Viet Cong soldiers had escaped to the nearest tunnel complex, which would lead outside the village into the jungle—and safety. The Golf Company grunts figured that they would eventually run across the lucky bastards who escaped and finally put them out of their misery. Fred Sanders had just begun to relax, and he spoke quietly to Dennis Toncar about having lined up the Viet Cong sentry for the first kill of the engagement.

Just when the snipers were feeling a sense of usefulness, another Viet Cong machine gun opened up, sending a flight of bullets through the brush just a titch above Toncar's head. Sanders and Toncar hit the deck and began digging with their bare hands into the sandy soil, trying desperately to hide under the incoming clusters of lead that flung themselves across the Marine lines in no particular pattern. The grunts braved the incoming fire to pop up sporadically and shoot quickly aimed snap shots back into the Communist bunkers. Dennis Toncar went back to work, with his M-14 rifle on semiautomatic firing rapid-fire groups of three to five rounds that coned with deadly precision into the Viet Cong positions. Knowing full well that the Marine small arms fire was insufficient to break the VC fire superiority, the skipper got on the radio to the 11th Marines Artillery Fire Direction Control back at An Hoa, requesting urgent fire support.

"Steel Curtain, this is Golf Actual. My troops under heavy fire vicinity AT915354 in northeast sector Antenna Valley. Give me one spotting round eight-inch gun with WP. Golf Actual will adjust fire. Over."

The captain and his troops huddled inside their perimeter and sporadically returned fire. The volume and accuracy of the incoming automatic weapons fire marked the enemy as one of the hardcore Viet Cong main force units that were turning the Que Son Valley into a Communist rest and refitting area. The enemy attack would have broken off long ago had the ambushers been a local Viet Cong guerrilla unit trying to shake up the Marines. These hardcore VC were the NVA-led and trained professional killers who would definitely stand and fight. Fred Sanders glanced up toward the Que Son Mountains, awaiting the artillery-spotting round that was presently spiraling down through the heavy winter clouds toward Golf Company's platoons of weary men.

Sanders and Toncar looked at each other the moment the terrible scream of the huge 8-inch howitzer shell tore through the sky toward the fractured perimeter. The round shrieked its arrival and flung its heavy mass three hundred meters over the Marine perimeter, clearing the enemy ambush by a good two hundred meters. So closely were the two combatant forces locked in deadly combat that the Viet Cong seemingly hugged the Marines to ward off the incoming artillery. The Golf skipper got back on the secure net to An Hoa and was immediately relayed to the 11th Marines Fire Direction Center.

"Steel Curtain," he said, "this is Golf Actual. My Six Position is static in perimeter a hundred meters west of enemy ambush. I have unknown numbers of KIA and WIA Marines requiring immediate medevac. Fire mission. Drop 150 meters from spotting round number one fired AT 915354. Fire WP spotting round number two using eight-inch gun. Golf Actual will adjust. Over."

The Golf captain had cut the range of the second white phosphorous spotting round by 150 meters. If the artillery adjusted the second shell impact just behind the enemy position, then the captain would call for a two-gun fire mission, danger close switching to HE (high explosive) rounds. In a few short minutes a second heavy artillery shell slammed to earth just over the Viet Cong main force positions. The Golf skipper wasted no time in calling a "fire for effect" mission, with each of the 11th Marines eight self-propelled guns firing an HE shell danger close into the chaos of the ambush site.

"Steel Curtain. This is Golf Actual. Fire mission. Drop another 50 meters. Repeat, drop five-zero meters to second spotting round at AT915354. Fire HE for effect 'danger close.' Repeat, enemy is a hundred meters east and locked up with Golf Marines in firefight. After fire mission run and secure, send immediate medevac my position. Approximately eight Marines KIA and WIA evacs. Golf Actual, over."

"Golf Actual, this is Steel Curtain Fire Control," came the response. "Running fire mission. Fire for effect eight-inch guns with HE. Target is VC ambush 200 meters drop from AT915354. Enemy emplaced 100 meters east your Six. Fire 'danger close.' Medevac is alerted. Estimate fifteen minutes ETA [Estimated Time of Arrival] your position after fire mission secured. Running fire mission. Steel Curtain, out."

Fred Sanders lifted himself up on one elbow and sighted in on a standing Viet Cong in a camouflaged pith helmet who wore a pistol in a leather holster strapped across his chest. His dark green uniform marked him as one of the North Vietnamese or Chinese advisors who helped plan the Viet Cong ambushes and defensive strategy in the Que Son Valley. Sanders knew he only had a brief moment to fire as the NVA officer waved, signaling his troopers to swing closed the flank of their effective L-shaped ambush.

The trigger took up smooth and clean as the M1-D bucked hard in Sanders's sweaty grip. When the scope settled back to the original point of aim, the Communist field commander was gone. Sanders's bullet had torn a gaping hole in the young officer's chest, and at no more than one hundred meters, the force of the .30-06 bullet had pumped the 173 grains of metal into his heart, expending 2,400 foot pounds of energy.

The venerable .30-06 bullet had a .308 diameter, which also would be utilized in the M-14's .308 NATO round. This bullet had the perfect ballistics and accuracy to cut through brush, logs, small trees, and light armor and still kill effectively with one shot. Later in the early spring, the Marines would be forced to equip their battle-proven riflemen with the caliber .223 M-16 rifle, which delivered less than a third the punch at a third of the range of the M-1 and M-14 rifles. Needless to say, Fred Sanders was getting pretty salty, and another Marine would have had to choke Fred to fuckin' death to get that old M1-D away from him.

The first artillery shell blasted into the Viet Cong ambushers and tore deeply into the earth, throwing heaps of vegetation and dirt high into the sky. The second round plowed into the general vicinity of the first shell a few seconds later. God in Heaven, it must have been a hellacious surprise for any of the ambushers who looked up or got out of their holes to run after the first shell impacted. The Marine 8-inch gun threw a 204mm shell almost eleven miles with enough explosive power to wound or kill any soldier within a hundred meters of its impact area, depending on the type of surface the round burst upon. In the rice valley, the earth was soft and muddy, laced with the runoff from the rice fields.

Fortunately for Fred Sanders and Dennis Toncar, the soft ground sucked up a significant amount of energy and shrapnel. The Marines were still terrified as they clustered in shallow, quickly dug holes as pieces of hot shrapnel big enough to cut a man in two whizzed overhead. The effects of a "danger close" fire mission were petrifying to the Marines near the impact area and absolutely murderous to the Viet Cong.

Sitting up to pepper the Marines with small arms fire, the Viet Cong soldiers had been caught dead to rights by the close artillery support from An Hoa. The 8-inch shell bursts had killed many of the VC riflemen by concussion. Others were literally ripped to pieces by the terrible explosions that threw earth and debris a hundred feet into the cold, gray sky.

As the second pair of rounds impacted, there was no more ambush site left to menace the Marines. Sanders hugged Toncar and let out a rebel yell in his glee to still be alive. Dennis Toncar, on the other hand, looked white as a sheet, but still managed to stroke the worn wooden stock of his M-14 rifle, which had delivered him and his partner from another catastrophe at the hands of the elusive and combat-veteran Viet Cong. The remaining VC had hit their escape tunnels and only left half a dozen or so riflemen to face the Marines once they realized that heavy Marine artillery was on the way. The Viet Cong and their NVA advisors were cagey and junglewise soldiers, and if anything could be said about them in the way of praise, it was that they were damn hard to kill.

Sanders took in a full breath of cool air and looked at the Marine wounded that were being carried on stretchers and in ponchos into the awaiting choppers. The tattered bodies of the Marine KIAs would be lifted out in another chopper after being tagged and bagged. After preliminary ID at An Hoa, the dead heroes would be flown to Graves Registration in Da Nang for the long flight home to the land of milk and honey.

Sanders and Toncar walked through the fire teams and rifle squads of hard-faced kids who were growing old in battle. The young Marine survivors of 2/5 were quiet and sat smoking cigarettes, reflecting on the general value of life. Fred Sanders knew that he would always shoot straight and true to protect these young men. These brothers in the most misunderstood war in American history had made a silent bond that in all ways—from this day on—the surviving warriors would honor their dead and serve the living. Sanders smiled, glad to be alive, and thought about the spoiled teenagers back in the States who were bored, driving around with their girlfriends, with full bellies, and a soft warm bed to sleep in. Sanders was proud of himself and his fellow Marine grunts. They had faced the bullets like men and had come out on top, with stronger understanding of freedom and liberty than the protected would likely ever know.

CHAPTER FIFTEEN

Snipers Called into the Arizona Sergeant Tom Casey and Ron Willoughby

While Fred Sanders and Dennis Toncar were fighting for their lives down south in the Que Son Valley, Sergeant Casey had been conscripted by Echo Company of the 2nd Battalion, 5th Marines, to patrol north into the Arizona Territory. Casey took his most seasoned sniper, Ron Willoughby, with him as team spotter. This company sweep was part of Operation Independence, which involved the entire 2nd Battalion, 5th Marines, in different sectors of their vast TAOR surrounding the combat base at An Hoa. The Arizona Territory was definitely "Indian country." The 2/5 had fought several battles along the banks of the Thu Bon River and its tributaries. The area's Viet Cong main forces were well-armed and eager for combat. The spring of 1967 began a new era in the evolvement of the Arizona and its potential horrors for any Marine units that found themselves outgunned or forced to camp out during the night with so many enemy troops operating in the vicinity.

One bright factor was that Sergeant Tom Casey's old classmate and close friend from the Citadel, Lieutenant John Fuller, had taken command of one of Echo Company's rifle platoons. When Casey grew weary of waiting for his chance in battle and had joined the Marines just shy of graduation, Fuller had stayed with the old grind and graduated. Then Cadet Fuller had opted for service in the USMC and reported to Quantico, Virginia, for Officers Candidate School and the Basic School. He was a bright star in the Marines and a very capable combat leader. Both Casey and Fuller had that inbred southern combination of courage, strength, and honor that had made their forefathers so feared on the battlefield.

Tom Casey and Ron Willoughby took their places in the long green-clad column that snaked out the airstrip perimeter wire and down the main road to Phu Loc 6 and Liberty Bridge. After an uneventful night at Phu Loc 6, Lieutenant Fuller lead his platoon into the lowlands and paddies that stretched west toward the river a mile distant. The Marine point scouts cut the paddy dikes in right-angled marches, turning at every opportunity to present less of a target to any enemy ambushers who would likely be shading their patrol route. Nothing ever entered the Arizona without the villagers, Viet Cong guerrillas, or regular main force patrols picking up the scent.

Casey and Willoughby stepped lightly and surely into the dark brown muck and goo of the paddies, which were filled up to the dikes with rainwater from the winter monsoons. The paddy footing was treacherous, and Marines fell and cursed no one in particular as they stumbled back into column. The strain on leg muscles and backs supporting heavy field packs laden with extra rations, machine-gun ammo, mortar rounds, and radios—not to mention the gear humped by the machine gunners—was wearing on the young men. The young Marines were forced to develop a toughness and endurance level never attained on any stateside maneuver. Some of the veteran grunt sergeants cursed and yelled at the FNGs (fucking new guys) whom everyone kept away from, hoping to ward off bad luck. Tom Casey was careful to protect the sights of his M1-D sniper rifle, which he had wound with a loose green towel. In the Marines, the combat rifleman has a respect for and reliance upon his rifle that borders on religion. Your rifle is your life in combat. The care with which Casey babied his prized M1-D Garand was testament enough to his time in the bush.

The sun had fallen like a torch cutting through the leafy branches of the trees lining the river. It caught the perspiring, chest-heaving grunts by surprise as they toiled through the filth and mire of the rice fields. The Echo platoon leader called out to his squad leaders to head for the base of the next shallow hillside and form a perimeter for the night. The tired grunts lifted their mud-encrusted boots like ghosts caught in slow motion as the bright orange orb of the sun began to burn itself out in the cool waters of the Song Thu Bon.

The squads trekked the last hundred meters up the jungled hillside and split up to form an elongated circle with each squad's combatants facing outboard to fend off an enemy attack. Willoughby broke out his entrenching tool and, as junior man to Sergeant Casey, bent his back digging a deep foxhole. The rest of the grunts picked spots around the perimeter that had natural fields of fire and dug holes for two men each. The holes, spaced approximately ten meters apart, were dug a bit closer than back at An Hoa, since there was no protective wire or mines to fend off Charlie. Finally, Willoughby tamped a flat parapet into the dirt and created a firing ledge to cover his body—leaving room to set out grenades and extra magazines.

Once the platoon had dug in, the Marines reached into their packs for C-ration meals that they opened with their bayonets and K-bar combat knives. The extra tins of bread or chocolate patties were crimped at both ends, and a heat tablet that looked like a small blue bar of rough soap was set in the can and ignited. The small furnace in the empty can was perfect for cooking the larger cans of ham and lima beans—better known as ham and mother-fuckers—that were detested by the grunts. I found the ham loaf with cheese excellent, though, and the beef with potatoes even better. There were small cans of peanut butter and crackers and a four-pack of cigarettes—usually Salems. Nobody smoked the Salems, but if a grunt got lucky, one of the village girls would trade a nonsmoking Marine a piece of pussy for two packs of Salems. Nobody understood why the Vietnamese loved Salems so much. Maybe it was the cool menthol smoke on an extremely hot day? In fact, we really didn't try to understand them, and maybe that was part of the United States' problem in Vietnam. We were totally unschooled in their customs, and although most Marines were pretty kind to the villagers, some men invariably personified the ignorant, ugly American.

After another half-assed meal in the field, the squad leaders assigned watches and checked the weapons and magazines of their troopers. Casey and Willoughby would take four-hour watches until first light. The sky had grown as black as an inkwell, and no one smoked or chatted as the sentries kept their eyes peeled and their ears open. The natural jungle sounds, which meant all was clear, thrummed along the paddies, and monkeys cried plaintively in the treetops. It was a pleasant enough environment to lull many men to sleep, but the terror of a sudden night attack by Viet Cong or mortars kept the young Marines on edge.

Suddenly, a Viet Cong sniper with a Moishin-Nagant scoped rifle fired two shots past Sergeant Casey's bunker. The heavy *thwock thwock* of the bullets in the surrounding brush made the noise signature of a heavy long rifle. The sniper was no doubt moving his position when the squad M-79 man came up alongside Casey's shoulder. Casey pointed out the direction of the sniper as best he could tell in the intense darkness. The grenadier loaded the weapon with a 40mm high explosive grenade and fired into the paddy. A bright ball of red and yellow light flashed about two hundred meters to the left flank. The grenadier fired several more rounds in a sawtooth pattern, covering the flats where the sniper would have emplaced himself to fire into the Marine perimeter. No further sounds came from the paddy, and in the morning a badly burned body lay in the mud in the direct line of the grenadier's fire.

On February 4, Tom Casey and Ron Willoughby set into a hasty perimeter to guard a "live" sidewinder missile that was accidentally torn off an F-4 Phantom's weapons pylon during a napalm run. The platoon commander had radioed An Hoa for an Explosive Ordinance Disposal (EOD) team that would be arriving by chopper to blow the missile before Charlie could turn it into a road mine and destroy another Marine vehicle. As Willoughby scoped the paddies with his binoculars, he noticed a hoard of Vietnamese running from a tree-lined village away from the Marine patrol. He and Casey worked their way around the shielding groves of bamboo trees into a spot where they thought they might make a clean shot if any of the Vietnamese were armed.

Just as Casey hoisted the sniper rifle to his shoulder to scan the large group of villagers, it appeared that some of the men were carrying rifles, but they were mixed in with women and children. Marine snipers did not shoot children, or women and children. Not ever! Casey took the rifle down and rose, turning back toward the perimeter bunkers, when another grunt tripped a booby trap. The Chi-Com grenade had been set inside a small tuft of brush, with a taut trip wire running across the footpath in the rear of the perimeter. The grenade exploded in a ferocious cloud of fire, laced with large chunks of shrapnel. The grunt was blown into the air, with terrible wounds gouged into his legs and torso. Pieces of shrapnel had flown across the twenty yards or so where Casey was approaching his foxhole, and several pieces of deadly hot metal slammed into his right leg, cutting deeply into muscle and sinew. Casey writhed on the ground in front of a petrified Ron Willoughby, who forced himself into action, holding his partner down while a corpsman ran over to check his condition. The red-hot shards of metal were still burning when Casey slipped into unconsciousness, unable to hear the lieutenant giving medevac the platoon's coordinates.

Both Marines were wounded sufficiently to be evacuated by medevac chopper to Da Nang and the 1st Medical Battalion, where skilled surgeons were busily performing miracles on youngsters who would probably have bled to death during World War II or Korea. Casey had the rough shards of shrapnel cut out, and his blasted leg was put into a new plaster cast. Sergeant Tom Casey hated to leave Corporal Willoughby and his sniper brothers, but he was twenty-four years old and bushwise enough to know that he and the other rifle pogue were lucky to be alive. No question about that shit!

CHAPTER SIXTEEN

Jayne Mansfield Visits An Hoa

While Tom Casey recuperated in the medical facility at Da Nang for a week, Ron Willoughby and the other members of the sniper platoon continued to patrol with the various rifle companies of the 5th Marine Regiment. Finally, a hurting but undaunted Casey received his Purple Heart Medal from a Marine colonel on the 1st Division staff. He returned to An Hoa on limited duty and met the new S-3 officer in charge of 5th Marines Regimental Operations.

Major Dick Esau brought considerable experience as a company commander, and proven leadership to the planning section of the regiment's tactical operations, which included the assignment of all of Tom Casey's snipers while they supported infantry operations in the field.

Operation Stone commenced during February 1967. It involved one rifle company from 2/5. No sniper teams were requested, as was often the case with some units that had not completely adapted to the deployment and utilization of snipers as "combat multipliers." The sniper teams increased the effectiveness and added a long-range selective arm to conventional infantry capabilities.

During World War II the German Wehrmacht (armed forces) had adopted a short-range (four-hundred-meter)

assault rifle similar to the M-16, the Sturmgewehr—
StG 43/44. The Sturmgewehr was produced mainly for
front-line units on the Eastern Front to provide fully automatic fire using a "Kurtz"—or short-case length cartridge—of 7.92mm pushing a 123-grain spitzer (pointed)
full-metal-jacketed bullet. The German infantry officers
had recognized the true value of sniping in the trenches
during the static defensive battles of World War I. German
sniping took on an ever more deadly role during the close-
quarter battles in Eastern European cities, from Warsaw to
Stalingrad and the vicious street fighting outside Moscow
during the frozen wintertime in Russia.

The United States had employed Marine snipers during 1917 at the Marne, Chateau-Thierry, and with the
deadly Devil Dogs at Belleau Wood. The terror and
death wrought by seasoned marksmen armed with tele-
scoped, match accurate rifles was devastating. Entire
German units surrendered after snipers killed their officers, as happened with the American marksman hero,
Sergeant York. The Germans used their finest marksmen, armed with the Mauser 98 rifle—fitted with a pre-
cisely manufactured telescopic sight, to cut down
essential enemy leaders—accompanying weapons crews
such as machine gunners or mortarmen. The overall effect of this stealthful but quick killing team was to create chaos and undermine the tactical effectiveness of the
enemy.

I regress into World War I and II sniping techniques
and utilization by the infantry to underscore the fact that
very few American officers appreciated the combat value
of the snipers' craft in Vietnam. Probably the fact that
the U.S. forces had become the most highly mobilized in
the history of combat led senior officers to rely mainly
on heavy artillery, tanks, armored personnel carriers,
helicopter gunships, fixed wing bombers (B-52s), and jet

fighters armed with bombs and rockets as the primary weapons in their arsenal.

But Vietnam was a jungle war where the enemy was almost impossible to "find-fix-destroy." The reality of warfare there was that no distinct battle lines were formed. This contributed to the difficulty of conducting purely conventional tactics. So Vietnam became one of the last great infantry wars where small units tracked each other down over the limitless jungled hillsides and mountains, meeting in brief but bloody firefights almost always broken off by the Viet Cong.

The United States Marine Corps had been the only U.S. branch of the armed services to continue to emphasize excellence with small arms, including rifle marksmanship, machine gunnery, mortar training, and combat training with the Korean vintage 3.5-inch rocket launcher. Improved high-tech weapons like the LAAW rocket system and the new M-79 grenade launcher were now employed in the rifle platoon. The Marines were well-schooled in close-quarter fighting and the use of every small (portable) arm in the rifle company arsenal. Yet an expert analysis of the weaponry carried and used in jungle combat by young Marine infantrymen revealed little improvement from the arms used by the American G.I. or German Wehrmacht grenadier of World War II. The conditions, however, were decidedly different. There had never been a war where the battleground favored the indigenous military forces more than Vietnam favored the Viet Cong.

The VC could hide from the Marines underground in tunnel systems dating from pre–World War II conflicts against the Japanese. The Viet Cong could retreat after a losing battle into neutral Cambodia or Laos, escaping pursuit by the Marine battalions closing in for the kill. The VC could, of course, slip into and out of the clothing and role of a peaceful noncombatant villager. The

Viet Cong and North Vietnamese were also not curtailed in their murderous conduct of war against the people of Vietnam since they were not signatories to the Geneva Convention. Their American Marine counterparts, excepting a few transgressors, played by the rules.

Sergeant Tom Casey knew the toughest assignment of his tour in Vietnam wasn't killing Charlie, but destroying the ignorance and rigidity of the Marine Officer Corps when ground commanders refused to employ snipers as a deadly asset to support line infantry units locking horns with the treacherous and evasive Viet Cong. Sometimes Casey would lie awake on his cot and stare into the dark evening sky at the thousand twinkling stars that pulsed so clearly he thought he could reach out and touch one. Those blinking celestial sparks were like the active thoughts racing through his brain—thoughts of his shooters cutting down Viet Cong officers as they moved through their trenchlines, invisible to regular Marine riflemen with iron sights on their rifles. A sniper using a high-illumination Redfield scope on 9× power could look clearly into the foliage and jungle shadows where the naked eye saw only a blur.

Casey knew his snipers could cut out the leaders, the medics, and the deadly Communist snipers with surgical precision. His men could take a lot of heat off the grunts once they rose to their feet to begin an attack across a soggy rice paddy with its open and dangerously exposed ground. Casey also felt assured that his veteran snipers—like Willoughby, Spanopoulos, Moore, Nickell, Kleppe, Flynn, Sanders, and Toncar—could kill a few extra Viet Cong soldiers once they decided to bug out and flee into the jungle before they hit their tunnel complexes. This war in Vietnam was one thankless, dirty son of a bitch. The grunts who did most of the fighting and the dying deserved every advantage the Marine Corps could provide for them.

Some officers were so naive that they thought snipers could crawl into enemy territory, kill Charlie by themselves, then walk out again like they were fucking Superman. No one ever went into the Arizona Territory alone, or even with a spotter, and engaged the enemy and lived to tell about it. The Viet Cong were the masters of the Arizona and the Kings of the Jungle. Nothing escaped their animal-like awareness, nor did they ever fail to hunt down a reconnaissance team or downed pilot once he was discovered either by villagers or an enemy patrol. Since South Vietnam had some eleven thousand hamlets dotting nearly every square mile of countryside, it was self-evident that no big-assed, white or black-skinned American soldiers ever walked into or out of Indian country without the Viet Cong likely knowing their fucking name, rank, and serial number.

Tom Casey was a realist concerning Marine sniping operations, knowing that a team of shooters could enhance any infantry operation. Whether employed defensively in an ambush hide or a blocking force, or on a patrol or while supporting an attacking sweep force, snipers added an accurate and devastating terror weapon that caused immediate disruption of the enemy's command and control.

Oh! I almost forgot to mention one of the saddest chapters in the history of American USO entertainment. Just after Casey returned to An Hoa, he and his partners attended a show next to the battalion mess hall. A huge Marine CH-46 helicopter had brought a legend of cinematic fame—and "buxomatic" renown—out of the clear blue sky.

Touching down on the strip, the Sea Knight chopper deposited an aging American icon, Miss Jayne Mansfield, who had starred as a busty delight in Hollywood films throughout the 1940s and 1950s. She was hustled into camp and displayed atop a wooden stagelike platform hastily built by the Sea Bees. Jayne had to be in her late forties or early fifties at the time. She was still buxom as hell, and mostly pouched out of her red halter-top ensemble. A lot of the young Marines, particularly the Mexicans and some of the blacks, had never heard of Jayne Mansfield, who at one time had been a pretty attractive dish and a screen rival of sorts of Marilyn Monroe. Anyway, Jayne smiled and talked to a crowd of about four hundred grunts and REMFs and captains, and one horny colonel who kept patting her on the back—probably trying to catch a glimpse of the famous cleavage. Finally, Jayne did a little song and dance routine, and all the troops up close to the stage let out this monstrous groan.

Casey was trying to figure out what the ruckus was about, and since he was standing in the rear of the Marines who had crowded to the front, he couldn't see very well. Not to be underestimated, Tom Casey pulled out his binoculars and focused in on the ugliest pair of cellulite-encrusted knees he had ever seen in his life. Jayne Mansfield must have known that she looked like shit, but Casey, being a decent type of man, thought she had a lot of guts just to come to Vietnam in the first place. Anyway, after most of the Marines had scoped out the fat and wrinkles on her legs, it was evident that there wasn't a whole lot to stick around for, so most of the troops just swore under their breath and moved slowly back to their billets.

Jayne Mansfield died in a car accident shortly after returning to the United States. Nearly everyone felt badly about her final performance in an otherwise outstanding— and I do mean outstanding—career. It just serves to illustrate how fucked-up America is—when one worn-out old movie star gets more publicity and sympathy for dying than thousands of fine American Marines and soldiers who actually are trying to stomp out the evils of Communism and save an ignorant third world people from slave-like domination.

On February 25, 1967, Tom Casey became the official platoon sergeant for the 5th Marine Regiment Sniper Platoon. Colonel Kenny Houghton became the new regimental commander of the 5th Marines two days later. Casey carried the regimental colors during the change-in-command ceremony on Hill 35. Later in the summer, during Operations Union I and Union II, Colonel Houghton would become one of the most celebrated battle commanders of the Vietnam War. The 5th Marines would later win the coveted Presidential Unit Citation for extraordinary heroism on the battlefield under his command.

CHAPTER SEVENTEEN

Gunny Mitchell Comes to Casey's Aid

On February 15, 1967, Operation Independence was secured. Sergeant Casey, just out of the hospital, returned to An Hoa on limited duty. He was glad to see Ron Willoughby and the rest of his snipers, but deep inside Tom Casey knew that the Marines had to sharpen their infantry skills to defeat the Viet Cong and the stealthy North Vietnamese. Casey felt that his Marines were often too impatient to make a kill, and that they failed to go with the tide of events, taking what opportunities Charlie gave them. Forcing a quick shot usually meant missing the target and compromising the sniper's position without thinking out the next movement in advance.

The Viet Cong snipers, on the other hand, always had a secondary hide or escape tunnel set up to flee any Marine counterfire or artillery support, which would likely find their position after they opened fire. The VC also employed better camouflage techniques, using all natural plants and dyes to blend perfectly into their environment. The Communists were well-trained by older veterans who had done extensive combat sniping and understood the effect of creating diversions with explosive booby traps to confuse their prey and cover up the noise of their weapons. The Americans took an unreasonable pride in making the long shot ending in a kill. The Viet Cong snipers polished themselves on close-quarter surprise tactics when an American patrol was sighted. Only one man would be targeted and killed, walking around a bend in the trail or topping a rise on a hill. The Marine point would often be shot in the head. The Viet Cong marksmen never worried about leaving secondary targets alone while they concentrated their primary fire on the point scouts or the radiomen, who were easily identified in a Marine column.

As Casey pondered the logistics of getting his snipers further trained, a memorandum from 1st Marine Division came into Headquarters Company of the 2nd Battalion, 5th Marines:

GUNNERY SERGEANT VERNON D. MITCHELL TRANS-FERRED TO 1ST MARINE DIVISION TO HEAD UP DIVISION SCOUT SNIPER SCHOOL AT HAPPY VALLEY RANGE. MITCHELL RETIRED FROM THE MARINE CORPS IN 1964. HE IS A 1955 NATIONAL INDIVIDUAL RIFLE CHAMPION AT CAMP PERRY, OHIO. IN 1958 MITCHELL WON NATIONAL SERVICE RIFLE CHAMPIONSHIP IN THE U.S. COAST GUARD MATCH WHERE HE SHOT RECORD SCORE WITH 15 OF 20 BULL'S-EYES IN THE SMALLER "V" RING. MITCHELL IS A COMBAT VETERAN OF WORLD WAR II AND KOREA. HE HAS REENTERED ACTIVE SERVICE AT REQUEST OF CMC. GYSGT. MITCHELL REPORTS TO 1ST MARINE DIVISION HQ, DA NANG, FEBRUARY 1967, TO BEGIN ACTIVE SERVICE.

BY DIRECTION
HQ USMC
WASHINGTON, D.C.

It was like the Almighty had answered Casey's prayers by sending the Marine Corps' greatest combat sniper to Da Nang to teach his Marines the "real art of sniping."

Gunny Mitchell had killed so many North Korean and Chinese soldiers on the frozen slopes of the Chosin Reservoir, all the way to Hagaru, that he had long ago lost count. Armed with a venerable M1-D sniper rifle, Mitchell and his spotter had terrified the hordes of Chinese troops sweeping up frozen ice ledges to attack the well-bunkered Marines. When an automatic weapons position needed to be neutralized or Commie leaders shot dead during an attack, Mitchell was always lurking beside the grunts' foxholes, picking his victims with a polished and discriminating eye.

In a story I related earlier, but which bears repetition, Gunny Mitchell's most famous encounter called for accurate shooting up a muddy slope when he and his partner were called to aid a confused U.S. Army unit that had bogged down under heavy enemy machine-gun fire. A distraught Army officer had all but given up any attempt to advance his unit due to strafing from an enemy machine-gun crew six hundred meters up a ridge. The North Koreans peppered his troops whenever they got out of their trenches to advance. Mitchell and his buddy took a few minutes to size up the situation, then asked the Army lieutenant to order some of his men to stand up and fire a few rounds at the enemy. The lieutenant took one look at Mitchell and his spotter, realizing they weren't bullshitting about their request. Mitchell and his partner snugged themselves into their rifle slings and as soon as the enemy machine gunners got their gun aimed and fired a long burst toward the Americans, the two Marine snipers squeezed their triggers one after the other, sending deadly bullets streaking uphill at the North Korean gunner and loader. The gunners' heads exploding horrified the Communist soldiers, who grabbed their packs and beat a frantic retreat up the hill and out of rifle range. Mitchell and his pal jokingly suggested it was likely safe for the Army to advance, but should they encounter additional enemy resistance, to please call first for assistance. As far as Marines were concerned, nothing compared to helping the United States Army out of the sorry-assed messes they continually stepped into in Korea. As Gunny Mitchell later always said, "Nothing fucks up a good war more than the Army! That's what Marines are paid to do—unfuck things!"

At their first meeting, Sergeant Casey knew that Gunnery Sergeant Mitchell had the experience in shooting, coaching, and, most important, in combat to create the kind of sniper school that would become a legend among the 1st Marine Division Snipers from the 1st, 5th, and 7th Marine Regiments. There would later be contingents of U.S. Army, Air Force, Navy, and Korean Marine Corps personnel who would attend the school to learn the principles of combat sniping prior to establishing their own sniper courses. Sergeant Casey had shot on the 2nd Marine Division Rifle Team at Camp LeJeune in 1964, and he knew what proper instruction standards were all about. Gunny Mitchell was still young enough, at forty-two years of age, to demonstrate proper firing positions and conduct live firing demonstrations for his students.

The first Marines Casey sent to the new Happy Valley school were the group of Fred Sanders, Dennis Toncar, Jim Flynn, Loren Kleppe, Vaughn Nickell, Ron Willoughby, and Tony Spanopoulos. Another team of newly arrived sniper candidates, including George Wilhite, Stanley Watson, Dave Kovolak, and Tom Elbert, would begin preliminary training under Sergeant Casey, going out on regular patrols and night ambushes around Hill 35. Casey was an expert at night ambush tactics, and he worked hard with his men to teach proper cover and concealment during dusk, just before nightfall, when the sniping is often the best. All told, he personally led some forty-eight night ambushes around the Chu Lai and Hill 35 Tactical Areas of Responsibility. His snipers learned instinctively to put themselves in the place of infiltrating Viet Cong sappers to realistically determine the likely avenues of approach, and then construct Marine ambush sites accordingly. As Tom Casey's father always said, "When the boys in the next pond are catching all the fish and you ain't, maybe you jus' picked out the wrong hole! If you can't beat 'em, join 'em."

Casey was a true field Marine with a quick, reasoning mind for warfare. Equating combat sniping in Vietnam with hunting squirrels and rabbits back home in the swamps and meadows of humid South Carolina, he knew the key to successful hunting was to be fully prepared and wait alertly along the trails where the game was moving. Vietnam was no different. However, Thomas Casey and his band of "13 Cent Killers" were the only Marine combat group that hunted the Viet Cong at night just as successfully as during the day. The VC hated the Marine night ambush operations because they denied Charlie the only time when he could move about with impunity.

When Fred Sanders, Ron Willoughby, and the rest of Casey's shooters arrived at Da Nang, they were trucked by six-by-six double-axle trucks to the Happy Valley Range next to the Sea Bee's rock quarry in the far western outskirts of the base. The 5th Marine Regiment snipers were issued the new Marine standard sniper rifle, turning in the old M1-D Garands of World War II and Korean War fame.

The new Remington Model 700 was a walnut-stocked, five-shot, bolt-action rifle with a match-grade, medium-heavy Douglas barrel. The trigger was a match Canjar setup with a crisp 2.5-to-three-pound pull. The walnut stock was uncheckered and cut into a modest Monte Carlo cheek piece that lifted the shooter's face up into the business end of a Redfield 3 × 9 power adjustable scope with an integral range finder that snipers seldom used in combat. Nonetheless, the Remington was a fine shooter, and after breaking in the bore, most sniper candidates could hold inside a one-inch, three-shot grouping at a range of a hundred meters. At three hundred meters, a good shot could cut three-inch-plus groups with Lake City Arsenal 168-grain match ammo. This level of accuracy might not win a match at Camp Perry or the Marine Corps base at Quantico, but the only marksmanship task in Vietnam was killing Charlie. That meant Casey's dingers had a target about ten inches from armpit to armpit, and maybe twelve inches vertically from the bottom of the throat down to the middle of the abdomen, to score a hit. Any Viet Cong or North Vietnamese who got holed by a 168-grainer doing over two thousand feet per second would have enough internal bleeding to water his garden back home. A chest-wounded VC would still have pools of hot sticky blood spilling out a wound channel big enough to stick a man's fist into or, to be anatomically correct, through the front of the sternum, bursting the heart before exiting out the back. Well, I think you have the idea. Any unlucky enemy hit by a .308 NATO bullet in the chest or abdomen would be DRT.

Sergeant Casey came to the logical conclusion that much of the painstaking rifle range training that many Marines felt was gospel was overly scholastic. Formal training deemphasized the realities that were life-and-death lessons in combat sniping and were not always encountered or addressed in range practice. Gunnery Sergeant Mitchell agreed. His "Rule number one" concerning engaging the enemy was that a sniper team would *never* engage any enemy unit that was too numerous for the snipers to quickly kill or to destroy their ability to fight. In other words, Mitchell and Casey preached that if a sniper team scoped out a Viet Cong or NVA unit that was anywhere near platoon size or larger, then the sniper had standard orders (SOP) to call for air or artillery support.

The Marine Corps had foolishly allowed some legends to continue unchallenged. Fantasies about single snipers who engaged large NVA units and killed them all with a bolt-action rifle and a spotter armed with an M-14. These remarkable Marines were supposed examples of gallantry under fire. However, as Gunnery Sergeant Mitchell often said, "Combat is about the 'Marine team,' and not about individual heroism." Any sniper team that fired on a company of enemy troops would be killed, absolutely, in less than ten minutes.

It's true that examples of storied heroism make for fine boyhood reading, like the myths about Ulysses, Hector, and Achilles in ancient Grecian lore. But in Vietnam the encouragement of tactics like "solo patrols" or sniping large units by a two-man sniper team were the type of idiocy that got Marines killed in real battle. Was it any wonder that the personnel that encouraged these ridiculous acts had never been in combat? Their romanticizing egos drove them to misadvise young Marines who might die because they imitated these fanciful combat actions.

Gunny Mitchell and Tom Casey, two of the most experienced Marine combat snipers ever to draw a bead on the enemy, both urged their snipers to act aggressively but prudently in the field. Live to fight another day was the order to follow. If that didn't make perfect sense, then why did the Viet Cong always break away when the Marine firepower coned into their hideout and things got too hot to handle? There was no possibility of winning the Vietnam War by attrition, due to the availability of millions of North Vietnamese replacements, not to mention the reality that Communist Chinese troops had already been killed in combat along the Demilitarized Zone. China was capable of sending vast hordes of well-trained, fanatical troops to North Vietnam's aid. As General Douglas MacArthur had warned, "You do not engage in a full-scale land war in Asia and survive." Evidently, the old saying, "One who fails to learn from history is destined to repeat it," was true and alive and well.

Mitchell and Casey both realized that the path to victory lay in fielding experienced Marine infantry backed by airpower, artillery, and well-supported by company weapons and dedicated sniper teams. Snipers fully trained to function as a "combat multiplier" would be working to extend the infantry arms capabilities, to annihilate the enemy by sowing terror and defeatism into his ranks.

Personal glory or heroic recognition has no place in modern infantry combat. Any great warrior will gladly tell a spellbound audience whose eyes are riveted on his Medal of Honor that there are always other Marines who were more deserving but unnoticed in the fire and hell of battle. All the great combat leaders—like Jim Kirschke, George Burgett, John Pindel, or the selfless savior of Operation Tuscaloosa, Jerry Doherty—will first praise the dying efforts of their unsung Marine grunts who do all the fighting and most of the dying. For years, Captain Doherty took much of the blame on his own shoulders for the blood spilled by Hotel 2/5 at the sandbar on Operation Tuscaloosa. But had it not been for Jerry Doherty's intrepid stamina and self-control under fire, it is likely that none of his men would have lived to fight again. As it was, Hotel 2/5 finally won the battle, if not the war. Many young Marines learned to appreciate the value of picking your ground and your battles carefully.

Gunny Mitchell and Tom Casey had the dual responsibility of training their snipers to be effective killers without encouraging them to throw their precious lives away in a stupid gamble to gain a moment's fame or their partner's regard. In Vietnam most of the heroes went home early—in a box.

Willoughby, Sanders, Toncar, Flynn, Spanopoulos, and tough little Vaughn Nickell split up into two-man teams to sight in their new weapons. The Remingtons were lighter than the M1-Ds by a couple of pounds, but the greatest surprise came in the optics used with the bolt rifle. The old M1-Ds had a 2.5-power, side-mounted scope that gave modest magnification out to six hundred meters. The Remingtons with the Redfield variable 3 × 9 power tubes gave the Marines a firing capability out to a thousand meters. It was rumored that the longest single kill in Vietnam was made at over 1,700 meters— more than a mile—but I personally thought that was bullshit, unless the shooter had used the Palomar telescope to sight the enemy with. Anyway, the Remington turned out to be an excellent choice of weapon for a sniper rifle perhaps due to the synergy of its parts working together, rather than any one characteristic, such as a highly accurate barrel or smooth trigger. This is akin to requiring all the infantry elements of a Marine battalion, including the sniper unit, to work together in harmony. Incidentally, it's the meaning of the Chinese word "gung-ho," or "to work together."

To familiarize themselves with the Remington, the snipers' targets were placed in a target butts at three hundred, six hundred, and a thousand meters. Willoughby, Toncar, Sanders, Nickell, Flynn, and Tony "the Greek" Spanopoulos went to work firing initial rounds to get on paper, then moving their elevation and windage knobs after each group of shots until they fired tight groups into the center black. Each shooter made single scratch marks on their elevation knobs to denote the correct setting for three hundred meters for actual fieldwork. Two scratch lines were etched on the elevation knob denoting a range six hundred meters, and three scratch marks were cut to indicate a thousand meters. In the event that the snipers would fire in the winter rainy season, the bullet would fall more at each range than the normal, dry weather sight elevation. The snipers were instructed to hold off above the target to compensate for a lower bullet strike.

In combat, both Gunny Mitchell and Sergeant Casey emphasized practical tactics like "holding off" and "incremental holds on moving targets," instead of attempting to adjust or fine-tune the precision scope, which is unnecessary to accomplish the combat mission: "Seek out and kill the enemy with a well-placed shot." A well-placed shot has more to do with terrain, weather, wind direction and force, and sun glare or target illumination, than merely firing a set course on a rifle range. The great combat marksmen—like Mitchell, Casey and the rest of the 5th Marines' handpicked snipers—were all natural shots, and most were seasoned hunters and stalkers.

Gunny Mitchell used to laugh out loud at the constant questions about long-range sniping. He told the story about the young Marine who had shouldered his way through a thicket of bamboo, taking up a prone position and sighting some enemy soldiers in a village a half mile away. As he lay in his hide, his binoculars flashed beams of sunlight that painted the faces of the Viet Cong sitting around the open fire. A few minutes later all hell broke loose as VC bullets slapped into the grove of green bamboo from close range. The Marine had not heard or seen the Viet Cong crawl around his position until they could fire into his flank with their AK-47s. The Marine beat a hasty retreat back to his squad and, covered with sweat, told the awful tale of his near death. The Gunny smiled and said that the man's mistake was to not first alert his squad members. His second mistake was to sit in his hole instead of working in close enough to kill the Viet Cong. Instead, the Marine had gotten careless and by flashing his binoculars, advertised his whereabouts to the whole fucking village.

Mitchell stopped speaking and eyed the group of youngsters, all hell-bent on destroying the Viet Cong by themselves on their first day in combat. "Boys, just remember this Vietnam is an old country," he said. "The Viet Cong have lived here all their miserable lives. They haven't driven fancy cars around the countryside, they've walked every foot of it. They know this land a hell of a lot better than us. They'll find you ten times quicker than you can find them. Do not take unnecessary chances. The Marine Corps has spent a lot of Uncle Sam's money on your training. I hate to see good beer or good money wasted. *Never underestimate the Viet Cong! The sneaky little bastards will likely be here after we are gone.* Be patient and take the good shots they give you. Make the bastards bleed for their country, then all this Commie horseshit may not mean so much to 'em."

Everyone had a smile on his face, then began to realize that this little Asian "police action" might last a whole lot longer than anyone would have guessed. Getting yourself killed over some eager heroic stuff was just plain stupid. Ron Willoughby and Loren Kleppe, for instance, remembered that there would always be chaotic battles like the fight at the sandbar on Operation Tuscaloosa, where anybody could get his ticket punched for a quick flight home. Living often had a lot more to do with luck than skill. In the big battles, there was so much lead flying and mortar and rockets slamming into Marine positions that Lady Luck randomly selected her chosen survivors, while the Grim Reaper knocked over the fallen with the crooked nail of a twisted claw.

Along with the 0700 to 1700 hours of range practice, the "13 Cent Killers" of the 5th Marines had classes on camouflage techniques and wind-reading skills. After two weeks of intense range and classroom instruction they were ready for qualification at a thousand meters.

The shooters fired their Remington rifles at twenty-inch bull's-eyes, managing to keep all their rounds comfortably inside twelve inches. The Gunny had the personnel in the butts trenchline walk targets stuck on long stakes from left to right and then right to left at a quick-time pace, while the snipers practiced moving leads and holding or "trapping" leads on the targets.

Most shooters, including Vaughn Nickell and big Jim Flynn, soon learned that it was a lot easier to take a standard lead and move your sights along with the target than to pick a spot and fire, hoping that the target fell into a "trap" where the lead was already figured into the bullet strike. The more the young Marines fired their rifles from each position—kneeling to prone, sitting to kneeling, kneeling to offhand (standing), offhand to prone with a sandbag support at a thousand meters—the more they appreciated the ugly truths of combat. First and foremost, the reality is that you train for combat in battle—not on the rifle range. Second, shooters soon learn that there is no best position, but the terrain will dictate how you must fight. Third, the quickest shot is not necessarily the best shot, but the quicker shooter will kill the slower shooter—all things being equal. Do not fuck off on the battlefield! Take a good position, align sights, breathe and hold, squeeze the fucking trigger gently, recover and fire again. Fourth, the sniper who performs these functions without becoming overly emotional, but rather, more mechanical, allowing his rifle to kill the enemy, will come out the winner and live for another day. The neurotic sniper or frightened rookie who always hesitates to get a better sight picture or screws with his equipment will invariably die due to indecisiveness.

Personally, I believe that a true "13 Cent Killer"

enjoys hunting the enemy so much that killing the prey is incidental to the stalk. Killing itself is painful in that it terminates the excitement of the hunt. A great sniper like Gunny Mitchell, Sgt. Tom Casey, Ron Willoughby, or Fred Sanders, takes great satisfaction in stalking his quarry. When the target is finally in the sights, then the hunt is over, because the professional does not often miss. Killing completes the ballet, or perhaps the "dance of death." There is a certain sadness to it because it must be replayed to achieve that superlative high adrenaline rush that comes from taking another's life. The dance is only of true value when the opponent is as good or better than you are.

The final lesson that Gunny Mitchell conveyed to us was that the Viet Cong snipers were not just as good as us, but better. Why? Because they didn't get to go home! Vietnam was their home. Their only chance to live was to be ever careful and stealthy in moving, creative in camouflaging, and selective in killing. I had witnessed many Marines shot in the head at close range by Viet Cong snipers who took the easy, close shots and then melted into the jungle.

Few Viet Cong marksmen came out alive in protracted shootouts with the seasoned "13 Cent Killers" trained by Gunnery Sergeant Vernon D. Mitchell and lead by Sgt. Thomas Casey. Out of all the skills the Marines had over the Viet Cong, only two stood out above all the others: exceptional shooting ability and indomitable courage and pride. These military virtues were the general hallmark of the United States Marine Corps in past wars and in tradition. These combat characteristics, like the battlefield heroics of wars long forgotten, were encouraged and revered by the two sniper legends, Gunny Mitchell and his favorite pupil, Sgt. Tom Casey.

CHAPTER EIGHTEEN

Great Leaders
Are Made, Not Born

Tom Casey's most endearing character trait was his practice of putting the safety of his men first. Born in humble surroundings in South Carolina's plantation country, he'd hunted as a child under the strict supervision of his father, learning that gun safety, hunting ethics, and just plain good manners were expected of him. In the South, people had an almost mythical respect for Robert E. Lee, Stonewall Jackson, Braxton Bragg, and George Pickett, and most South Carolinians also had reverence for the Confederate battle flag that flew above the state capitol at Columbia.

Tom Casey learned early in life to respect a man not for his wealth, but for his character and his deeds—particularly in battle. All his life, he trained himself for an eventual appointment to the South's great bastion of military training and discipline—the Citadel. There, as a cadet, he met future Marine heroes like his closest friend John Fuller, who would be awarded the Navy Cross for extraordinary bravery while leading Echo Company, 2nd Battalion, 5th Marines, on Operation Newcastle in March 1967. Casey knew the risks of becoming a professional Marine NCO, but he accepted the dangers as "business risks," and always personally led his snipers into battle, if he could escape the staff officers and their dependence on voluminous technical advice from all quarters. Modern warfare had achieved such rapidity in communications that general officers were constantly tempted to conduct operations from the rear, sacrificing the objectivity and spontaneity that exists only on the front lines. And Casey had been taught that a true military commander led his troops into battle making the hard decisions that cost lives on the spot.

It was Sergeant Casey, of course, along with Gunnery Sergeant Mitchell, and Sergeant Douglas DeHaas, who implemented the planning, organizing, and execution of a uniform curriculum of sniper training that would eventually be adopted by the rest of the U.S. Armed Forces. Among those three, Mitchell is no doubt the single greatest authority on sniping and the initial driving force behind the combat effectiveness of Tom Casey's 5th Marine Sniper Platoon.

Gunnery Sergeant Vernon Mitchell was a walking, talking encyclopedia of tactics for snipers. He was skilled in the utilization of supporting arms, such as air power and, particularly, artillery fire support. Casey realized that Gunny Mitchell offered an opportunity to plumb the depths of jungle warfare tactics employing snipers with modern long-range weapons in infantry combat. Mitchell had experienced intense and desperate combat against the Japanese in the South Pacific in World War II, and the North Koreans and Chinese later in Korea. While Gunny Mitchell didn't doubt the willingness of the Japanese or the North Korean and Chinese commanders to fight bravely and readily sacrifice most if not all of their soldiers to gain a victory over the Marines, he also knew that coordinated infantry tactics could stall and eventually destroy almost any enemy attack.

Vietnam was an altogether different situation from any war the Marines had previously fought. The Viet

Cong and North Vietnamese were masters of camouflage, silent movement, ambush tactics, and, most important, escape and evasion. Both Mitchell and Casey
knew the Marine grunt companies were the most
aggressive soldiers on earth when used in the assault.
However, some conditions in terrain and weather ham-
pered the best-run assault operations and favored the
quick retreating gunmen of the Communist hit-and-run
rifle squads. It was reputed that a well-trained Viet Cong
main force infantry platoon of not more than twelve to
sixteen soldiers could ambush and pin down an entire
American rifle company long enough to inflict very
heavy casualties. Then the stealthy Viet Cong, often with
their North Vietnamese advisors and weapons experts,
would melt away as quickly as they had attacked, leaving the panic-stricken Americans sputtering into their
field radios, calling for artillery and air support.

Mitchell realized that one answer to small unit survival lay in training teams of expert Marine sharpshooters commanded by skilled NCOs and officers using
highly advanced jungle combat tactics that could defeat
Viet Cong using similar tactics. An old slogan began to
make the rounds among the 1st Marine Division Snipers:
"If you want to kill Charlie, you learn to fight like Charlie!" Mitchell and Casey had trained the first of many
groups of snipers at the Happy Valley range in what
would come to be regarded as the most distinguished
sniper training school established during the Vietnam
War. Utilizing one-week refresher courses for snipers already in the field, and two-week inclusive courses for
new snipers and experienced expert riflemen chosen
from Marine infantry battalions, Mitchell trained
around three hundred Marine snipers during 1967. All
Marine snipers had the basic infantry 0311 Military Occupational Specialty and received a secondary MOS of
8541 Scout Sniper upon graduation from the 1st Marine

Division Sniper School. No doubt there were several informal or battalion level sniper schools that taught the same marksmanship and basic jungle tactics; however, the true Marine Scout Snipers had to complete the divisional school before they were officially sniper trained, receiving the sniper 8541 MOS.

It seems appropriate, here, to mention that since the Vietnam War has ended, every veteran I meet was either a sniper, a Force Recon Marine, a SEAL, or an Airborne Ranger. Where were all the fucking cooks hiding? The Marine Corps Rifle Team shooters who served in Vietnam as military policemen or motor transport NCOs and the like were not snipers, nor did many of them experience any combat action that I ever heard about. The cold hard truth is that there were probably no more than fifteen hundred snipers trained to operate during the entire Vietnam War, including the Army's excellent 9th Infantry Sniper School, the SEALs' sniper program, the 101st Airborne, the Korean Marines 2nd Brigade Blue Dragons, and the shooters from the 1st, 5th, and 7th Marine Regiments, which comprise the 1st Marine Division. The 3rd Marine Division fielded some of the finest combat regiments during the Vietnam War. I would rank these Marines alongside any fighting force in the world: the fabled striking 9th Marines, the 4th Marines of the old "China Sailors" fame, and the 3rd Marines "Herd." The 1st Battalion of the 26th Marine Regiment of heroic Khe Sanh survivors fought alongside my battalion of the 5th Marines and were OPCON (Operational Control) to the 1st Division, but were actually part of the 5th Marine Division.

(This critical examination of the skills and combat actions learned and displayed by the heroes of the 5th Marines Sniper Platoon in no way diminishes the overall gallantry and sacrifice exhibited by the United States Army, Navy, Air Force, and our allies, such as the efficiently brutal and ruthless Korean Marine Corps killers from Hoi An.)

The second truth for the misinformed student of Vietnam history is that 1967 marked the beginning of the highest-intensity pitched battles between Allied and Communist forces during the war. By the beginning of 1968 it was a foregone conclusion that the Communist-led factions, even with the addition of highly trained and well-armed North Vietnamese Army divisions, could not stand against U.S. Marine regiments or U.S. Army Infantry divisions in fixed battles. After TET in early 1968, the Viet Cong were broken, and the North Vietnamese Army refused to stand and fight like their predecessors in 1967. Therefore, I will venture the opinion that the Marines and their Army brethren fighting down south in the II and III Corps areas of South Vietnam had victory in their back pocket. A combined invasion of North Vietnam by an Army-Marine team would have ended the war if the American political leaders only had the balls to implement the plan.

CHAPTER NINETEEN

New Snipers
Report to Chu Lai

While Sergeant Casey prodded his shooters at 1st Marine Division Sniper School at the Happy Valley range, new troops reported to 5th Marine Headquarters at Chu Lai to fill the ranks of the understrength sniper platoon. All these new men were expert riflemen and fresh from Staging Battalion Jungle Warfare School at Camp Pendleton, California. They included Corporal Vernon Smith, tough little Eddie Rackow, who had been raised in the hot and dirty oil fields of the Midland-Odessa, Texas area; Big Steve Englebrecht from Los Angeles, California; and Kenny Barden from Jackson, Mississippi; and they were all eager to join the snipers.

George Filyaw, who'd been to Vietnam early in 1965, assigned to Motor Transport, evidently hadn't gotten enough action being ambushed on supply convoys and wanted to join the infantry. He was from North Carolina and fit the general description of a Marine sniper, being a country boy who'd grown up hunting and reveling in the big piney woods of the South.

Big Steve Englebrecht was a big-boned German lad of over two hundred pounds. Out of all the young expert marksmen, he was probably the best rifle shot. He'd posted a score of 236 in his rifle qualification at the Edson Range on the Marine Corps Recruit Depot in San

Diego during his final qualification round, ending three weeks of intensive marksmanship training. He fired so accurately on the five-hundred-meter-long A course that the PMIs (Primary Marksmanship Instructors) had considered keeping him as an instructor. However, Vietnam was looming big on the planning charts, and all 0311s (Basic Riflemen) were expected to serve at least one tour of duty in the rice fields before coming home to instruct new recruits. Big Steve was easygoing and very intelligent. He went to Vietnam without any presupposed ideas one way or the other. Probably above all things, Big Steve and his fellow snipers would develop a deep sense of loyalty and sacrifice for the other members of the sniper platoon.

This sense of honor was hard to comprehend for the harried civilians back home who concentrated mostly on improving their lifestyles regardless of the impact on others. Vietnam would indeed become an honored place where young men of special character and ideals would learn the true meaning of comradeship and brotherly love. Without the overt support of much of the American public, most Marines learned to fight for each other and the honor of the Marine Corps.

The new snipers had no earthly idea that their very lives would depend on the words and deeds of their Marine brothers in the very near future. The big battles of 1967 were still waiting to be fought to the bloody end. Kenny Barden and the others busied themselves with shooting their new Remington model 700 bolt rifles and running short patrols with the Marine infantry units in the Chu Lai area. They would not commence their specialized sniper training until Sergeant Casey returned from Happy Valley. Barden showed his potential as a brave and true Marine infantryman right from the start of his tour at Chu Lai by stealing beer and clothing supplies from the U.S. Army.

It's a well-known fact that the United States Marine Corps has forever been placed on the tail end of the supply chain when it comes to the issuance of new gear—particularly weaponry and uniforms. The first Marines in Vietnam wore Korean War boots before the modern jungle boots became available, and they packed the 3.5-inch rocket launchers of Korean War fame into combat while the Army had new rockets such as the LAAWS (Light Antitank Assault Weapons) designed specifically for Vietnam. Even Marine trucks, tanks, and rifles were surplus and inferior in quality compared to standard Army or Navy issues. This discrimination in equipment priority was actually a motivational challenge for the Marine Corps. Every Marine prided himself on his toughness and combat readiness training, particularly in the area of rifle marksmanship. The fact that Marines got the short end of the stick when the gear was issued created a fierce pride that the Corps didn't need the best gear, helicopters, or artillery pieces because the Leathernecks were so much better trained and led that they could achieve much more with less.

Marines like Kenny Barden, who was a hell of a fine shot and knew how to joke around with the best of 'em, also took a perverse satisfaction in nightly missions of pilfering jungle boots, beer, C-rations, and any other extra supplies that Army personnel abandoned on pallets near the airfield. Kenny Barden and his closest partner, Patrick Montgomery, from Dallas, Texas, figured that if the United States Army didn't have the time or inclination to guard their gear better, then it was a fact that the bastards didn't really need it!

In the Marine Corps, shortages of supplies always existed, as when U.S. Navy ships deserted the just landed Marines without supplies on Guadalcanal because of the rumor that the Japanese Navy was right around the corner, steaming down the slot to kick their asses. The

Marines always made do by adjusting to the situation at hand and improvising methods to make ends meet. As every Marine was instructed in ITR (Infantry Training Regiment) after boot camp—in the event you're attacked and run out of bullets, raise your rifle and aim at the enemy, yelling "Bang, bang, bang" at the top of your fuckin' lungs. The idea being that Marines never surrender and never complain about the shortages of gear.

I guess if Uncle Sam thought the Marine Corps was as soft as the Army, they'd see that we received more stuff. We always figured, "Fuck 'em if they can't take a joke," and when we run out of bullets, the entrenching tool works wonders on enemy chests, legs, and faces. The point is that the Marine troops are conditioned, or brainwashed, into the fanatical belief that battle is serious business and that the toughest, most vicious, brutal bastards will eventually prevail.

The young snipers with Big Steve Englebrecht, George Filyaw, Kenny Barden, Pat Montgomery, and scrappy little Eddie Rachow had no idea how brutal Vietnam combat would become when the big battles played themselves out and left the paddies soaking in American blood. The Marine commanders hadn't even imagined the names of the desperate fights as yet, but Tuscaloosa, Independence, and Newcastle had all been bloody orgies of ruthless killing. These first combat tests of Marine Corps resolve would pale in the crimson glow of Operations Union I, Union II, Swift, Essex, and the final carnage in the fiery hell of Hue City. Little did the youngsters know that their short breaking-in period of relatively light combat patrolling would end as abruptly as it had begun in the rain-swollen rice fields of the An Hoa Basin.

Sergeant Casey walked down the firing lines at the Happy Valley range to see what the snipers who gathered together were watching with such intensity. He broke through the loose clutch of troops who stood with gaping mouths, holding their utility covers in their hands.

Gunnery Sergeant Mitchell sat before them, facing downrange and with his knees brought up to his chest. He leaned back slightly in a relaxed position, like a kid curled up on a couch watching television. Mitchell held an ancient (.45 caliber) Colt 1911 pistol in both hands, and squinting down the worn barrel slide, fired round after round at something way downrange. Sergeant Casey squinted into the dying sun and heard the pistol bark sending a 230-grain hardball bullet arching over the smoothly packed dirt. The heavy bullet tore into a bright shiny metal fruit can a hundred meters away. Each shot forced the muzzle of the pistol six inches into the air, and Gunny Mitchell let out a war whoop as the rounds tore through the can, making it hop right and then left a yard into the air. Casey had never seen anyone shoot a .45 automatic pistol at that distance before and wondered what the hell Gunny Mitchell was trying to prove. When the seven-round magazine ran dry, the Gunny got gingerly to his feet and turned around, smiling at the twenty-odd Marines who stood there, dumbfounded.

The Gunny took the clip out of the pistol and thumbed the slide stop, bringing the slide back into battery. He holstered the pistol and wiped the sweat from his face with the sleeve of his utility jacket. "Boys," he said, "you have all been taught that this old 1911 pistol ain't good for nothin' but killing rats in your bunkers. But what are you gonna do if you run out of rifle ammo and the chinks think maybe they've got your ass dead to rights? All snipers should carry a pistol and learn to shoot it accurately at over a hundred meters. If any of you don't think this old 'slabsides' will kill your young ass, just walk downrange and I'll convince you it can. Learn to master your weapons! All of 'em! Improvise and make the other son of a bitch die for his country. You got to remember, you men are Marines. The meanest sons of bitches in the valley!"

All the snipers turned on their boot heels and wordlessly strode back to evening chow on the last day of Division Sniper School. They had seen with their own eyes why the deadliest warriors in the world had been the Marines fighting the Japanese in the island hell of the Pacific, and again in 1950 against overwhelming hordes of North Koreans and Chinese in Korea. It started to sink into the hearts and minds of the young shooters of the 5th Marines that they were an important legacy of the legendary battle heroes of the Corps. It occurred to many of them that their contribution to the battle prowess of the Corps would be no less important than those that went before them.

The first task in becoming a great warrior is training your mind and body for combat, and then allowing your natural courage and stamina to carry you to victory. Finally, with each victory comes renewed confidence and further achievement. As my father once said after World War II, "The U.S. Marines didn't get to be called the 'Devil Dogs' because they ran away in battle. After their aggressive bloody campaigns against the Germans in World War One, everybody knew they were special warriors."

Sergeant Tom Casey gathered his snipers and praised their shooting skills at the range. He also admonished them about any foolish inclination to think they were bulletproof. Casey told his men that new recruits were waiting on Hill 35 in Chu Lai. There was no extra time left to get the newly trained sniper teams back into the field patrolling with the rifle companies. The level of combat activity was growing dramatically. There were fresh reports of North Vietnamese Army battalions now operating in the Arizona Territory, and the NVA 2nd

Division was reportedly contacted in several sectors of the Que Son Valley west of Chu Lai. Casey advised the snipers to pack their gear and clean their rifles thoroughly before taking a mid-morning hop (flight) to Chu Lai. Each Marine was now officially sniper-trained and would receive the secondary MOS 8541 "Scout Sniper" upon his return to base.

Everyone felt proud and pleased that they'd shot well and learned so much technical information. Wind estimation and effects of the weather, map reading, camouflage, leads and holds, ballistics, and firing positions swirled through every youngster's head. The older snipers knew that the game was just beginning, and now the classes would be held along jungled green hillsides and sun-glinting rice paddies. Victor Charlie (the Viet Cong) would be out there trying to run their asses out of Indochina, just as he'd done to the French. Viet Cong marksmen who had sniped a hundred men and were never spotted lurked in the humid jungle. This new phase of the Vietnam War would pit the young Marine snipers against much better adapted and more seasoned enemy marksmen. This time the stakes would be for real. The action would be for pride and professionalism, but mostly it would be for blood. No quarter would be asked and none given.

Sunrise came early. The snipers were trucked to the airfield and boarded a C-123 Air Force transport for the twenty-minute flight to Chu Lai. No one said much as the ten Marines slid into the cargo hold's web seats along both sides of the fuselage. The engines revved up as the camouflage-painted transport shot down the runway full of rations, bullets, boots, and snipers, and tucked its tail. The plane lifted off the skid-marked tarmac and climbed into the bright sunlight of another deceptively glorious day in Vietnam.

CHAPTER TWENTY

Night Patrol
with Bravo 1/5

Operation Newcastle would kick off on March 23, 1967. Sergeant Casey had enough time on Hill 35 to get his four teams of trained snipers into the bush on several road sweeps and combat patrols with elements of the 1st Battalion, 5th Marines. The 1/5 still occupied the Chu Lai TAOR, and regularly swept the paddies north toward An Hoa from Hill 51. The Marines of 1/5 began to request snipers on a regular basis for support during hazardous patrols, especially west of their base camp into the Que Son Valley. Ron Willoughby, Vaughn Nickell, Jim Flynn, Big Steve Englebrecht, Denny Toncar, and the hero of Tuscaloosa, Loren Kleppe, all were honing their sniper training in the Valley of Death south of the Que Son Mountains.

Charlie 1/5 had requested two of Sergeant Casey's most experienced sniper teams to accompany their battle-tough grunts into the Que Son Valley south of the Coal Mines to support Bravo Company. On the night of March 20, 1967, Loren Kleppe and the giant Fofo Tuitele, from American Samoa, teamed up with Vaughn Nickell and Tom Elbert, joining the grunts south of Hill 51.

Fofo Tuitele would prove to be one of the kindest men in the sniper platoon, probably because he was strong enough to squeeze the living shit out of anybody else. Like the great rhinos and rogue elephants of the African savanna, Fofo had no natural enemies except Victor Charlie. The straight-shooting Samoan giant had learned to respect as well as fear the animal-like surprise tactics of his compactly built foe. Watching Fofo run to the point of a patrol when Charlie hit hard from an invisible ambush site was like watching a giant bear try to beat back a slinky pack of wolves. Tuitele had a jutting chest hanging over trunklike legs that churned like a wild stallion when he broke through the slick surface of the rice paddies.

The nights were still cold, and most Marines wore short rain ponchos over their flak jackets to cut the sharp wind. The road from Hill 35 ran north until it branched off to the west. The four snipers glassed the long strung-out column of grunts marching south before joining the patrol as it jumped off into the Que Son Valley to the west.

There were two squads of Marines from Bravo Company, with one attached machine-gun team and a Navy corpsman. The snipers took their orders from the staff sergeant who led the patrol. The grunts seemed eager to find the Viet Cong troops who had been harassing Marine convoys along the switchbacks of Highway 1 running from Chu Lai to Hoi An and finally up to Da Nang. Most of the basic Marine supplies like food and ammunition moved by truck south from the port facilities at Da Nang to southern combat bases like An Hoa, Hill 51, Hill 35, and Chu Lai.

The Viet Cong, masters of the night, had employed every imaginable type of homemade bomb and explosive device to hopefully destroy or at least cripple the long green columns of Marine six-by-six trucks as they churned up the muddy roads, often without the luxury of mine-sweeping units at the point. The patrol from 1/5 was a combat interdiction force that was hopeful of catching the enemy mining the roads or surprising Viet Cong demolition details in the field. The patrol had to operate at night since the wily VC would never dare show themselves so close to a major highway during daylight.

The Marine column snaked through fields that turned into giant mud bogs, which made the hiking extremely tiring and noisy. It was rumored that the Viet Cong soldiers could detect an American Marine smoking a cigarette at night up to a quarter mile away. It was obvious that the Marines had to move to higher ground, where good fields of observation were available, if the enemy was to be sighted. Viet Cong point scouts were the best in the business at sniffing out Marine ambushes and stopping their comrades before falling into a trap of murderous Marine firepower.

At night the VC probably would not employ any flankers because of the difficulty in managing their troops, but the Viet Cong would not necessarily march in column either. Since the guerrillas knew every foot of the terrain, they would more likely employ a wedge formation, with their point scouts far ahead of the main body. If the VC point ran into an American patrol or ambush, the main body of soldiers would melt away and rendezvous later at a predesignated ambush point to await any Marines forming a hasty pursuit force. In the thick jungle, the professional Viet Cong main force almost never exposed their entire force. The Marines might see one or two fingers of a probing hand, but never the clenched fist that was held stubbornly in reserve, waiting to pounce on the overly aggressive Marines. The older, more seasoned combat leaders knew how to envelop their ambushers and employ multidirectional firepower on the Viet Cong positions before moving into the assault phase of any engagement.

The Marines of Bravo Company 1/5 were bushwise veterans who were learning how to utilize terrain and position to anchor their units in the event of a sudden skirmish. Sometimes at night things got so mixed up that some Marine units had actually been tricked into a short deadly firefight with elements of their own units. The Viet Cong would open fire on one Marine column, which flanked closely alongside its neighbor, from inside the two columns. When the Marines returned fire, the VC slipped hurriedly into escape tunnels and listened as the grunts shot at each other until cooler heads figured out the enemy was long gone. The necessity of using trickery and deception in jungle warfare was an attempt by the VC to gain superiority in night fighting tactics by shoring up their lack of firepower and close quarter fighting skills.

During the first two years of the war, the Viet Cong had yet to win a decisive battle. Their battalions were incapable of overpowering the Marines fighting head-to-head in a conventional battle. The old guerrilla strategy of hitting the Americans quickly and withdrawing into the jungle, leaving a few Marines to bleed out and die, would have to suffice until the better armed North Vietnamese divisions could pour across the South Vietnamese borders from their marshaling points along the Ho Chi Minh Trail. The Que Son Valley would eventually become the tactical operating headquarters for the NVA 2nd Division; specifically, the veteran NVA 21st Regiment of crack infantry battalions, with their deadly antiaircraft batteries, would contest the best the Marines could muster during the entire year of 1967. The series of hard-fought battles in the 5th Marines' TAOR was no doubt the most intense period of nonstop combat during the Vietnam War after the bloody battles of Operation Prairie on the Demilitarized Zone were concluded.

Loren Kleppe and Vaughn Nickell both carried M-14

rifles. The Remington 700 sniper rifle with its high-intensity, range-finding telescope, would be of little use in the pitch-black expanse of rice paddies that lay shimmering before the column as it trudged along. Only the silent moon cast a faint glow across the water as ripples from the Marines' plodding boots made wavy beams of white moonlight shimmer over the inky pools.

Finally, after two hours of steady humping through mush and mire, the four snipers tucked themselves into a hillside ravine that ran along the crest of a hogback ridgetop for a half mile. The paddies looked like shimmering rectangles of moonlight slivers sparkling for miles into the far expanse of jungled hills that made an ebony streak across the landscape.

After an hour of waiting, the patrol made a situation report to base at Hill 35 and got Sergeant Casey on the other end of the radio net. A "Nothing sighted" short message squawked into the mike back at sniper headquarters, and Casey raised the map of the eastern stretches of the Que Son Valley up into the light. He knew that any Viet Cong sapper unit or demolition patrol would have to come from the west out in the central valley, and that his Marines appreciated that they were likely to find the Viet Cong farther west. It was also a likelihood that the VC would become more active just after midnight and until dawn broke over the Que Son Mountains clustered around An Hoa to the northwest.

Casey spoke directly to the platoon sergeant from Bravo Company and suggested the combined patrol work farther west, keeping to the high ground until morning. The staff sergeant from Bravo 1/5 was as eager to interdict the enemy as Casey. He'd plotted a lengthened patrol route, sweeping five klicks westward and circling back in a wide arc.

Next, Casey rang up the artillery section at Chu Lai and reported the patrol route extension that Bravo would be running into the valley. All harassment and interdiction fire missions into the patrol's immediate sector were secured for the night. The batteries of 105mm and 155mm howitzers stood silent in their sandbagged revetments, awaiting the call for "Fire mission" from any of the Marine patrols already maneuvering in the field.

The Bravo sergeant had served in combat for a long cold year in Korea and was very bushwise, even on a dark cloudy night. He shot a compass azimuth and ordered the troops to saddle up and move off the ridgeline and down into the valley. The point scouts, the most seasoned infantrymen, took a compass heading of 263 degrees due west, stepping off into the inky black night. After a slow, painstaking march across undulating rice fields and over slippery mud-mushy dikes, the patrol halted near a silent village. It was another of the nameless myriad of thatched huts cloistered around a common square lost in a sea of rice fields. The Marines knelt silently while the point scouts approached in low crouches until a large dike was reached seventy meters or so from the ville.

All of the Que Son Valley, including the northern coal mines at Nong Son running west to the Song Thu Bon, which then snaked north toward 2/5 Headquarters at An Hoa, was known as Indian country. This zone of operations was considered a "free-fire zone" at Marine Headquarters in Da Nang. This specific area of Quang Nam Province was presumed to be controlled by the Communist forces of the People's Liberation Army (the Viet Cong). All villages were likewise presumed to be friendly to the enemy, and as such, any area in the Que Son Valley west of Highway 1 was enemy territory, and enemy soldiers could be fired upon at will by any Marine unit in the area. Unfortunately, this "free-fire zone" also put the women and children in the local villages at risk. Most Marines considered the villagers who inhabited the

"Communist areas of control" to be unwilling to relocate, and thereby complicit. Personally, Casey and the snipers hated to fire into crowded areas, but orders were orders, and war wasn't referred to as "hell on earth" for no reason.

Naturally, patrol leaders had their general orders to follow. Civilians were not to be targeted. Neither were children or agricultural beasts of burden, such as water buffalo or cattle, to be killed indiscriminately. However, every Marine commander—and particularly the sergeants who led most combat patrols—recognized that any villagers who got in the way of the enemy during a firefight would most likely get chewed up and spat out just like the Viet Cong riflemen.

The Bravo sergeant who'd been in Korea had seen how the Viet Cong and the NVA troops used civilians as shields to break off an engagement when the overwhelming power of superior Marine rifle and machine-gun fire coned into their trenches and tore their soldiers apart. The North Vietnamese were worse still, and had a long history of putting Viet Cong guerrillas in front of their regular infantry when attacks were staged against the airbase at Da Nang or the perimeter lines at Chu Lai and An Hoa. Charlie was just one deceitful little bastard. When Marine patrols got their chance in the batter's box, the grunts and their machine gunners would tear into the enemy with a blood lust that was violent and savage beyond imagination.

The snipers, on the other hand, were the long-range surgical arms of the Marine infantry strike force. Snipers didn't consider the realities of hand-to-hand combat or the possibility of getting their uniforms shot off at close range. Patrolling with Bravo 1/5 would open the eyes of many of Sergeant Tom Casey's "13 Cent Killers" until they would finally become just another killer looking for their daily fix. One thing you could surely count on in

Vietnam's wartime jungle madness—everything eventually reached its own "lowest common denominator" with respect to combat motivation and retribution. Either you killed efficiently and without mercy, or you got yourself killed by the other side's merciless sons of bitches. Jungle combat was just one mean-assed heartless motherfucker, and the ironic part of it was, that's just the way the Marines liked to play the game.

The point scouts turned away from their cover and concealment behind the large earthen dike to wave the rest of the patrol members forward. In their haste, they failed to observe a team of VC sentries run a belt into their antiquated but quite deadly Chi-Com wheeled machine gun that covered the eastern approach to the village. Just as the scouts waved their arms forward and back in quick short motions, trying to signal their buddies through the black expanse of the rice paddy, the VC squeezed off a short burst of rounds that tore one Marine's arm to pieces. Hitting the ground behind the dike, the point scout could feel the hot sticky goo from his shattered arm pulse out through a half-dozen holes and down the side of his utility jacket. Temporarily forgetting about the situation in the village, the Marine yelled out for the corpsman, who was hunkered down fifty yards behind the point scout.

The Viet Cong machine gunners held their fire and waited, knowing the gallantry and fearlessness of the young Marines would shortly push them into action. The Korean War veteran signaled with a flat hand palm down for his men to stay down and keep silent. He whispered to the senior squad leader to lead his riflemen around the edge of the paddy dike wall and open fire, peppering the village when they came abreast of the main huts. The sergeant knew that a raking cross fire would run any stragglers out of the village proper. It also might kill every son of a bitch in the village, but that wasn't his concern right now. He had a badly wounded point scout just fifty meters away who was gonna bleed out if the corpsman couldn't get to him soon.

As the lead squad moved around the dike in a looping left envelopment, the snipers closed ranks. At Loren Kleppe's signal, they rained down accurate plunging fire from their hard-hitting M-14 rifles on the Viet Cong gunners, who backpedaled, withdrawing into spider holes that ringed the periphery of the village.

Vaughn Nickell and Fofo Tuitele's first shots sliced into the machine gunners, wounding them superficially in the arms and sides. The .308 caliber bullets struck with such devastating force that the gunshot VC were out of commission even with slight wounds. The M-14 and the Remington 700 bolt-action sniper rifles had tremendous impact energy and would strike targets at ranges up to five hundred meters and longer with over three times the force of the newly issued M-16, with its puny caliber .223 bullet. The seasoned combat troops all knew from deadly experience that you didn't take on a bunkered enemy with a .22 caliber weapon that wasn't deadly past three hundred meters, when the M-14 was accurate and powerful way past five hundred meters and hit like a freight train in comparison. The Marine .308 NATO bullets tore through thatch and wood into the tattered remains of the village. Livestock were scattered about, with punctured carcasses leaking blood, and gore still dribbling into pools in the narrow dirt streets.

Sensing that the Viet Cong were done in or had finally "didied" (Vietnamese slang for run away), the Marines rose as one and headed through the mud and blood leading to the smoking thatched roofs of the shot-up huts that miraculously remained standing. Just as Loren Kleppe reached the VC machine-gun position, he spied an earthen cover leading to a small bunker. The lid was ripped off the hole, exposing the two machine gunners who had spilled the first Marine blood. Kleppe just stared at the Viet Cong, who were clad in dirty, tattered green shirts and black cotton trousers.

The VC had light green soft jungle hats covered with leaves and grasses. Their backs had bunches of grass and plants like ferns tied into cartridge belts that held a half-dozen AK magazines in pouches in front. An AK-47 rifle was found in the bottom of the earthen hole. The bigger man, who appeared to be the gunner, had a Chinese Tokarev semiautomatic pistol on his hip in a worn military leather flap holster.

Everyone was so fascinated by the two prisoners at the bottom of the hole that they momentarily forgot about the shot-up point scout who lay behind them at the first paddy dike. The Navy corpsman had followed his basic hospital training and first treated the wounded man to stem the flow of life-giving blood from his shattered arm. A tourniquet was tied at the elbow using a web rifle sling from one of the grunt's proffered rifles. A bayonet still in its scabbard twisted the web sling tight enough to cut off the blood flow from the man's heart. Battle dressings were wound tightly around his biceps and shoulder wounds, clogging them with the stream of American blood that had sprung sprinklerlike from the rents in his tender flesh. The Marine was lying on his side, deep in shock, with his torn-up arm held up in the air like a solemn banner of courage by another point man.

The staff sergeant had gotten on the radio back to Hill 35, where Sergeant Casey was monitoring the patrol's progress. A medevac chopper was already in the air with an ETA of six minutes. If the young grunt scout could just hold on another twenty minutes, he would be safe at the medical center in Da Nang.

Everyone spread out to search and secure the village, except the patrol leader, the corpsman, and the second point scout remained with the youngster who clung desperately to life in the filth and mud of another fucking no-name village in the Que Son Valley. This latest Marine casualty was courtesy of a bold pair of poorly armed Victor Charlies who had nonetheless known exactly how to fire an obsolete Chi-Com machine gun, which proved that the quality of an army's weapons did not necessarily define their fighting spirit.

The second, smaller Viet Cong prisoner looked around, and seeing that the Marines were scattered throughout the village, made an attempt to escape. He waited patiently until the wounded man groaned again, desperately begging for relief from the agonizing pain shooting from his arm into his chest. The instant the Marines busied themselves with their wounded comrade, Charlie leaped from the shallow bunker and ran with his hands still tied behind his back, weaving toward the smoke and chaos in the village.

As the Viet Cong machine gunner ran in a lurching hobble toward the smoldering safety of the burning thatch roofs, the corpsman drew his pistol and ran the prisoner down in less than twenty steps of his hurdling stride. Incensed at the precarious plight of his wounded patient, the usually peaceful and intelligent profile of the Navy medic became frosted over with a cold, remorseless hatred developed from watching too many of his Marines die in cruel circumstances at the bloody hands of the Viet Cong. The corpsman grasped the etched grooves along the back of the pistol's slide and, racking the slide back and letting go, chambered a 230-grain .45 caliber military ball bullet. He glanced for a moment, a red glaze over his eyes, at the silent body of the young Marine point scout now departed to a warrior's heaven, never again to see his homeland or his family. The pain was just too much for the young corpsman to bear as he leveled the pistol's muzzle against the fleeing man's temple. He jerked the trigger, sending the heavy bullet spiraling and churning through bone and brain and exploding out in a gush of mushy sprayed pulp that saturated the walls of the nearby hut with sticky crimson. Then the corpsman fell to his knees and sobbed, unashamedly covering his face with both hands while the smoking barrel of his pistol lay unattached and unmindful in the dirt at his feet.

The patrol leader gave the command to torch what was left of the village. All the pigs, buffalo, chickens, and dogs were already long gone on their journey to VC Pet Heaven. The sergeant faced the east and saw the first tinges of light glow over the jungle and the paddies, which were starting to churn and resonate with the sounds of crickets, flies, and grasshoppers. The medevac chopper was spinning down from the sky too late to save the young American point scout, who lay still, his blood-encrusted arms hugging his dead body as though he could awaken and stand up and the nightmare would be over.

In Vietnam, the professionals knew the nightmare never ended, and the thirty-seven-year-old Korean War staff sergeant wondered how long men would fight these senseless little wars for corporate greed and power while young patriots like his point scout paid the taxes with their lives. The patrol leader sighed heavily and lit his first Camel of the new day. He cast a sullen eye over his filth-covered troopers, who stood alert and ever ready to follow their leaders into hell itself if necessary. The four snipers had grown a little bit harder and a bit more cautious. This Vietnam thing would go on a long time unless the Marines finally got to flex their muscles and kill every fucking thing in Vietnam. Every man was glad to be alive, and looked around at his buddy, not really understanding how some men bought the farm and died in battle while some lucky others couldn't even kill themselves, no matter how many stupid things they did.

The troops snapped out of their brief moment of reflection as the sergeant's gruff voice broke the morning air. "Saddle up and move 'em out to base. I guess we done all the damage we can do tonight! Just as well get on back home before these bastards send their whole army after us. Snipers up! You shooters did a crackerjack job last night when the shit hit the fan! You boys can patrol with old Sergeant Merryweather anytime. When we split up, tell your Sergeant Casey that I think his snipers are dead-eye dicks."

The old sergeant turned his weathered face into the sun, and the last remaining point scout moved out as the rest of the patrol picked up the pace toward home base.

CHAPTER TWENTY-ONE

5th Marines Push into Antenna Valley

On March 15, 1967, Sergeant Casey had another urgent request for snipers to accompany a battalion-size sweep into the Que Son Valley. Evidently, word of the outstanding success of Loren Kleppe and Vaughn Nickell's foray into the valley on a roving night ambush had reached the commanders of the 3rd Battalion, 5th Marines. Casey picked the team of Kenny Barden and Tom Elbert to accompany either Kilo, Lima, or Mike Companies of 3/5. Barden would be the spotter and Elbert would act as shooter, carrying the Remington M-700 rifle while Barden lugged the automatic M-14.

Ken Barden was a transplanted southerner who had been born in Pennsylvania, his father a U.S. Navy pilot stationed at the Philadelphia Naval Yard. Barden graduated from J.E.B. Stuart High School in Falls Church, Virginia, in 1966. He had distinguished himself as a high shooter in boot camp at Parris Island, South Carolina, and like Tom Elbert, had been handpicked for the sniper platoon. Barden also had another piece of family history that would motivate him to become one of the outstanding snipers in the 1st Marine Division. His father had flown U.S. Navy Dauntless dive-bomber planes off the carrier *Intrepid* during the World War II battle for Leyte Gulf and later in the Solomon Islands.

The senior Lieutenant Barden had rolled out of the long glide of the bombing run and scored a direct hit on a Japanese battleship, which eventually sank the behemoth in a caldron of flames and smoke. Lieutenant Barden later scored another direct hit on a Japanese carrier. Barden's dad was a modest man who, like a lot of his World War II contemporaries, seldom talked about the war. When he did tell a story, though, he always spoke about the bravery of his flightmates and the heroes of the great naval battles in the South Pacific who had given their lives for democracy. But despite the old lieutenant's failure to mention his own battle prowess and heroism, he had a hard time convincing his son, or any of little Kenny's pals, that his Navy Cross didn't mean he was a hell of a pilot and a heroic warrior.

Sometimes in the afternoon when his dad was at work, young Kenny would stare at the Navy blue ribbon with its white bar running vertically down to the medal and imagine himself cutting across a smoke-filled battleground littered with casualties and bravely assaulting the gun positions of the villainous Red Chinese or Soviets. In his dreams, Ken was always part of an aggressive U.S. Marine infantry platoon that would never consider surrendering until the final objective had been reached and the enemy soldiers laid out stiff and cold in pools of Commie blood.

In the 1950s and the early 1960s, America was still turning out youngsters who cared deeply about the security of their country. These patriotic, competitive, but unselfish youths were the stuff that the Marines of Vietnam fame were made of, and Kenny Barden and his buddies were typical of that breed. When your father is a true war hero and teaches his kids to love and respect his nation's fallen warriors, there grows a deep sense of resolve to carry on the banner of freedom and become honored in the eyes of your elders. In contrast, it seems to me, the liberal permissiveness of the public school system plots to undermine the patriotism and pride that welled up so strongly in young people like Kenny Barden. As a result, I don't believe that today's youth compares.

Tom Elbert toted the Model 700 Remington sniper rifle under his right arm, the scope covered by a green towel wrapped loosely over the front objective lens. The towel was hanging down toward the barrel crown, which angled toward the dirt at his feet. Kenny Barden packed the 7 × 50 millimeter binoculars and carried a full haversack of rations, cigarettes, dry socks, extra ammo, and a poncho to fend off the nightly winds and rain. Barden carried the heavy automatic-selector-equipped M-14 spotter rifle to provide breakaway firepower in the event that he and Elbert were ever cut off from the grunt patrol's main body and had to fight their way out.

The M-14 was a very accurate rifle, and it was durable in the mud and muck. Its iron sights were the same type as the World War II adjustable peep sight used on the extremely successful M-1 Garand. In fact, the M-14 was a modifield M-1 rifle with less moving parts and a flash suppressor to lessen recoil. The 7.62 × 51 millimeter cartridge performed as well as the older Springfield .30-06 caliber cartridge employed with the M-1. The main failure of the M-14, however, was the inaccuracy of fully automatic fire, due to the weapon's relatively light weight and inability to fire a long burst with controllable muzzle climb. The old World War II Browning Automatic Rifle (BAR), with its heavier bipod and greater bulk and weight, fired on full auto in steady, manageable bursts that pushed the weapon directly back against the automatic rifleman's shoulder. The BAR never jumped or climbed out of control like the lighter weight automatic M-14.

These new weapons systems made Ken Barden wonder just what the hell was wrong with the old M-1, M-1 carbine, and BAR of Guadalcanal and Pelileu fame. It was a fact that practically every U.S. manufactured weapon used in the Vietnam War was copied from World War II German weapons or other systems that had been battle proven. The American M-60 machine gun, for example, was copied in its air-cooled, belt-fed, bipod-fitted design from the German's standard World War II MG-42. And the flat-shooting main cannon on the M-48 tank surely looked like the German Panther tank's exquisite 88mm gun.

Barden and Elbert joined the grunts of Lima 3/5 from a jumping-off point at Hill 10 just north of Chu Lai. The line company troops spread out into two long columns with platoons abreast, splashing through the bloated mud of an endless patchwork of rice paddies. The dikes were slick, and no matter how hard Barden and Elbert tried to stay on top and keep their equipment dry and functional, they kept sliding into the goo and stink of the urine and feces fertilized water. The older veterans, who had been with 3/5 for six months or longer, bore the deep sores and scars from cuts and gouges sustained in forced marches through the filth of the paddies. The smallest cut or nick would fester in a matter of hours and become a weeping mass of puss and infection the next day. Some Marines had sores that had grown as large as marbles on their calves and forearms, where their bodies were continually exposed to the pools of germs and scum riding the surface of the placid-looking bowls of rice sheaves.

Suddenly, the Lima point scouts crested a shallow hill and the young company commander called, "Snipers up!" Barden and Elbert flipped the cigarettes out of their mouths into the paddy water and double-timed up the thickly vegetated slopes of the hillside. The skipper told

Tom Elbert to pick out a depression and tuck the sniper team into the hillside and scope out the approaches to the valley where a small village was visible. It was presumed to be under Communist control, and the outward-facing huts were protected by a curving ditch that skirted the thick bamboo stands running along the main group of hooches until they disappeared in a mist of ground fog and drizzle. The skipper then gave orders to his point fire team to circle the village from the left front and hold up until the automatic weapons teams could be brought forward.

The four point fire-team scouts spread out into a column and hustled down the hill's muddy slope until the flat pastures below were reached. The team kept spread out, watching for mines and booby traps as they cut across the main dikes, closing in on the far periphery of the sleepy-looking village.

Tom Elbert had shaken out his gear and got his hasty sling looped out, ready to fire. A handful of 168-grain Lake City Arsenal match boattail bullets lay in a tight cluster inside his bush hat. The weather was damp, with more monsoon sheeting rains forecast for later in the afternoon. In I Corps, the heaviest rain usually fell in late afternoon and tapered off to a hard downpour throughout the murky nights. Sniping was diminished by the darkness of cloudy late afternoons and the constant rain, which intermittently pelted the snipers with such force that their rifle scopes misted up and were practically useless. Elbert kept the thick green Marine shower towel draped over his scope's objective bell lens. When the time came to shoot, he would dial in the approximate elevation called out by his spotter, Kenny Barden. The rifle would be shouldered, and at the last moment the towel would be rolled back so Elbert could squeeze off a shot.

From out of the mist and rain, Barden spotted three

Viet Cong riflemen walking through the rectangles of rice paddy dikes, coming straight for the sniper's hide. The grunts had already passed the village and were circling far to the left flank of the main huts, trying to get at a ninety-degree angle to the snipers before they opened fire. Elbert watched Barden lower his rain-splattered glasses and point out the location of the Viet Cong by chopping his knife hand down in the direction of the enemy line of march. Barden spoke quietly, not two feet from Elbert's head, as the shooter slipped into his sling and eased into a tight cross-legged sitting position. The barrel of the Remington M-700 fell naturally on the lead Viet Cong scout. Elbert's range-finder indicated the enemy distance at around four hundred meters and closing.

"I guess we got four hundred to four-hundred-fifty meters to shoot over to hit the first dink," Barden said. "What does the range-finder indicate?" Barden was no amateur at estimating ranges, but he knew that the Viet Cong soldiers would appear closer than they actually were because the snipers were looking down off the top of the hill, cutting off the trough of the valley below from observation.

Elbert twisted the elevation knob until his Redfield scope registered three-hundred-meter battle sights. He turned the power band on the rear of the scope to a 6× power setting for what he thought would be a pretty standard straight shot into the lead VC. "Kenny, I think I can hold off a foot over the leader's head with three-hundred-meter range on my elevation knob and still hit him square in the chest. The wind is kicking up in gusts, so I'll aim above his left shoulder and bring the shot into his body."

Barden raised his binoculars and guessed the wind gusts weren't over ten miles per hour. At four hundred meters, shooting downrange, the heavy .308 caliber

NATO match bullet shouldn't drift over six inches. Even if a gust pushed the round ten inches, it would still tear into the enemy's right chest or arm. Either way, Barden figured that as fine a shot as Elbert was, at this close range the enemy leader was a definite DRT. Barden unsnapped the keeper on his green web sling and assumed a tight prone position, to follow up after Elbert fired the first round.

"I've got the leader targeted now. Approaching three-hundred-fifty meters dead ahead. I've got no more than ten miles per hour of half value wind. When he steps onto that flat dike, I'm bustin' his ass!" Elbert said, giving the play-by-play as Ken Barden's grip grew sweaty on the pistol grip of his M-14.

Barden pushed up hard on the twenty-round magazine and set the M-14's selector on semiautomatic fire as his iron sights picked up the second VC. He held a six o'clock sight picture on the Viet Cong soldier's head. Just as he eased his rifle off safety and began taking up the trigger slack in the two-stage military trigger, Elbert's Remington exploded in a violent blast of fiery red smoke, sending the heavy boattail bullet whacking through the right chest and lung of the Viet Cong point man. The bullet broke the two right ribs just under the VC's nipple and blew the air from his lung in a hammerlike blow that expanded through bone and tissue, making a fist-size exit channel out of the man's lower back.

The Viet Cong gunner never saw what cut his slender body almost in two. He was tossed violently backward into the rice paddy, where he sprawled, awaiting his final mission orders to VC Heaven. The second VC knelt as the heavy round from Elbert's rifle slammed into his buddy. His time on earth was also rapidly drawing to a finale, as Barden broke his first shot, sending a 150-grain ball bullet arching skyward off the sniper's hillside bunker. The second bullet flew well under Barden's aim point on the Viet Cong's head and hit him flush in the vitals. The bullet tore into the VC rifleman's guts, ripping his bowels to shreds and breaking his spine at the tailbone as it cut its way out of the Commie DRT's lifeless body. Barden's shot had hit so squarely that the Viet Cong's flimsy body was completely doubled up by the impact, a white chunk of splintered spine reaching out of his back like some ghostly apparition trying to escape the blood and madness.

Tom Elbert looked at Ken Barden and mutely raised two fingers, signifying two kills with the first three shots. Barden had reacquired his binoculars and watched the third Viet Cong soldier turn and run a wild zigzag back into the safety of the village. Both Barden and Elbert had enough combat savvy to stay down and let the drama below unfold. Any bushwise Marine never counted on the Viet Cong to be predictable. The Viet Cong, on the other hand, counted on the Americans to be predictable, and that's why they could always expect an American assault once the first deadly shots had been exchanged.

Elbert saw the grunts coming out of the treelines in skirmish formation, shooting rifles and machine guns into the village. The thatch walls and roofs of the huts splintered as the heavy automatic fire tore mindlessly through the hooches. Barden watched as one Marine rifleman knelt and, with a well-placed shot, cut down the third Viet Cong, who had temporarily been fortunate in escaping the accurate killing shots from the snipers' hideout.

Barden shouldered his rifle and fired a half-dozen rounds into the village for good measure. Sometimes it was hard to obey strict fire discipline when the grunts got carried away firing up a ville or busting up a Viet Cong ambush. The really hardcore veteran grunt line companies in the 5th Marines were a lot like the Tartars of Genghis Khan. When the bloodletting began, they just went nuts, killing everything from chickens, pigs, cattle, water buffalo, to Viet Cong soldiers, including their family members if they got in the way. It was hard to control the adrenaline and be selective when some of your closest friends had been killed or just shot to pieces. Often after a grunt point scout had been mutilated or killed by a booby trap, his buddies required little excuse to get even.

Elbert looked at Barden and back along the village rice fields again. Smoke was rising from several huts as the assault line of grunts shot their way across the fields toward the terrified peasants left alive inside the huts. Two Viet Cong riflemen suddenly burst out of a copse of tall bamboo trees about fifty meters from the village, running directly toward the sniper's position atop the shallow hill. The Viet Cong didn't seem to understand that their two companions lay dead along the shallow rice paddies below, covered with mulch and blood.

Elbert glanced at Barden and felt the electricity running from Barden's devious mind into his trigger finger. This shit was too good to be true! Tom Elbert opened the bolt of his Remington and ran another cartridge smoothly into the chamber. He shouldered his Remington and tracked the weaving progress of the Viet Cong escapees as the pair ran headlong into his sights. Barden wasn't waiting for permission to fire this time. He tucked into the hasty sling and snugged his left hand up toward the sling swivel. He flicked the M-14 off safety with the back of his trigger finger, taking a tight bead on the second man's chest. "Jesus, Elbert, look at these crazy assholes," he said. "They sure don't have long before they can join up with their dead buddies. You kill the leader and I'll take the next guy!"

Elbert just nodded. He was completely engrossed in keeping his crosshairs aligned and gently squeezing the trigger. The second after Elbert's rifle fired, flinging another killing round through the first hapless Viet Cong, Barden broke his next shot and knocked the trailing soldier to his knees. A second pair of quick snap shots made certain they could all join up later in Heaven for an eternal game of mahjong. Elbert turned, facing Barden, who was taking his upper arm out of the sling. He held up four fingers, and a giant grin spread over Elbert's face. He knew he was becoming a true Marine "dinger, asskicker, and name taker." On the other hand, Kenny Barden just laid his M-14 down and let the barrel cool off as the two snipers watched the first assault line of Lima Company 3/5 fan out and enter the no-name village, or more accurately, what was left of it.

Barden looked over the battlefield and realized that the entire engagement probably had not lasted over twenty minutes, though during the shooting it had seemed like an eternity. He wondered why he didn't feel any remorse for the dead Viet Cong, and realized that he had only done his job the way he was trained. The young snipers felt damn proud. So far as they were concerned, they'd struck a blow against the hordes of ruthless Communist enslavers of a free and peaceful South Vietnamese people who surely never asked for this sorry fuckin' war.

The column of grunts came out of the burning chars of huts that still blazed in the center of the village. The grunts were smeared with dirt, sweat-laden smoke, and they were bone tired. These Lima Company killers were the most terrifying soldiers on earth when they went into the attack. They had just killed over a dozen Viet Cong, and fired about two thousand rounds to do it. On the other hand, Barden and Elbert had killed four confirmed enemy soldiers with only five bullets.

CHAPTER TWENTY-TWO

Casey's Friend Dies a Hero's Death

Tom Casey and John Fuller were not only best buddies at the Citadel in the early 1960s, but both men openly expressed a desire to become professional officers. Not any branch of the United States Armed Forces would do for the two southerners whose lineage traced back to the Civil War. Tom and John not only helped each other academically, but also rivaled each other in a friendly way to excel in military science. John Fuller showed true genius in tactical thinking, and Tom Casey knew he would someday become a high-ranking officer in whichever branch he chose.

Casey was a natural leader who always put his classmates' welfare ahead of his own. Fuller used to joke that some day Tom Casey would make himself into a great sergeant major and would probably outrank Fuller unless John made it to general officer. In the United States Marines, a sergeant major is a titch below the commandant in true authority. The commandant is by tradition just below God, who rumor has it always signs all heavenly documents as God Almighty, USMC Retired.

The Citadel was an institution where love of country and respect for the professional soldier was exalted. During the Vietnam War, most of the college's graduates served in Vietnam, usually in a combat command billet, due to their leadership abilities and their fierce tradition of southern military pride and sacrifice.

I believe that the 1960s was a period when American youth separated themselves into two classes of people: men and boys. The men followed the leadership of our nation into the hell and turmoil of Vietnam, never complaining that the civilian leadership of America was just a notch above organized crime. However, the general officers and senior commanders were for the most part honorable men, and many combat leaders like Marine generals Bruno Hochmuth, Herman Nickerson, Lewis Walt, Donn Robertson, Robert Cushman, and Victor I. "Brute" Krulak were highly professional and cared deeply for their country and their Marines.

Tom Casey and John Fuller were cut from this same mold. Just like the Marine divisional commanders in Vietnam, they would earn their spurs on the battlefield, where the training manual gets thrown out the chopper window and the leader with the best trained, most courageous do-or-die hardcore sons of bitches always comes out on top. The key to their success had more to do with the subtle art of motivating men during periods of high stress, when discipline and resolute action define victory or defeat. The ability to bond and create a synergistic whole out of a bunch of individuals, and then focus their individual minds into one team, was the real trick. Some men—like Robert E. Lee, Stonewall Jackson, Chesty Puller, and Smedley Butler—had the charisma and natural persona to lead others even if they were heading for the bathroom.

The young warriors at the Citadel were getting the harsh training skills in close-order drill and combat exercises and maneuvers. Casey and Fuller exemplified the foremost skills in effective leadership: bravery, clear decision-making, steadfastness under pressure, and standing up for your men regardless of the personal consequences. The idea of standing up for principles whatever the outcome or punishment is the single character trait that separates the career soldier from the career politician. The professional soldier must lead his men, and if necessary die an honorable death with them. The politician, on the other hand, must learn to adapt to changeable situational ethics, and like the color-shifting chameleon, always plan his escape, even if his decisions have doomed others. Tom Casey and John Fuller often sat up late into the night to ponder the fate of their beloved nation if the politicians were ever actually given complete control over wartime activities. Little did our two heroes know that soon they would both be fighting for their very lives in a snakepit of political intrigue and deceit where the President of the United States concentrated more on selling helicopters than on winning the war.

The 2nd Battalion of the famous 5th Marine Regiment was called to action once again in late March 1967. Lieutenant John Fuller led the Marines of 3rd platoon, Echo Company, 2/5, into the river-bound jungle fortress controlled by the Viet Cong at their operational headquarters in the Arizona Territory. The Song Thu Bon and Song Vu Gia rivers enclosed a ten-mile-wide corridor of Communist control that had never been successfully interdicted. The Marines had made combat forays into the Arizona Territory continually since the An Hoa combat base was made operational by the 5th Marines in November 1966. The well-armed and dedicated Viet Cong main forces, along with a growing number of North Vietnamese tactical planners and logistical operations officers, held tightly to the network of trails and riverine highways that the People's Liberation Army utilized to move men and supplies farther south to continue the military pressure on South Vietnam and its patchwork of regional capitals and army detachments.

The Marines held a growing belief that an overwhelming ground attack into the Arizona Territory could destroy the effectiveness of the enemy supply efforts in Quang Nam Province. This offensive action would relieve pressure on the Marine base at Da Nang as well as the other hard-pressed Marine Corps bases on down the coast to Chu Lai.

The 2nd Battalion, 5th Marines, began Operation Newcastle on March 23, 1967, utilizing the rifle companies of Echo, Foxtrot, Golf, and Hotel to attack the river-fed bastions of the Viet Cong from the An Hoa combat base and the firebase at Phu Loc 6. Once the swollen river was reached, the lead rifle companies of Echo and Foxtrot would cross the Song Thu Bon. Hotel would follow in trace with extra ammunition and medical supplies and cross the main tributary of the river. The Marines would ford the fast water aboard the giant metal monsters of 1st Amtracs. Once across, Hotel would operate as a Sparrow Hawk reserve force and fill in any gaps. If it became necessary, Hotel's Leathernecks would fight their way into any breach, while the other sister companies swept ahead, trying to box in the enemy. The sweep companies crossed the river northwest of An Hoa and maneuvered toward the Communist-controlled sector three miles distant.

This was the same region that my fire team had occupied on the blocking force along the Thu Bon River during January 1967. The infantry had run crossing patterns trying to drive the Viet Cong into the river. I could well remember the inky dark night lit by the luminous flares from the battery of 105mm howitzers back at An Hoa. Corporal Kirby, John Lafley, Gary Woodruff, Gerald Burns, John Jessmore, and I had tucked ourselves into our bunkers, awaiting any attempts by the enemy to cross the river to escape the grunts of Echo and Foxtrot. Finally, we had sighted a dozen fleeing Viet Cong riflemen, in their haste entering the river crowded into small fishing boats. We had a heyday firing up the surprised Communists, who died quickly in a torrent of bullets, never getting off a return shot in their defense.

Echo Company's 3rd platoon, led by John Fuller, crossed the river safely and without incident. Once west of the Thu Bon River, the rifle platoon assumed point duty for the entire battalion and maneuvered across wet fields and rain-gorged rice paddies in a southerly route toward a group of hostile villages that formed the nucleus of Viet Cong activity in that area. The 3rd platoon moved carefully, realizing that they had entered a free-fire zone and all Vietnamese males were presumed to be hostile. Lieutenant Fuller's standard operational orders required his men to return fire only if fired upon. However, if the point scouts spotted armed enemy soldiers or encountered men running from a likely explosive device or booby trap, the Marines would take the Viet Cong perpetrators under fire unless they immediately surrendered.

Several huts came hazily into view across long stretches of shallow rice paddies. Few villagers were observed by the Echo point scouts, which meant that the other Marines in the column might likely be walking into an ambush or some kind of trap. When the hairs on the back of the point scouts' necks pricked up, all hands thumbed the selector switches of their M-16 rifles onto full automatic fire to disburse any ambushers as they closed on the village.

Lieutenant Fuller had just ordered his men to form into skirmishers to provide maximum firepower directed at the village front in the event Viet Cong snipers or automatic weapons crews opened fire. Less than fifty meters from the quiet village of Dai Khuong, all hell broke loose as the false walls of several thatch huts collapsed, affording the Viet Cong gunners clear fields of fire into the shocked Marine platoon. Before the Marines could hit the deck and sight their weapons to return the incoming fire from automatic rifles, mortars, and 57mm recoilless rifles, Fuller was hit by a rifle bullet. He had moved into range with the lead squad from 3rd platoon, and now his men were scratching into the paddies, looking for cover, while their leader shrugged off the intense waves of pain from his wound.

Fuller clawed his way atop a narrow paddy dike where he could see the flickering muzzle blasts of the enemy weapons and hopefully direct his Marines' rifle and machine-gun fire back on the enemy in their well-camouflaged positions. As he yelled encouragement to his men, a second bullet tore through his body, causing him to bleed internally as he lay sprawled in the mud under the whizzing madness of the firefight. Even with two bullet wounds causing Fuller to lose consciousness intermittently, he still maneuvered himself, with the aid of a corpsman, toward his radioman, who lay pinned down by enemy fire. Fuller had hopes that he could call in artillery fire and move the Viet Cong out of their well-entrenched bunkers before any more of his Marines were killed in the angry cross fire. Bullets continually raked the paddies and slammed into the soft mud around the young men clinging to life in a precarious deathtrap.

Lieutenant Fuller, turning pale from blood loss, slipped into another state of unconsciousness just as he reached the radioman. His final words of encouragement motivated the radioman to call in an urgent artillery fire mission, "Danger close." The Marines huddled in the dirt found new spirit and arose as one under the controlled fire of the platoon machine gunners and M-79 wielding grenadiers. They assaulted the village after the artillery fire tore into the Communist bunkers and tunnel systems. The grunts splashed through the shallow mud and muck, firing their rifles from the hip, while the grenadiers fired round after deadly round from their 40mm "blooper guns." The loud fiery explosions of M-72 LAAW rockets savaged what remained of the smoking skeleton of the once scenic village, now cloaked in a geyser of smoldering flame.

The radioman cradled the head of the young Marine hero who had suffered two bullet wounds and yet still fought off the Grim Reaper long enough to save his men, his brothers, his fellow Marines.

Lieutenant John Fuller died on March 23, 1967, in a nowhere village in no-man's-land thinking only of the welfare of his men. I have often asked myself how America constantly produces heroes like John Fuller and Tom Casey, who was John's best friend. I wonder how they decide to risk their lives for the Marine Corps and their men. I only know that great leadership inspires great deeds by common men on the field of battle.

Lieutenant Fuller was posthumously awarded the nation's second highest award for extraordinary heroism in battle: the Navy Cross. Personally, I think Fuller should have received the Medal of Honor for extraordinary heroism under fire, but then, the Marines were confused about who deserved and who received medals in Vietnam anyway. The infantry troops knew who the real heroes were, and John Fuller's reputation ranks right up there at the top. He will always be recognized as the kind of Marine officer who fought for the right reasons: to destroy the enemy and protect the sanctity of his lifeblood—his men.

THE PRESIDENT OF THE UNITED STATES
TAKES PLEASURE IN PRESENTING

THE NAVY CROSS

TO 2ND LIEUTENANT JOHN L. FULLER, JR.

For service set forth in the following CITATION:

FULLER, JOHN L., JR.

Citation: For extraordinary heroism in action against insurgent Communist (Viet Cong) forces while serving as Platoon Leader, Third Platoon, Company E, Second Battalion, Fifth Marines on 23 March 1967. During Operation NEW CASTLE, Second Lieutenant Fuller's platoon was maneuvering toward the fortified village of Dai Khuong (1), Quang Nam Province, when they were undertaken by intense small arms, mortar and recoilless rifle fire from a well-entrenched enemy force. Moving with the lead squad, Second Lieutenant Fuller was wounded by the initial burst of fire. Unmindful of his wound, he stationed himself to direct fire on the advancing enemy and while positioning and encouraging his men, he was struck again by enemy fire. Although suffering from a severe loss of blood, he courageously began maneuvering toward the radio position of the platoon, with the intention of directing artillery fire on the enemy, knowing it would save the lives of the other Marines. In his advance toward the radio, he received his fatal wound; however, his profound sense of duty and determination enabled him to reach the radio, but he lost consciousness and subsequently died of his wounds while attempting to call in the artillery fire. Inspired by his apparent calm, valiant fighting spirit and dynamic leadership, his Marines went on to defeat the Viet Cong in this fierce battle. Second Lieutenant Fuller's daring initiative and his undying devotion to duty reflected great credit upon himself and upheld the highest traditions of the Marine Corps and the United States Naval Service. He gallantly gave his life for his country.

CHAPTER TWENTY-THREE

Buddy Bolton and John Culbertson Team Up at Sniper School

By the end of March, Sergeant Tom Casey had eleven teams of snipers going out to all the dispersed rifle battalions in the regiment. The "13 Cent Killers" were starting to make a name for themselves as skilled scouts who could provide accurate long distance covering fire for patrols, as well as destroy enemy officers, automatic weapons personnel, and even enemy snipers once a firefight began to get confusing. Ken Barden and Harold Moore, Ron Willoughby and Denny Toncar, Tony "the Greek" Spanopoulos, Loren Kleppe, and tough Vaughn Nickell provided some of the most steadfast and deadly marksmanship skills in I Corps. When the grunts got pinned down or ambushed so close that the average rifleman could only guess at his target, the snipers provided the surgical precision shooting that cut down Viet Cong officers, medics, and other snipers, relieving pressure on the infantry to form an assault line and overwhelm the enemy.

Some battalions, like the 1st Battalion, 5th Marines, were convinced of the combat effectiveness of the sniper platoon. The officers of Col. Pete Hilgartner's 1/5 kept Tom Casey inundated with requests for sniper teams to accompany the line (infantry) companies on combat operations. Even the Marines of 3/5 used the snipers on several occasions to provide the long arm of the infantry on forays into the river-fed hell of the Arizona Territory. But the 2nd Battalion, 5th Marines, was another story.

The 2/5 always maintained a high level of expert riflemen, and the grunt officers, almost to a man, believed that their own highly trained scouts were better suited for rapidly advancing operations than the snipers. Parts of the Arizona Territory with its mile-long stretches of open paddies interspersed by low-lying dikes and only a few trees made for ideal sniper utilization. Many of the officers of 2/5 had relied regularly on artillery fire missions when engaging an enemy force at any distance greater than five hundred meters, unless the grunts could cut off the escape routes by enveloping and forming a rapid blocking force.

I was with the 2nd Battalion, 5th Marines, breaking in as John Lafley's assistant point scout, and felt that I marched with the finest infantry in I Corps. Almost all of the Hotel Company grunts had earned their spurs on the DMZ at Con Thien in mid 1966, and these veteran Marines were the epitome of "Marine combat riflemen." Nevertheless, when a quota went out from 1st Marine Division to all the other infantry regiments, the 1st, 5th, and 7th Marines were obligated to fill the required manpower slots whether they liked the proposition or not.

In Hotel Company, 2/5, we had very senior company officers, staff NCOs, and squad leaders with much combat experience. I think most officers felt that "if it ain't broke, then don't go fixin' it" made sense in this instance. Regardless, several expert riflemen were handpicked to report to the newly formed 1st Marine Division Sniper School at the Happy Valley range in Da Nang under the command of Gunnery Sergeant Vernon D. Mitchell.

My platoon commander, 2nd Lieutenant John Pindel,

called me into his office and gave me orders to report to Marine Corps Base in Da Nang for two weeks of TAD (Temporary Assigned Duty) at the Happy Valley range near the Sea Bees rock quarry on the western edge of the giant base. I would join several other shooters from the 2nd Battalion, 5th Marines, and sniper candidates from the other regiments. My shooting partner turned out to be a young Marine from Indiana named Dennis O. Bolton. I later learned that Buddy Bolton had already been assigned to the 5th Marines Snipers under the command of Sergeant Tom Casey. Several other snipers, including Vernon Smith, Eddie Rackow, Big Steve Englebrecht, Kenny Barden, and George Filyaw, would all receive their formal divisional schooling in April. If successful, they would be officially classified as U.S. Marine Scout/Snipers with the MOS (Military Occupational Specialty) 0311/8541. If they failed to qualify in marksmanship skills or personality and occupational temperament, they would be reassigned to an infantry unit.

I was an excellent shot and had high hopes that by impressing the hell out of the instructors at the sniper school, I could obtain a transfer to the 5th Marine Sniper Platoon. After all, I'd shot with the snipers off the perimeter of Phu Loc 6 and had met Sergeant Casey, Ron Willoughby, Vaughn Nickell, and Fred Sanders, and felt that I could be an important part of the Marine Corps' deadliest and least understood detachment: the scout-snipers.

Buddy Bolton and I flew with several others to Da Nang in a Lockhead C-130 Hercules. We landed without mishap and were driven up the rough-hewn slopes of the Sea Bees rock quarry and base camp at Happy Valley. We were billeted in standard olive drab Marine Corps tents at the top of a windy hill overlooking the rifle range, which ran out to a thousand meters across a shallow valley where the target butts were emplaced.

Buddy Bolton and I spent the first week almost exclusively in class inside a big open-sided tent. The Marine Corps' finest rifle instructors had been handpicked by the commandant and sent to Vietnam from Camp Pendleton to establish a formal sniper program for the 1st Marine Division. Foremost among them were Gunnery Sergeant Mitchell, perhaps the finest shot in the Marine Corps, and Sergeant Tom Casey, who had shot with Gunny Mitchell in the East Coast Matches in 1964. He felt that Mitchell had the finest overall credentials to instruct combat marksmanship due to his sixteen years of competitive shooting on Marine Corps Teams, and the fact that he was a combat veteran of both World War II and Korea. In Korea, Gunny Mitchell was one of the top shooters and snipers in the newly commissioned 1st Marine Divisions Sniper Platoon. Mitchell had the combat savvy, the competitive shooting experience, and perhaps most important the temperament and skill to instruct and mold highly motivated youngsters into deadly combat snipers.

Sergeant Douglas DeHaas assisted in teaching the professional courses in rifle marksmanship, map reading, weather analysis—including reading the wind—camouflage, ballistics, sniper tactics, targeting high-value enemy assets on the battlefield, and finally, providing a "combat multiplier" for the infantry in a firefight. DeHaas was twenty-four years old and hailed from Iowa. He was a top marksman and a gifted teacher, with the temperament of a man much older and wiser. Together, Mitchell and DeHaas tutored each of the eighteen sniper candidates in reading the wind and working through draws, down valleys, over saddles, and up steep hillsides in map-reading exercises that would have grown boring if the young Marines hadn't known for certain that they would someday likely save their lives. One thing we had to admit about Marine Corps schools was the practical, no-bullshit facts that were covered over and over until they became rote. It's a known fact that in combat the Marine who reacts correctly will come out alive, but if you have to stop and figure it out, you're probably DRT (dead right there).

Buddy Bolton and I bonded like brothers. Even though we were Marines, I felt Buddy had an honesty and almost childlike simplicity to him that was both refreshing and a constant reminder that very few of us were over twenty years of age, though many of the snipers had the look of hardened combatants many years older than their chronological age. Buddy was the kind of young man you would instantly like and learn to trust with everything you had, even your most precious possession—your life. He never complained and had an openhearted spirit that used to be found in small towns across America. Buddy wasn't a killer, but he was a patriot who set out to do what he thought was his duty to America. Like myself and most other Marines whom I met, he never thought that President Lyndon Johnson or Robert McNamara could ever have anything but our best interests at heart. So fucking much for youthful enthusiasm and the dangers of becoming a true believer! However, the fact that Bolton and I and most others were misused during the war in Vietnam sure as hell doesn't mean that we were idiots. All my life I have maintained that Buddy Bolton and all the rest of us who fought believed we were fighting for the destruction of world Communism and the preservation of freedom for an impoverished people. And I believe that the greed and corruption of political and industrial America was the scum that ruined the broth. Even thirty years after Buddy Bolton was shot dead in a rice field northeast of Phu Loc 6 in the Arizona Territory on April 19, 1967, I still think of what a fine American citizen he would have made if he had lived. All I ever wanted in life was to be a United States Marine and serve with men of honor like Tom

Casey, Kenny Barden, Fred Sanders, Ron Willoughby, and Buddy Bolton. The true indicator of a man's worth is dictated by the kind of friends he surrounds himself with. In my case, I couldn't dream of being part of anything more noble than the United States Marines, the "13 Cent Killers" of the Vietnam War.

The second week of sniper school, Buddy Bolton and I coached shooters from the 2nd Marine Brigade of the Korean Marine Corps. These stocky fighters were terrifying in their stubborn resolve in combat. They prided themselves on their own brand of efficient combat brutality, which scored high marks with the Viet Cong and any North Vietnamese units that were unlucky enough to tangle with the ROK (Republic of Korea) Blue Dragons. Bolton and I also helped train the SEALs, who swam a lot better than they shot. The U.S. Army sent a contingent of cracker-jack-sharp Rangers. These troops were so well-prepared in every facet of marksmanship that they needed little of our help. We did, however, envy the Army Rangers for their tiger-striped jungle utilities and the rest of their excellent quality gear. The Marine Corps issued a lot of well-used gear like helmets, packs, magazine pouches, canteens, flak jackets, and web gear, but the Remington Model 700 bolt-action rifles were in top condition, which was truly all most of the young snipers gave a damn about.

The Marine shooters shot considerably better than the handpicked men from the other services. Then again, marksmanship is not a skill in the Marines, but rather it is a religion. Bolton and I had taken the religion to heart and shot some outstanding strings from three hundred meters out to a thousand meters, using a sandbag rest from a prone position. Again, as I've said before, the stories about snipers making thousand-meter-plus shots from standing (offhand) positions, and also killing moving enemy soldiers and the like, are the wildest bullshit any sniper could ever dream up. Don't believe it! My average kill in Vietnam was no more than four hundred meters, with the longest at around seven hundred. I always tell my shooting buddies that if a target is a thousand meters away and worth taking, then the sniper should get off his ass and walk closer, just like any competent hunter. The average range for firefights in Vietnam was inside two hundred meters, and in thick jungled mountains like Hills 861, 881N, and 881S, the lethal range was more like twenty meters. As my father used to say, "Son, figures don't lie, but liars sure as hell figure!"

After two weeks of classes and very extensive range training, we shot for qualification at a thousand meters. Everyone eventually passed and became sniper qualified, receiving an 8541 MOS from the division school. I'm not refering to Marines designated company sniper or self-proclaimed sniper, but to the official 1st Marine Division Sniper School trained shooters. Those sniper-trained marksmen who served after graduating from the school started their own highly successful programs, like the SEALs and the Air Force Air Police. The Korean Marines' 2nd "Blue Dragons" Brigade also set up their own sniper platoons.

In a sense, it was ridiculous for the Koreans to bother with sniper training, because no Communist forces in Vietnam ever wanted to go up against them, especially if they had already had their troops shot up, butchered, tortured, or maimed by the little warriors from the Land of the Morning Calm. Even today, after more than twenty years of continuous Tae Kwon Do training and finally becoming a Master instructor, I believe the Koreans are the toughest fighters on the planet—with the exception of my Marine friend, Corporal Billy May from 1/5, who was blown up by a mine on Operation Jackstay in the Me Kong Delta in 1966.

The explosion affected Corporal May's mind, and afterward he believed himself indestructible. A fierce giant, Billy May's fingers are bigger than bananas, and his neck looks like a telephone pole. Billy spits tobacco like lightning, shits thunder, and likes nothing better than beating up squids and doggies. I call Billy every week not only because I truly love the man, but also because I need reassurance that he's not pissed off at me.

Buddy Bolton, John Fuller, Billy May, Tom Casey, John Lafley, Luther Hamilton, and the countless brave Marines who risked everything to wipe the evils of Communism off the map will always remain as my heroes and patriots of the highest order. Many Korean martial-arts masters have also served as my teachers and become friends. These fierce warriors have proven that it's not the man in the fight, but the heart and fight in the man that matters. The 5th Marine Snipers under Sergeant Tom Casey exemplified "heart and spirit," and as their tales of sacrifice and bravery unfold, I can only hope people appreciate and understand the value of their service.

CHAPTER TWENTY-FOUR

Big Jim Flynn and Tony the Greek Go on Patrol

Having previously recounted many of the ambushes and firefights involving young Vaughn Nickell and his initiation into the crude and cruel world of the combat sniper, I must include an incident involving another "cherry"—Tony "the Greek" Spanopoulos.

Both Nickell and Tony the Greek arrived in Vietnam in late 1966. After being posted to the deadliest sniper platoon in Vietnam—the 5th Marine Snipers—Ron Willoughby, Big Jimmy Flynn, and the other snipers got Vaughn and Tony into a poker game. Another sniper had just received a "Care package" from the States that contained, among other tasty items, a bottle of Jim Beam whiskey.

Now, everyone knew that the teenage Nickell and his young partner, Tony the Greek, didn't drink or gamble. They had arrived in Vietnam as relative virgins, to be thrust into a lascivious den of iniquity with hardened killers like Willoughby, Flynn, Denny Toncar, and even Tom Casey, who overlooked most of the rear echelon highjinks as long as the kill ratios stayed high in the field. Work hard and play hard. It was the Marine Corps tradition!

Ron Willoughby got the newcomers seated alongside a canvas cot covered by an olive green Marine Corps blanket pulled tight to make a poker table. The cards were shuffled a few times, for luck. Willoughby had a gleam in his eye that he got whenever there was some kind of hell about to be raised, or when an unlucky new Marine was about to be initiated into a "ball busting" trick that was played to humiliate the newly arrived snipers. He looked at Big Jimmy Flynn and, winking like a sly fox, began explaining the rules.

As Willoughby put it, "The rules are real simple, gents. If you fold or lose a hand, you not only cough up your bet, but you gotta take a shot of whiskey. Just one shot, mind you! I don't want you boys getting drunk or any shit like that."

Big Jimmy Flynn started laughing and almost rolled out of his seat on the next cot. Willoughby's eyes were wide with anticipation as the cards were dealt onto the green wool blanket. After three losing hands in a row, Vaughn Nickell was seeing stars and nodding his head like a typical drunk; in his case, a first-time drunk. Willoughby continued to deal the cards, and for some amazing reason, maybe bad luck, Nick and Tony the Greek continued to lose, raise the mandatory shot glass of whiskey and drain it in one gulp, like real men. Willoughby kept up the banter, telling both young snipers that they were behaving like real Marines and in time their luck would change.

By the fifth shot, Vaughn, completely wasted, pulled himself erect and staggered in short jolts toward the door of the hooch. He flung open the wood screened door, launched himself into the rain and slipped into a bog of oozing mud. Vaughn, who'd been a high school track star, got to his feet and ran weaving wildly down the company street, sliding through the muck and mire of the red clay.

When Nickell failed to return, Willoughby and Jimmy Flynn got worried about the possibility that he might fall facedown in a mud puddle and die, so they went to look for him. Willoughby was worried that the intoxicated young man would get apprehended and foolishly tell an officer or staff NCO that he—Willoughby—and Flynn had aided his relative state of mental instability. Rounding the corner of the staff duty hut, Willoughby and Flynn heard the distinct sounds of someone yelling and splashing around in water. Upon closer investigation, they stared in surprise as Vaughn Nickell smiled up at them from the tarp-lined pool forming the battalion's water supply. Nickell yelled with glee and kicked his boots, still crusted with mud, in the air. He flopped helplessly around like a beached porpoise, splashing mud and dirty red water into Willoughby's and Flynn's no longer grinning faces. Could courts-martial be the outcome of this poker game gone mad? Willoughby grabbed Nickell by the arms, hefted him out of the shallow reservoir and hustled back to the hooch, where Flynn assisted in pouring copious quantities of coffee into Vaughn Nickell's booze-contorted mouth.

Later that week, Jimmy Flynn was ordered to go on a night ambush with Sergeant Casey and serve as spotter. Flynn was an excellent shot, and in the field he was, like the other snipers, "all business." He did worry that Sergeant Casey might have heard something about Vaughn Nickell's "poker initiation," and he was prepared for an ass-chewing if the subject came up. When it didn't, Flynn exalted in Casey's ignorance of, or perhaps indifference to, his duplicity in the inebriation of Vaughn Nickell. Flynn ended up getting a couple of probable kills on Viet Cong sappers from the 400th VC Sapper Battalion, who were trying to infiltrate the defenses around Hill 35 north of Chu Lai.

Sergeant Casey always took time to personally instruct each sniper under his command by taking them into the field. Like most combat leaders, he believed that classroom tactics and war games were fine training, but nothing could come close to instilling combat instincts like real patrolling or night ambushes. The snipers of the 5th Marines benefited greatly from having a leader who was not only unafraid to personally train his men in the field, but in the case of Sergeant Tom Casey, actually reveled in it. In total, Casey took his Marines on forty-eight night ambushes and half again as many daylight patrols. If the snipers of the 5th Marines learned anything of value from his leadership style, it was that skill is earned the hard way on the field of battle. There ain't no shortcuts, and one small mistake can get your sorry butt sent home early in a casket.

On March 13, Jimmy Flynn and Tony the Greek joined Charlie Company of the 1st Battalion, 5th Marines, sweeping the paddies below Hill 51. Tony Spanopoulos was only twenty years old and hailed from Palisades, New Jersey. He had a thick "Jersey" accent and took a lot of ribbing from the others, but he proved to be a fine shot, and had balls big enough to bowl with. By the morning of the second day, he and Flynn were moving in column twelve klicks south of Hill 51 when they reached a bend in the trail that abruptly wound along the edge of an extensive system of rice paddies. Suddenly, an enemy sniper fired from what seemed a long distance across the paddies. The snipers went to ground, along with the grunts who called for "Guns up," to position their M-60 machine guns ready for action at the front of the column.

Unbeknownst to the fast-moving infantry, which had fanned out wide into skirmishers to defend against the possibility of an ambush, the errant sniper bullet had slapped into Jimmy Flynn's elbow, chipping away at bone and sinew. Then the same bullet traveled unspent through the leg of another Marine, completing a kind of two-for-one trick shot that was as unusual as it was deadly.

Flynn went down hard, grimacing with the agony of shattered bones protruding from a gaping bloody hole in his utility jacket, as shocked as he was hurt. Rolling to his side, he looked for Tony and yelled, "I'm okay, partner. Just find that son of a bitch and kill him for me!"

Young Tony didn't know what to do since Flynn had the sniper rifle and the shot was out of range for the iron sights on the pathetic M-16 the spotter was forced to carry. The corpsman came in a quick dash, his free hand holding his helmet tightly on his head. Flynn's arm was placed in a splint, with several battle dressings holding the sliced-up tissue hanging from his elbow together until he could reach the battalion aid station. Tony took the Remington from Flynn just as the helicopter appeared over the treeline to spirit the wounded sniper and the wounded grunt back to An Hoa and then on to Da Nang for emergency surgery. Flynn had received the "million dollar wound" and would be transferred back to Great Lakes Naval Hospital in Illinois, never to return to Vietnam.

Just before the medevac chopper lifted off, Big Jim Flynn yelled out to Tony the Greek, "Find that fucker and make him hurt, man. I'll see you back home after the war is over. Keep your head down, partner. Stay alive!"

The chopper's turbine engine throttled up, and the olive drab bird whirred into the sky, muffling another hidden shot from the Viet Cong sniper. This one took the platoon commander, Lieutenant Jewel, down with a wound through the arm. Another Marine was down and wounded superficially as Tony hastily took a fire team of four riflemen and edged along the trees toward the left flank of the platoon, looking for the Viet Cong sniper. There was no doubt in any of the Marines' minds that this VC "dinger" was no rookie. He had seriously wounded Jimmy Flynn and Lieutenant Jewel, and scared the living shit out of the third wounded man.

Tony Spanopoulos tracked the berms and shallow hills that faced the stricken platoon of Marines, awaiting another shot from the sniper. The Marines guessed correctly that he was moving his hide after each shot. Tony glanced hard at the likely terrain features that he felt he would employ if he were the Viet Cong shooter. Then another shot rang out, and a bullet cracked through the air just over Tony's head. Spanopoulos glassed to the front toward a small grassy mound that bordered the rice paddies to his right flank. He knew the sniper had to be there. Tony leveled his Remington at the shallow mound some six hundred meters distant, mentally counting off the mills of elevation that he would need to adjust his sights to eliminate the enemy threat, and finally left his sights set at three hundred meters and held off a meter over the target.

As he sighted on the top of the small hillock, he anticipated that the sniper might appear anywhere along the crest or down the side of the mound. By holding off a meter higher, he could assure himself of a body shot with three-hundred-meter battle sights still on his rifle. Tony knew if he got an extra second, he could turn the scope's elevation knob to the six-hundred-meter mark and likely be right on the target with a six o'clock hold. He was afraid that any time wasted with the Remington off his shoulder might cause him to miss the opportunity to kill the Viet Cong. This is why any seasoned sniper must learn "leads and holds" for his particular rifle, so that holding off can be practiced and employed in quick target acquisition when no time is left to fiddle around with elevation and windage screws.

Spanopoulos thought he saw a dark green shape emerge and then quickly disappear from the left side of the mound. He turned the power ring on the Redfield scope up to 9×, then peered into the reticule to scope out the terrain. Sure enough, a canvas tarp or the inside of a poncho lifted slowly above the dirt and stands of sparse grass. This Viet Cong sniper was smart, all right. He looked for another Marine target through his scope lens from inside the tarp cover that shielded his form from the Marines. It was evident to Spanopoulos that the VC sniper was banking on the fact that no Marine snipers were attached to the patrol, which would have left him fairly safe, tucked away in his blind and protected from the naked eyesight and bare iron sights of the grunts' rifles.

Tony got a knot in his throat as he placed the crosshairs just a couple of feet over the canvas rag shelter hiding the Communist sniper. Remembering his trigger time on the Happy Valley range, the Greek took in a full breath, allowing it to escape slowly through his lips until his heart relaxed. He took up the trigger slack ever so gently and maintained the sight picture, boring a hole through the canvas cloth with his mind's eye.

Kablaam! The rifle discharge caught Tony momentarily off guard as sniper school training had taught him. He then rode the rifle's recoil, and when the barrel of the Remington settled back on the target, the canvas cover was blown off and a bloody shape like a smashed melon lay crushed over to one side of the hill. The round had pierced the hide and smashed into the sniper's rifle, causing the Greek's thin metal jacket to explode and literally cut the Viet Cong's head into shards of brain and skull covered with a shiny gelatinous spray of blood.

The Charlie Company skipper had witnessed the rifle shot, and ordered his point scouts to advance toward the mound of earth while his machine gunners covered the advance. Nothing more was heard from the Viet Cong sniper. His oozing remains were left for the birds to pick clean while the Marine column saddled up and moved carefully toward the patrol's next checkpoint.

Tony the Greek had made an outstanding kill, but was saddened knowing he would likely never get to tell Big Jimmy Flynn that he had shot the sniper. Spanopoulos was growing pretty salty, and on this patrol learned one basic lesson of war. When you face off with the veteran Viet Cong snipers, you must always employ stealth, and above all use extreme patience. Some VC shooters would lie dog all day just to catch a Marine patrol, and after making one killing or wounding shot, would fade away like smoke into the eternal night of the jungle. To kill the VC, the Marine snipers had to think and perform like the Viet Cong. In truth, Vietnam was not only the Communists' country, but it was their jungle and their war.

CHAPTER TWENTY-FIVE

The Snipers Get Rescued by Grunt Mortars

On April 6, 1967, Operation Boone commenced in Quang Ngai Province some thirty miles south of Hill 35 and south of Chu Lai. Tom Casey sent two sniper teams to hook up with Charlie Company of the fighting 1st Battalion, 5th Marines. The snipers were assigned to Charlie's Headquarters platoon, and they humped all day before reaching a giant hill just outside of Quang Ngai City, nestled alongside Highway 1. The hill was named Buddha Mountain, and headquarters set up a tight perimeter near the crested peak. There was also a contingent of RVNMC (Republic of Vietnam Marine Corps) Marines and ROK (Republic of Korea) Marines present, which added a sinister and deadly flavor to the allied forces tucked into their own defensive earthworks. In particular, the RVNMC Marines were nothing like the regular Vietnamese Army or Popular Forces. Indeed, the Vietnamese Marines were some of the best trained, highly motivated soldiers in the Vietnam War. Much of the credit for the training and development of the RVNMC Marines went to seasoned U.S. Marine officers like Major Jim Johnson, who helped mold the little fighters in the image of the United States Marine Corps.

The Korean Marine "Blue Dragons," whom I've mentioned before, were all professional soldiers and dedicated fighters. They were among the most ferocious killers in the Vietnam War. Their methods were almost medieval, and included the interrogation and torture of prisoners right on the battlefield where they had surrendered or were, unfortunately for them, captured. The Koreans were Asians, of course, and on several occasions explained to the Marine shooters at 1st Marine Division Sniper School that they had scant interest in the protection of Vietnamese civilians but clearly understood the evils of Communism, since their own country was constantly threatened by the North Korean Communists. The ROK Blue Dragons also explained, to Kenny Barden, Gene Davis, George Nash, and Pat Montgomery, that the Americans falsely believed they could win a psychological battle for the "hearts and minds" of the Vietnamese villagers. The Koreans spoke forcefully, stating that any village inhabitants who fired on Korean troops or aided the Communists were immediately destroyed. If the civilian population got in the way during a firefight between Korean Marines and the Viet Cong, then that was unfortunate, but did not deter the ROKs from their duty of wiping out the VC. Furthermore, the ROKs felt that any Viet Cong who surrendered was less than honorable, and any treatment was acceptable as long as the Koreans extracted the information they required for operational intelligence.

I thought the Korean attitude toward combat made perfect sense. At least they didn't pussyfoot around, like the South Vietnamese Army and Popular Forces. And when the shit hit the fan, you couldn't ask for better comrades to watch your back than the Koreans. They never cut Charlie any slack, and when a firefight got chaotic, the Blue Dragons from the land of Summer Fire and Winter Ice fought brutally, like the soldiers of the Great Khan himself. Nothing was left alive in their bloody wake as the Blue Dragons spread mayhem and terror across the South Vietnamese countryside.

On Buddha Mountain, Ken Barden and Dave Kovolak split off from the second sniper team of Pat Montgomery and Stanley Watson. Both teams joined the long green column of grunts snaking off the lower fingers of the mountain and winding out into the rice valley like a cobra leaving its lair. The snipers were positioned with one team near the point, to support the grunts if the point scouts were ambushed. Pat Montgomery and Stanley Watson marched in front of the Marine commander, so he could dispatch them to any sector of the column when they were hit.

The grunts carried light haversacks, and many wore their utility shirts open at the chest with the sleeves rolled up for comfort. Their web belts, however, were hung heavily with spare canteens, magazine pouches, bayonets and K-bars, battle dressing pouches, and an occasional pistol holster. Some Marines wore map cases crammed with loaded M-16 magazines, with the shoulder strap crossing over the chest and the pouch holding as many as a dozen twenty-round mags, dangling at the hip ready for easy access. After a period of six months in the bush, most Marines adopted more practical personal styles of carrying their gear. The uniforms were always the standard loose-fitting jungle utility shirt and trousers bloused over jungle boots at the boot top. Flak jackets were always worn, even if the temperature was 120 degrees. Helmets were inscribed with hometowns, months and days left on a Marine's tour of duty, or some personal message like "Born to Kill" or "Vietnam Sucks." Commanders put up with all the nonmilitary bullshit as long as the grunts did their job, and make no mistake about it, the only job the grunts and the snipers had was to seek out and destroy the enemy.

Kenny Barden sloshed through the heavy mud in the

paddies and slipped climbing up a dike that was so caked with slimy mud it looked like a freshly iced chocolate cake. As he and Dave Kovolak rounded a thick stand of bamboo and waist-high grass that edged the trail leading out of the rice paddy, several rifle shots cracked in the distance and bullets whizzed by, skipping off the placid water.

Barden and Kovolak went down on a knee and tried to locate the direction of the enemy sniper fire. Kovolak fumbled with the leather case holding the 7×50 millimeter binoculars that he used to spot with, finally bringing the glasses up to his eyes. His hands trembled as he tried to focus the glasses, sweeping the far treelines and slowly looking for enemy movement or any other odd feature. Without warning, another pair of rounds cracked past the point fire team's position and didn't miss the snipers by a hell of a lot.

It was always unnerving when a pair of well-camouflaged Viet Cong marksmen shot at the snipers. The problem grew more severe until the enemy was finally located in his hide. Then all fears would be forgotten as the Marines fired back. Usually after a firefight was over and the snipers had a moment to reflect on the insanity and near death they had endured, many Marines would sit and stare at their still living and breathing buddies and ask themselves, Just how the hell did we survive that shit and not even get a scratch? Man, God must really be lookin' out for our young asses! Thank Heaven the Almighty signs his name "God Almighty, USMC (Retired)."

Just as Barden and Kovolak were starting to get their bearings and feel a moment of relief, the dreaded command "Snipers up!" echoed over the rice paddies. The two snipers grabbed their gear and ran weaving up to the point, praying they wouldn't get shot. The grunts were firing sporadically at the treeline stretched out in a long dark smear four hundred meters up a shallow rise in the terrain where the jungle reached the edge of the paddies. Barden scoped the jungle with his scope on 9×, while Kovolak swept his binoculars back and forth, pausing momentarily to wipe the sweat from his eyes. Another shot rang out, and Barden caught the short white flare of the muzzle blast deep inside the treeline. The Viet Cong sniper was clever and had retreated a few meters into the dark shadows of the jungle's overgrowth, where the muzzle blast and report would be much harder to detect than firing in the open.

Kenny Barden had three-hundred-meter battle sights on his scope, and he tracked over to the spot where the flash had emanated and took careful aim, holding off a foot above the target to compensate for the approximate 450 meters in range that Kovolak estimated. Barden held his breath and took up the trigger slack, firing a heavy match FMJ bullet into the lightly camouflaged position. If the Viet Cong wasn't hunkered down behind a log or some heavy obstruction, he was highly vulnerable.

Barden knew the .308 NATO bullet with its heavy 168-grain weight had a good chance to pierce the cover and concealment and score a hit.

The snipers loved the Remington bolt rifles mostly because the .308 or 7.62 × 51 millimeter round was ballistically extremely accurate and would hit the target with sufficient energy to kill an enemy sniper or penetrate moderately heavy cover out to a thousand meters. The M-16 that the grunts were forced to carry after their outstanding combat-proven M-14 rifles were confiscated, fired a puny 55-grain bullet that sped from the muzzle at such extreme velocity that it blew up on impacting any heavy cover. The M-16's .223 caliber bullet wasn't capable of providing a third of the impact energy that Marines had learned to trust firing the M-14, with its .308 NATO cartridge. The grunts continued to fire away with their

Mattel Toy M-16s, which at 450 meters were incapable of killing a fucking dog, much less a man.

Barden lifted and cycled the bolt handle, pushing another round into the Remington's chamber. He still had the barrel aimed in the general area of his last shot while he scanned the dark green shadows of the jungle, looking for any sign of the Viet Cong. He figured there were probably two snipers in the hide since the Viet Cong usually worked in pairs or in a three-man unit called a "cell." Just as Barden took up the slack for his second shot, hoping for a bit of blind luck since he couldn't see the sniper, a fiery burst of Marine 60mm mortar fire flared in the paddy a few meters short of the sniper's last position. Like clockwork, more mortar rounds fell in the same area. The skilled Marine mortarmen with Headquarters Company walked the rounds through the dense foliage, blowing the limbs, leaves, vines, and bark from the trees into the air. The half-dozen mortar shells impacted along a thirty-meter-wide area that centered on the exact spot where the sniper had fired. The mortar teams of Lieutenant Colonel Pete Hilgartner's 1st Battalion, 5th Marines, were the finest in the 1st Division.

Barden looked at Dave Kovolak, who just shook his head and muttered, "That fucker is gone forever to Gook Heaven, Kenny. Hell, man, you just might have shot his ass before those mortar rounds tore the place up. Guess we'll never know."

Barden cycled the bolt, ejecting the live round out of the chamber. Then pointing toward the treeline, he said, "Now that nobody in particular can claim that asshole as his confirmed KIA, everyone will start saying they killed the little bastard. I'll bet he got clean away after his last shot, man. Those Viet Cong snipers are slick as bacon grease—at least the ones who stay alive are!"

The company commander yelled out for the troopers to get off their butts and saddle up for the return march to Chu Lai. The Viet Cong were given no such orders to return to their base. Instead, they spread the thick leafy jungle plants apart not far from their original hideout where they had opened fire and watched the Marines depart just like they had come—none the wiser.

CHAPTER TWENTY-SIX

The 5th Marines Make Their Summer Offensive

When Kenny Barden returned to Chu Lai, he laid out his gear, and after removing his utility trousers made a startling discovery. All the old veteran grunts who were the champion humpers of I Corps had told him and Dave Kovolak, along with the other rookie snipers, not to wear their skivvy shorts into the bush. Both Barden and Kovolak had guessed it was some kind of dumb ritual or a quicker method to get your trousers back on if you got shot at while taking a crap. Anyway, Barden and the others had all worn their skivvies on stateside duty and even into the field on training missions. None of the snipers believed the "old crusty dudes" would ever stoop to give sound advice to the snipers. Barden just figured they were probably fucking with his mind.

During the last patrol with Charlie 1/5, Kenny and Dave both had severe problems with chafing along their inner thighs from the constant immersion in filthy rice paddies and the incursion of mud and abrasive particles of sand. Their thighs, on closer examination, were rubbed more than raw. Spots of fresh blood clotted in deep abrasions were like "road rash" from falling off a bicycle or motorcycle and shining up the asphalt with their legs. Just the barest touch set off pangs of misery, and both Barden and Kovolak lay dormant and spread-eagled on their cots, letting the air dry out the wounds. Neither man dared to wash the tender area that had been tormented during a week of constant humping up hills and down into rice paddies full of the germ-ridden shit from a thousand water buffalo, not to mention the rice harvesters themselves.

Finally, in utter agony, Barden and Kovolak hobbled arm in arm like two invalids with ball (testicular) cancer, across the camp to the infirmary. The Navy corpsman listened to the two knuckleheads' lame excuses for a short minute and then ordered the boys to bare their privates. After sponging the effected areas with hydrogen peroxide to kill the bacteria, the corpsman grinned at the two numbies and dolloped on a copious quantity of antibacterial gel that burned even worse than the hydrogen peroxide. Barden and Kovolak commenced a newfangled sniper's folk dance, hopping in circles around the sick bay, crying and begging for the ointment to calm down and stop frying their legs. Just to be cute, the corpsman had splashed a bit of hydrogen peroxide onto the young snipers' balls for good measure.

Sometimes even corpsmen get bored with the routine of their jobs and seek to liven up the situation in a harmless way if the circumstance presents itself. No corpsman could ask or pray for a more deserving pair of bozos to show up at the infirmary during a boring shift than the two Marine heroes just back from confronting the enemy in the bad bush of Quang Ngai Province. The corpsmen were usually the saviors of the combat-wounded Marines, and their tales of bravery under fire are unequaled. This caper, however, would live in infamy as "the case of the burning balls." For many years the battalion's corpsman would have a good hearty laugh at the expense of the "skivvy humpers." The most remarkable thing was that Barden and Kovolak would laugh about it too—once they realized they were going to live!

After getting out of the infirmary, the two young snipers threw all their skivvy shorts away. The local Vietnamese wouldn't even wear them. Later, when it got dark, the two "walking wounded" men with the "burning balls" slunk into the local village to purchase a "forty pounder," which was an oversized quart of whiskey that contained forty ounces instead of the usual thirty-two. The Marines nipped away at the booze as they walked back to the sniper tent, and in the morning they found themselves laid out under a clump of bamboo trees. They were still drunk and feeling no ill effects from their recent abrasive jaunt into the hinterland as the morning sun started to beat down.

Within a half hour the two malingerers were sweating profusely and their heads throbbed like someone was hammering a gong between their ears. Barden looked up with bloodshot eyes and tender inner thighs at Kovolak, who first smiled and then threw up what was left of the "forty pounder" into the grass and collapsed into the dirt. Ken Barden, being a man of intelligence, made a mental note never to drink another forty pounder on an empty stomach and to immediately turn himself in to the battalion shrink if he ever again entertained the thought. Having finished his mental preparations for safeguarding his future health, Barden bent low from the waist and threw up. Then he unceremoniously joined his partner sprawled out on the ground.

Later that day Barden and Kovolak reported with Tony Spanopoulos, Vaughn Nickell, Ron Willoughby, Dennis Toncar, Loren Kleppe, and the rest of the remaining snipers to the company office. There, Captain Babich gave the men their preparatory warning order to prepare for a major operation that would be regimental in scope and designed to interdict and destroy recent North Vietnamese infiltration into the Que Son Valley. Charlie 1/5 and their attached sniper teams had been making increasingly stiff contact on patrols and sweeps in the area.

Captain Babich explained to Sergeant Casey that most of the sniper teams would be parceled out to the various rifle companies for the operation. He also read the list of eight snipers who would attend 1st Marine Division Sniper School on April 23, 1967.

Kenny Barden, Carroll Gene Davis, George Nash, Patrick Montgomery, Eddie Rackow, Alex Levandoski, Steve Englebrecht, and Vern Smith reported directly to Gunnery Sergeant Vernon D. Mitchell at the Happy Valley range for a week-long seminar to rezero rifles and get their mental attitudes back in shape.

Mitchell was as gifted in motivational psychology as he was in teaching shooting. He talked to the young snipers about the tendency to get cocky and think they were "bulletproof" just before they got killed. Mitchell said the veteran sniper should become expert in sensing the proper situation to ambush or stalk. He told them to never allow youthful exuberance to get the best of good common sense and sound judgment. The Gunny related a story about a fellow Korean-era Marine sniper who ran up an impressive string of kills and began to believe that he was too sharp to be killed. Finally, the Gunny said, a situation presented itself where the arrogant Marine sniper got an opportunity to take an easy shot at a North Korean sentry who acted like he didn't think there was even a war going on. The sentry turned out to be a "bait," and after the Marine shot him dead, another North Korean sniper hidden in a clump of foliage nearby shot the American right between the running lights. Mitchell impressed on the snipers that the Marine Corps was a team and that no one was any more valuable than anyone else. The heart of the Corps is the rifleman, and the sniper's duty is to back his play with accurate, aimed fire, removing any threats to the infantry's advance.

Gunny looked over at each sniper and added for emphasis, "No single Marine ever won a battle. Remember, the Commies can make 'em faster than we can kill 'em, so you've got to pick your shots carefully and kill the officers, weapons crews, medics, and above all, the enemy snipers. The Viet Cong snipers have operated for thirty years against the Japs, the French, and now the Americans. They know every inch of the land and they are resourceful and deadly. Make a mistake with a Viet Cong sniper and it may be your last. This concludes your training, and I can only admonish you men to be careful. Good luck."

That pretty much said it all, and the eight snipers packed their gear to head back to the new headquarters at Tam Ky. Operation Union I had officially kicked off on April 21, 1967, and the snipers looked forward to working with new rifle companies and some of the legendary company commanders in the 5th Marine Regiment.

When the snipers got back to their headquarters at Tam Ky, Sergeant Casey held a meeting and read some of the first operational assignments for sniper teams going out to the rifle companies. The teams were often switched, with some snipers working for the first time with others who had been longstanding partners with another shooter. Casey constantly drummed in the philosophy that all the snipers were trained the same way in tactics and shooting skills. It did not matter who worked with each other since this was strictly business and, personalities aside, they all had the same mission: find and kill the enemy.

Ron Willoughby was teamed up with Dave Kovolak, in place of Ken Barden. Perhaps in this case personality did enter into the decision-making, inasmuch as Willoughby was a fairly straight arrow and an NCO. Barden was teamed with Carroll Gene Davis, a giant Oklahoman who was a former college football star. Although Barden was a fine shot and showed much promise, no one really knew exactly what Kenny Barden showed promise for besides stealing Army supplies, requisitioning liquor, and being the platoon comedian. Barden just laughed the whole affair off since he also had high confirmed kill numbers in the platoon. Little Vaughn Nickell had finally gotten over the trauma of killing his first Viet Cong, and he turned into the most reliable and unselfish member of the sniper platoon. Casey teamed Vaughn up with Bill Wills, and the fourth team was composed of the gentle giant Harold Moore and the veteran Loren Kleppe.

These four teams would be attached to the various rifle companies on operation and provide long range sniping, observation, security, and accurate surgical destruction if a full-scale battle was joined. Since the enemy was growing in presence and boldness in the entire Que Son Valley, it appeared to Marine commanders, like regimental commander Colonel Kenneth J. Houghton, that the timing was right and the weather would permit a regimental-scale assault on the base camps of the North Vietnamese Army's veteran 21st Regiment.

The 21st NVA was the most highly active combat arm of the North Vietnamese Army 2nd Division, located south of Da Nang. The 2nd NVA Division also ranged north into the Arizona Territory and the surrounding An Hoa Basin, including Charlie Ridge and Dodge City. The 2nd Battalion, 5th Marines, had been locked in deadly territorial battles with elements of the NVA 2nd Division since the Thu Bon River's sandbanks were spattered with blood on Operation Tuscaloosa. Operation Union I would hopefully destroy the 21st NVA Regiment, or at least put them to flight to refit in Laos, as had happened with the Viet Cong Main Force R-20th Regiment earlier in January.

On April 25 the United States Army sent their untested 196th Light Infantry Brigade, represented by a rifle platoon and a weapons platoon commanded by a 1st lieutenant, to relieve the 5th Marines Headquarters section on Hill 35 just north of Chu Lai. Sergeant Tom Casey had been maintaining a security force of not more than two squads of Marines. Casey had run nightly ambushes and repelled Viet Cong sapper attacks on a regular basis when they attacked the 11th Marines artillery gun pits.

Casey met the Army officer and rendered a sharp salute, mostly for proper interservice relations since the Marines never saluted in the forward combat areas. The Army lieutenant gathered his gear together and followed Casey into the command bunker. Turning serious, the new lieutenant asked, "Sergeant, will you please conduct a detailed tour of the defenses before dark. My NCOs need time to set up our automatic weapons and post the pickets and sentries."

Casey just stared ahead and tried not to break into laughter. The Marines manned their bunkers just like on any other perimeter, and deployed what automatic weapons they had available, balancing out the defenses and giving close attention to the likely avenues of approach.

Casey watched as an entourage of soldiers brought bedding, blankets, communication gear, rifles, grenades, and a map table into the crowded bunker. He piped up from between the stacks of rations and equipment and gave the new lieutenant the lowdown: "Sir, the Marine sentries know this area well. The Viet Cong usually attack in the late morning hours with suicide sapper attacks directed at the artillery park. Our nineteen Marines repel them with M-60 fire, grenades, M-79s, and LAAW rockets. I usually lead my snipers out on a fixed position night ambush and try to catch the VC as they approach the perimeter wire."

The lieutenant seemed to bite his lip and clench his

jaw while looking out the bunker's hatch with a nervous twitch. He stepped out of the hatchway and, after eyeing the perimeter wire, exclaimed, "Sergeant, I can't possibly see how we can defend this hill with only ninety soldier⌐. My God, some of those NVA sapper units really do blo⌐ themselves up to breach the wire. How can we ever stop all of them?"

Tom Casey had heard all he wanted to hear. "Well, sir, for starters I'd get your senior NCOs to post your men now. Secondly, I'd get some artillery concentrations preregistered to counter an all-out attack. Thirdly, I'd have some of your men patrol at night to shake up the gookers. A night ambush every once in a while would be a nice idea also. Good luck, and I'm certain you'll do fine. I have to catch the next chopper out to Tam Ky, but if things really get sticky, you could always call us back, sir."

Casey saluted and, turning on his heel, made his way to the helipad and the waiting chopper. As the UH-34 spun up in a cloud of red dust, he prayed that God would watch after the doggies from the 196th. He knew it would take more than a few Marines to correct what was wrong with that outfit. Maybe a little time in the bush would help. Casey smiled and slowly shook his head as he gazed at the patchwork of colored fields and paddies flashing under the chopper's whirling rotor. Time could help things work out, but probably not with the Army's propensity to fuck things up.

Casey wondered just what the hell was taking the Army so long to take over the Marine positions in I Corps. Vietnam was the first war where American planners and the Joint Chiefs had used the Marines not just as an assault force, but as permanent defensive units operating from established bases like Chu Lai, Tam Ky, An Hoa, Da Nang, and further north at Phu Bai, Dong Ha, and Gio Linh. The U.S. Army also had the outstandingly aggressive troopers of the 101st Airborne Division and the equally battle-hardened "Herd" of the famous 173rd Airborne Brigade flying all over I and II Corps, fighting the desperate battles that regular Army infantry troops apparently couldn't handle. The Army had the biggest helicopter air force in the world and more artillery than Napoleon. Why was the undersized Marine Corps tasked to contain the infiltration of hundreds of thousands of North Vietnamese, Chinese, and even Russian troops and advisors? Casey guessed that the politicians weren't asking any more of the Marines in Vietnam than it had of the heroes of Guadalcanal, Iwo Jima, Tarawa, and Peleliu. Nonetheless, the Marines were up against some very combat-savvy divisions from North Vietnam, aided by the local populace and supplied by the local farmers. The NVA was perhaps the most underrated army in modern times, but Casey doubted if any of the wounded survivors of the French fortress of Dien Bien Phu would call the Communists unresourceful or ineffective.

As the chopper set down in a storm of dust at Tam Ky, Sergeant Tom Casey knew he had a lot of work to do to get his sniper teams ready for the big battles that he was certain were brewing up in the bloody caldron of the Que Son Valley.

Appendix

5th Marine Regiment Sniper Platoon in Vietnam
From October 1966 at Chu Lai to 1968 at Hue City

Allison, Ricky D.	OK	WIA BS	Dec 67/Nov 67
Barden, Ken	MS	WIA	Mar 67/Feb 68
Bean, Arthur R. D.	AZ	WIA	Jun 66/Dec 67
Berry, Martin	IN		Dec 66/Dec 68
Billingsley, Larry			
Black, Uliston J.	AK	WIA	Sept 66/Sep 67
Bolton, Dennis	*IN*	*KIA S*	*19-Apr-67*
Brown, Calvin	IN		Dec 66/Jan 67
Carter, Dennis	IN		
Carter, James D.	TX		
Casey, Thomas	SC	WIA 2/4 BS	Jun 66/Jul 67
Culbertson, John	H 2/5	WIA 3PHM	Mar/May/June 67
Davis, Carroll Gene	OK		Feb 67/Mar 68
Draper, Allen	IL		May 67/Jun 68
Dredern, Jim	MS		Mar 66/Apr 67
Elbert, Thomas	OH		Jan 67/Feb 68
Englebrecht, Steve	CA	WIA VCG	Mar 67/Mar 68
Filyaw, George	NC		Mar 67/Feb 68
Flynn, Jim	IL	WIA 3/13	Oct 66/Mar 67
Henshall, Eric	AZ		
Howell, John W.	IL	WIA	Apr 67/May 68
Hudson, Jim	GA	WIA	Dec 66/Jan 67
Josey, Randall	LA	WIA	
Kleppe, Loren L.	IA	WIA	Oct 66/Nov 67
Kovalak, David J.	MI		Jan 67/Feb 68

Kump, Robert	CA	WIA	Sept 66/Sep 67
Levandoski, Alex G.	WI	WIA	Feb 67/Apr 68
Mendoza, Ramon	AZ		Dec 66/Jan 68
Milliagan, Robert	PA		Oct 66/Nov 67
Monroe, Charles	AZ	*KIA S*	*3-Jun-67*
Montgomery, Patrick	TX		Feb 67/Mar 68
Moore Jr., William J.	PA		
Moore, Harold G.	CA		Oct 66/Nov 67
Nash, George	IN	*KIA*	*6-Sep-67*
Nesbitt, William	IL		
Nickell, Vaughn	IN		Oct 66/Sept 67
Rackow, Eddie	TX	WIA	Mar 67/Apr 67
Sanders, Fred W.	TN		Oct 66/Nov 67
Smith, Verne R.	WA		Mar 67/Apr 67
Spanopoulos, Anthony	NJ		Sep 66/Oct 67
Toncar, Dennis	OH		Oct 66/Nov 67
Tuitele, Fofo	CA	WIA BS	Nov 66/Dec 68
Watson, Stanley	MT		Jan 67/Feb 68
Wilhite, George	KY		Jan 67/Feb 68
Willoughby, Ron	OH		Oct 66/Nov 67
Wills, William H.	OH		Oct 66/Nov 67

5th Marine Scout / Sniper Platoon
Operations / WIA (Wounded in Action)
KIA (Killed in Action)

Month	WIA	Operations	Dates	KIA
Jan–67	Culbertson 2/5	Tuscaloosa	3/18, 5/15, 6/9/67	
Feb–67	Casey 2/4	Independence	2/1–2/6	
		Desoto	2/6–2/11	
		Rio Grande	2/18–2/24	
Mar–67	Flynn 3/13	Newcastle	3/22–3/26	Fuller 3/23
Apr–67		Boone	4/1–4/8	Bolton 4/19
		Union I	4/21–****	
May–67	Culbertson 2/5	Union I	****–5/17	
		Union II	****	
Jun–67	Barden 6/6	Union II	****–6/5	Babich 6/2
	Culbertson 6/9	Bai Loc	6/13–6/18	Monroe 6/3
		Adair	6/19–6/25	Graham 6/3
		Calhoun	6/25–****	
Jul–67		Calhoun	****–	
Aug–67		Pike	8/1–8/3	
		Cochise	8/11–8/28	
		Yazoo	8/27–****	
Sep–67		Yazoo	****–9/5	
		Swift	9/4–9/15	Nash 9/6
		Shelbyville	9/21–9/28	
Oct–67		Baxter	10/19–10/21	
Nov–67		Essex	11/5–11/12	
Jan–68	Barden	Hue City	1/31–****	
Feb–68	Englebrecht	Hue City	All Feb	

Compiled by Sergeant R. W. Willoughby
Assistant NCOIC / 5th Marine Snipers
Chu Lai, An Hoa, Da Nang, Hue City, Vietnam
1966–1968

SERGEANT JOHN J. CULBERTSON
U.S. Marine Corps 1965–1971

Sergeant Culbertson was born in Oklahoma City, Oklahoma, on May 27, 1946. He is a graduate of Northern Arizona University, where he earned a bachelor's degree in business administration in 1972. He was enlisted in the Marine Corps in 1965, completing recruit training at MCRD, San Diego, California. During his distinguished career in the Marine Corps, Sergeant Culbertson served with Hotel Company 2/5 1st Marine Division, at An Hoa, Republic of Vietnam, from December 1966 to July 1967 as an 0311 Marine Rifleman. While in Da Nang, he completed the First Marine Division's Sniper School, where he earned his secondary MOS of 8541. Sergeant Culbertson was also quarterback for the All-Marine Football Team in Quantico, Virginia, in 1968. Sergeant Culbertson was honorably discharged from the Marine Corps in 1971.

Today Sergeant Culbertson is a distinguished author, whose books include *Operation Tuscaloosa* and *A Sniper in the Arizona*. In his book *Operation Tuscaloosa*, he recounts his experience as a point man for the lead squad of Hotel Company, 2/5, where they nearly wiped out an entire battalion of VC troops. This book pays tribute to those Marines who gave their lives to make that victory possible.

Sergeant Culbertson's military awards include three Purple Hearts, the Combat Action Ribbon, the Presidential Unit Citation, the Navy Unit Citation, the Meritorious Unit Citation, the Vietnam Cross of Gallantry with Palm, the Marine Corps Good Conduct Medal, the National Defense Service Medal, and the Vietnam Service Ribbon.

Sergeant Culbertson is married to Mrs. Diane D. Culbertson. They have a daughter, Mary Ashley Culbertson, age 27.

Glossary

A-4 Sky Raider—Single-engine USMC attack jet. Medium-size and subsonic.

Actual—The commander of a platoon, company, battalion, etc.

AK-47—Main VC fully automatic battle rifle in 7.62 × 39mm.

Ambush—A covert attack method employed by both VC and Marines by firing on an unawares enemy from seclusion, often employing booby traps or mines.

Amtrac—Marine tracked armored personnel carrier, troops loaded through rear ramp door.

An Hoa—The ancient French fortress that comprised the westernmost logistical base of the Marines. Thirty miles southwest of Da Nang.

Arizona—The rice paddy territory of Dai Loc and Duc Duc provinces in South Vietnam stretching west and southwest from Da Nang.

Arty—Artillery used in fire support missions.

ARVN—Army of the Republic of South Vietnam.

Assault line—Marine attack formation with troops advancing abreast.

AT—Artillery target coordinates giving exact map locations on USMC topographical maps.

Azimuth—Compass heading toward an objective or target.

Back azimuth—180° opposite compass heading to an azimuth. This points to where a patrol has been.

Ball, ammo—FMJ (full metal jacket), usually weighing 150 grains in 7.62 × 51mm standard NATO bullet.

Bandolier—A linked belt of machine-gun ammo often worn across the chest.

Battalion—A Marine combat unit composed of four rifle companies and a headquarters company.

Battle dressing—A rectangular three-by-five-inch (approximate size) medical dressing carried into combat by Marines.

Betel nut—Narcotic seed nut chewed by Vietnamese villagers that colors teeth and gums blood red.

Blue Leader—The radio code of the first platoon commander of Hotel Company.

Boondocks, boonies—The jungle or bush outside An Hoa's perimeter.

Boots, jungle—Special canvas tops attached to lightweight leather boots with steel-shank protective soles.

Bouncing betty—A U.S. mine that pops into the air at waist level when triggered before detonation.

Cap—To "cap" an enemy is to bust a "primer cap" when firing a weapon at Charlie. To kill an enemy.

CH-46—Sea Knight helicopter, capable of lifting a rifle platoon. Twin engines.

Charlie—Victor Charlie, the South Vietnamese Communist soldier and the Marine's main foe in the Arizona.

Checkpoint—1. Any number of sentry-guarded entrances to An Hoa Combat Base; 2. The exact positions on a topographical map that a Marine patrol must intersect and radio in to headquarters.

Chi-com—Any weapon or explosive manufactured by the Chinese Communists.

Chieu hoi—A term used by VC or North Vietnamese to proclaim their unconditional surrender.

Chow—Marine slang for mealtime, or to eat "chow."

Claymore—Directional mine armed with plastic explosive and a ball-bearing-studded face. Antipersonnel defensive mine.

Clip—Marine slang for "to cut down" with rifle fire.

C-Med—Charlie Medical Facility at Da Nang. A surgical unit.

CO—Commanding officer.

Colonel—The commander of Second Battalion, Fifth Marine Regiment. Actually, his rank is lieutenant colonel, but in the field colonel is used exclusively.

Concertina—A circular rolled barbed or razor wire used in constructing a perimeter defense.

CP—Marine command post.

C-rations—The standard U.S. government canned meal, ready to eat in the field.

Crimson Leader Actual—The radio call sign of the battalion commander of the 2/5.

Dai Loc—Province in the Arizona.

Da Nang—The giant Marine base and seaport on the China Sea, thirty miles north of An Hoa at the inception of Highway 1.

Deck—The floor or ground. "Hit the deck" is a command to get down, usually under fire.

Defilade—A cut or low spot in the ground. Used as cover and concealment.

Delayed fuse—Artillery shells or bombs with delayed fuses that penetrate the ground before exploding.

Demo—Demolitions, usually C-4 plastic explosive. To "demo" a tunnel is to blow it up.

Deploy—To order troops into a specific battle formation.

Deputy—The deputy commander of the First Marine Division was a brigadier general.

Di di mau—"Run away" or "escape" in Vietnamese.

Dike—A built-up wall with a footpath above a surrounding rice field. Dikes are roads for the rice farmer.

Dink—A Vietnamese or Viet Cong (dinky).

Division—In Vietnam the USMC fielded the First, Third, and Fifth divisions. Each division is composed of three regiments. The Fifth Marine Regiment was part of the First Division. The Twenty-sixth Marines were part of the Fifth Division.

DMZ—Or the Z. The demilitarized zone dividing North and South Vietnam.

Doc—Medical personnel or corpsman.

Duc Duc—Rice basin north of An Hoa Combat Base.

Dung lai—To halt or order to stop in Vietnamese.

Enfilade fire—Rifle or machine-gun fire from a 45-degree angle from either front cutting across a position.

Envelop (right or left)—A tactic where a flanking fire team or squad encircles the enemy on its periphery while a base squad maintains fire superiority.

Evasion—Tactics used by the VC to avoid contact with Marine patrols.

F-4—A twin-engine jet fighter/bomber used by Marine air wings for ground support for infantry units. The McDonnell Douglas F-4 Phantom.

Field—The field is any area outside the main base where combat readiness is mandatory.

Field of fire—The radius that an automatic weapon can cover in an arc from port to starboard.

Firebase—Phu Loc 6 was the main artillery support base and Marine-guarded hill at the entrance to the Arizona some six miles north of An Hoa.

Firefight—An engagement of small units employing mainly rifle fire and small arms.

Fire in the hole!—The correct exclamation or preparatory warning before discharging explosives. A warning shouted when tripping a booby trap or mine.

Fire mission—An artillery mission fired to support troops in the field, or H and I fire.

Fire pit—Artillery revetments to segregate guns to lessen fire hazards.

Fire team—The basic building block of the Marine rifle squad. A fire team contains a leader, two riflemen, and an automatic rifleman (M-14 with selector). A squad contains three fire teams.

Flag officer—A U.S. Marine general officer.

Flak jacket—The fiberglass-paneled cloth jacket (vest) worn by Marines as protection from shrapnel.

Flank—The side of a unit, where it is weakest.

FO—An artillery forward observer, who can adjust artillery fires onto a target.

Foxtrot—A sister company to Hotel. In the Second Battalion, Fifth Marines there are four rifle companies; E (Echo), F (Foxtrot), G (Golf), and H (Hotel).

Frag—Fragmentation grenade. The U.S. M-26 grenade was the standard fragmentation grenade. The U.S. M-34 was made with white phosphorus ("Willy Peter").

G-2—Intelligence division of a Marine divisional staff. The intelligence officer is the G-2 billet.

Garbled—Radio communication that is indecipherable.

Golf—A sister company in 2/5.

Go Noi Island—A main force headquarters in the Arizona on the Song Thu Bon to the northeast of An Hoa.

Grazing fire—Flat-trajectory rifle or machine-gun fire aimed low to the deck against bunkered enemy troops.

Grid square—An area on a topographical map comprising 1,000 meters and defined by four coordinates. Six coordinates define the area to 100 square meters. Eight coordinates to 10 meters.

Groundpounders—Infantry troops. Grunts.

Grunt—Slang term for Marine infantry troops.

Gung ho—Marine spirit and enthusiasm.

H-34—Sikorksy UH-34 resupply and medevac chopper, used as the main Marine workhorse.

Halozone—Water-purification tablet.

Ham and motherfuckers—The most reviled C-ration meal, which you could not give away—even to the dinks.

Hamlet—Small village in the Arizona with less than 100 population.

Hawk—Very cold climate or high wind.

H and I—Harrassment and interdiction artillery fire. Sometimes called "we don't give a shit what we hit" fire. Designed to alter and hamper enemy movement.

HE—High-explosive shell or bomb.

Honcho—Native leader or village hetman.

Hot area—Dangerous, enemy-controlled landing zone strafed by enemy fire.

Hotel—Company in the 2/5.

HQ—Headquarters. The 2/5's HQ was at An Hoa. The First Marine Division's HQ was at Da Nang.

Hump—To walk a long distance on patrol or operation, usually loaded down with ammo and gear.

Illumination—Night artillery fire used to illuminate an area using a phosphorus filament suspended by parachute.

Incendiary—A shell that burns upon impact. White phosphorus shell.

Inchon—South Korean port where the First Marine Brigade made a historic landing.

Incoming fire—An enemy round of artillery or mortar round fired into a USMC position.

Indian territory—Hostile area controlled by enemy forces.

Infiltration route—One of the network of trails used by North Vietnamese troops to enter South Vietnam from the north, Laos, or Cambodia.

K-44—Chinese Communist battle rifle.

K-bar—World War II–vintage USMC combat knife.

KC-130—Main U.S. Air Force transport plane with four engines and rear ramp loading. Carries a combat-ready rifle platoon.

KIA—Killed in action.

Kit Carson Scout—An NVA soldier who defected and scouted for Marine patrols.

Klick, click—A unit of distance equal to 1,000 linear meters. Commonly used gauge for estimating distance in artillery-compatible gradations. One kilometer.

Kwajalein—South Pacific atoll assaulted by Marines in World War II.

LAAW—Light Antitank Assault Weapon, contained in collapsible, disposable, fiberglass tubes.

Land mine—Various types were constructed by the VC, especially utilizing undetonated U.S. bombs.

Liberty Bridge—Linked An Hoa to firebase Phu Loc 6 across the Song Thu Bon some six miles north of An Hoa in the Arizona.

LP—Listening post or sentry post, fielded at night to provide warning of an enemy attack.

LZ—Landing zone for helicopters.

M-1—World War II main battle rifle. Air-cooled, clip-fed, semiautomatic, shoulder-held rifle in caliber .30 MI. Occasionally used by VC and stolen from the ARVN. Arguably the finest battle rifle ever fielded by the United States.

M-1/M-2 .30-caliber carbine—U.S. air-cooled, magazine-fed, shoulder-held, World War II–vintage carbine, .30 caliber. Favorite weapon of officers and South Vietnamese due to light weight. The M-2 version is fully automatic.

M-2 .50-caliber machine gun—U.S. air-cooled, belt-fed, fully automatic, pylon- or tripod-mounted heavy machine gun, .50 caliber.

M-14—The standard USMC main battle rifle. Air-cooled, magazine-fed, shoulder-held, semiautomatic rifle in 7.62mm NATO.

M-26—The standard U.S. fragmentation grenade with coiled wire filament-encased fragmentation spool.

M-60 machine gun—U.S. air-cooled, belt-fed, fully automatic, shoulder-fired standard infantry machine gun, 7.62mm NATO, with bipod and replacement barrels.

M-60 tank—Main U.S. battle tank, equipped with 90mm main gun and .50- and .30-caliber machine guns. Weight: 58 tons, approximately.

M-72—Light Antitank Weapon (LAW) rocket. A plastic

tube extended to fire a shaped, charged rocket that would penetrate eleven inches of concrete or heavy logged bunkers. Replaced 3.5-inch rocket launcher.

M-79—U.S. shoulder-held, 40mm, single-shot grenade launcher with range around 400 meters.

III MAF—Marine Amphibious Force. The senior headquarters of Marine operations in Vietnam's I Corps area. Troop strength was eighteen infantry battalions.

MAG—Marine Air Group.

Mamma-san—The older mothers and grandmothers in a peasant village.

Medevac—Medical evacuation, usually by H-34 helicopter, although CH-46 Sea Knights were used on TUSCALOOSA.

MG—Designation for machine gun.

MIA—Missing in action.

Mike Mike—The radio code for artillery piece defined by caliber in millimeters. Example: 155 Mike Mike is a 155-millimeter howitzer.

Mortars—U.S. mortars are 60mm portable mortar, 81mm mortar used in the field only from fixed positions, and 4.2-inch mortar fired from firebase at Phu Loc 6. The main VC mortar was the 82mm Chinese infantry weapon.

MOS—Military Occupational Specialty, or job description. Marine infantry was 0300. A rifleman was 0311.

Moshin-Nagant—Russian bolt-action rifle in 7.62mm, of World War II vintage.

Napalm—Jellied gasoline in canisters dropped from jets. Sucked all available oxygen into its fireball.

Net—Radio network.

Number one—Vietnamese slang for "the best."

Number ten—Vietnamese slang for "the worst."

NVA—North Vietnamese Army regular soldiers.

Ontos—Marine tracked attack vehicle sporting six 106mm recoilless rifles and .50-caliber spotting rifle.

OP—Observation post.

OPCON—Operational Control. Delta 1–26 was OPCON to 2/5 during Tuscaloosa on January 27–28, 1967.

Paddy—The rectangular rice fields bordered by dikes and footpaths.

PF—Popular Forces, the Vietnamese National Guard.

Plunging fire—Rifle and machine-gun fire aimed down onto target from a position higher than the enemy.

Point—Lead Marine in a rifle squad on patrol. Lead element in a company column.

Point detonating fuses—Shells or bombs that explode on impact.

Police—To clean up or sanitize.

Probe—To attack a defensive perimeter line to analyze weapon placement.

Punji stake—A sharpened bamboo stake smeared with excrement and/or urine.

Racks—Bomb racks, where aviation ordnance is hung on the aircraft underwing or belly; Marine slang for bunk or bed.

R and R—Rest and relaxation. A short-term leave from combat duty.

Rear area—The combat base or any secure area outside the Arizona.

Recoilless rifle—The 106mm rifles on the Ontos fired

perforated cased shells that blew the gases out the rear breech ports, reducing recoil.

Recon—To patrol looking for enemy movements in order to collect information. Recon patrols avoid combat if possible.

Red Leader—The radio code name for the Second Platoon commander of Hotel Company.

Regiment—USMC unit composed of three rifle battalions and a headquarters. The 2/5 was a rifle battalion in the Fifth Marine Regiment.

Repeat—Radio fire mission coordinates and important facts are often repeated for clarity.

Scuttlebutt—Rumors or unfounded facts passed between Marines.

Sea Bees—U.S. Navy combat construction workers. They built the airstrip and most of the base at An Hoa.

Sea Knight—The CH-46 helicopter used for troop insertion and medevac on Operation TUSCALOOSA.

Short round—An artillery shell fired short of the target. This is a grave danger when firing over a unit of Marines toward the enemy.

Short-timer—A Marine with less than sixty days remaining in-country.

Skirmishers—A frontal attack formation with the squad in staggered line.

SKS—Simonov Soviet- or Chinese-made semiautomatic 7.62 × 39mm rifle. This is the standard VC infantry weapon and is accurate and reliable.

Slack—Any easy treatment by the Marines toward anyone. This seldom happened.

Snuffie—A private enlisted Marine.

Spider hole—An enemy fighting hole camouflaged to the eye.

Square away—To make orderly and neat, specifically uniforms and equipment.

TAOR—Tactical area of responsibility, or battalion operational area.

TO—Table of organization.

Topo—Topographical map showing elevation of hills, valleys, and contour lines.

Top sergeant—First sergeant or senior enlisted man in a rifle company.

Trail—A well-used path linking villages or leading through the jungle. Often mined or booby-trapped.

Utilities—Green Marine combat uniform made of lightweight cotton. In Vietnam, combat utilities were called "jungles."

Vaporize—To blow an enemy to pieces.

VC—Viet Cong soldier.

Volley fire—When an entire Marine squad or platoon fires in rhythmical cadence together.

Waste—To kill without mercy.

White Leader—The radio code name of the Second Platoon commander of Hotel Company.

WP—White phosphorus artillery shell or grenade.

XO—Executive officer, second in command of a rifle company or battalion.

XRAY—Letter X in radio call signs.

Zap—To shoot or hit with a bullet.

Zero—To bring a rifle's sights into alignment at two hundred meters for accurate battle dope.

Zilch—Nothing, no luck.